T0265494

Bounce Back

Bounce Back

The Ultimate Guide to Financial Resilience

Lynnette Khalfani-Cox

WILEY

Published by John Wiley & Sons, Inc., Hoboken, New Jersey.
Published simultaneously in Canada.

For general information on our other products and services or for technical support, please contact our Customer Care Department within the United States at (800) 762-2974, outside the United States at (317) 572-3993 or fax (317) 572-4002.

Wiley also publishes its books in a variety of electronic formats. Some content that appears in print may not be available in electronic formats. For more information about Wiley products, visit our web site at www.wiley.com.

Library of Congress Cataloging-in-Publication Data is Available:

ISBN 9781394205165 (Hardback)
ISBN 9781394205172 (ePub)
ISBN 9781394205189 (ePDF)

Cover Design: Paul McCarthy
Cover Image: Getty Images: © Maria Toutoudaki

SKY10059807_111023

To my sister, Debby. Losing you has been the most painful emotional challenge of my life.

While I try to bounce back every day, I will always miss you and love you—forever.

Contents

Acknowledgments

I'm incredibly grateful to a host of people who have supported me in various ways, inspired me, and made this book possible. To my husband, Earl: you are such a bedrock of security, stability, and happiness for me. When I think of all the things you've had to endure and bounce back from, I am in awe of your strength and character. I adore and appreciate you beyond measure, honey. To my parents, Lucille and Michael: thank you for doing your best and pouring good values, plus a love of God, into me and my sisters. To my siblings: Cheryl, Debby (RIP), Denise, Hope, and Tiffany: you are each so special and precious to me in your own way. I love you. To my sister-friends—from the fabulous LaTrice V. to the phenomenal Bali Chicks (you know who you are!)—I cherish your friendship and the way each of you consistently demonstrates the value of sisterhood. Lord knows we've all been through things. Yet despite our respective struggles and challenges, you all possess a rare combination of grace, grit, and determination that is so admirable. Let's hang onto that—and to each other. To my children: Aziza, Jakada, and Alexis: know that I love you more than words can express. I am so very honored to be your mother and incredibly proud of each of you. My biggest wish is for your happiness. Finally, but definitely not least, a huge thank you to every person who allowed me to interview you for *Bounce Back*. To both the subject matter experts and those who are experts of their own lived experiences, I will forever appreciate your candor, time, and willingness to share. This book came alive thanks to your input and stories.

About the Author

Lynnette Khalfani-Cox, The Money Coach®, is a personal finance expert, speaker, and author of numerous money-management books, including the *New York Times* bestseller *Zero Debt: The Ultimate Guide to Financial Freedom*. Lynnette has been seen on more than 1,000 TV segments nationwide, including television appearances on *Oprah*, *Dr. Phil*, *The Steve Harvey Show*, *Good Morning America*, *The TODAY Show*, and many more. A former financial news journalist, Lynnette now co-owns TheMoneyCoach.net LLC, a financial education company that she runs with her husband, Earl Cox. Together, they offer financial education consulting services, courses, and workshops.

As a subject matter expert on many personal finance topics—including credit and debt, saving and budgeting, paying for college, homeownership, and entrepreneurship and wealth building—Lynnette helps organizations of all kinds develop and roll out high-quality financial literacy programs and campaigns. She also creates financial education curricula and provides strategic counsel to companies, nonprofits, government agencies, or educational institutions that want to launch financial content, products, services, apps, or other tools. For her financial literacy work, Lynnette was honored with the Muriel F. Siebert Lifetime Achievement Award by the New Jersey Coalition for Financial Education.

Before starting TheMoneyCoach.net in 2003, Lynnette was a *Wall Street Journal* reporter for CNBC, where she covered business and personal finance news. Lynnette spent nearly 10 years at Dow Jones & Co. Inc. working as a reporter, bureau chief, deputy managing editor, and personal finance editor. Prior to her work at Dow Jones, Lynnette was a correspondent for *The Philadelphia Inquirer*, a writer, and an assistant producer for WTXF (FOX-TV) in Philadelphia, and a writer for the Associated Press in Los Angeles.

Lynnette earned her bachelor of arts degree in English from the University of California, Irvine. She also holds a master of arts degree in broadcast journalism from the University of Southern California as well as a certificate in FinTech (Financial Technology) from Cornell University. Lynnette is a native of Los Angeles who spent 20 years on the East Coast but now lives in the greater Houston area with her husband.

Other books Lynnette has written include:

- *The Bounce Back Workbook*
- *Perfect Credit: 7 Steps to a Great Credit Rating*
- *Your First Home: The Smart Way to Get It and Keep It*
- *Investing Success: How to Conquer 30 Costly Mistakes & Multiply Your Wealth*
- *The Money Coach's Guide to Your First Million*
- *Zero Debt: The Ultimate Guide to Financial Freedom*
- *Zero Debt for College Grads: From Student Loans to Financial Freedom*
- *The Identity Theft Recovery Guide*
- *College Secrets: How to Save Money, Cut College Costs, and Graduate Debt Free*
- *College Secrets for Teens: Money Saving Ideas for the Pre-College Years*
- *Free Pre-College Programs*
- *Millionaire Kids Club Book 1: Garage Sale Riches*
- *Millionaire Kids Club Book 2: Putting the 'Do' in Donate*
- *Millionaire Kids Club Book 3: Home Sweet Home*
- *Millionaire Kids Club Book 4: Penny Power*

Foreword

In times of adversity and hardship, we often find ourselves searching for guidance, support, and a glimmer of hope to help us navigate the challenges that life throws our way. The COVID-19 pandemic was undoubtedly one such period, testing our resilience, determination, and ability to bounce back from setbacks. It is during these moments that we need mentors and resources to provide us with the tools and inspiration to rise above our circumstances and find our way forward.

Lynnette Khalfani-Cox, lovingly known as "The Money Coach," has emerged as a beacon of light for individuals and families facing financial burdens, helping them overcome overwhelming debt and regain control of their lives. Her personal journey, which led her to pay off more than $100,000 of consumer debt, has become an inspiration to countless people seeking financial freedom and a fresh start. She has been a role model for me.

Now, in her latest book, aptly titled *Bounce Back*, Lynnette dives deep into the art of recovery, offering practical strategies, profound insights, and heartfelt encouragement to those who have experienced setbacks, especially during these trying times. This book is not just another self-help resource; it is a lifeline for those in search of a road map to reclaim their lives and thrive.

One of the most captivating aspects of *Bounce Back* is Lynnette's ability to speak from personal experience. Her journey from overwhelming debt to financial success brings a relatability that few authors can replicate. She has walked the path of financial struggle and triumphed, making her insights invaluable for anyone hoping to do the same. Lynnette understands the emotional toll that life's various setbacks can take on us and uses her own story to show us that there is always a path forward.

Through her appearances on numerous television programs and her role as a keynote speaker at conferences, Lynnette has touched the lives of many, imparting her wisdom and empowering others to take charge of their financial destinies. In *Bounce Back*, she distills her knowledge into practical steps that can be applied by anyone willing to put in the effort. From strategies to recover from financial stress to moving beyond failed relationships, Lynnette offers a comprehensive toolkit to help readers regain control of their lives and build a solid foundation for their future.

Although Lynnette is known as "The Money Coach," *Bounce Back* goes beyond mere financial advice. It delves into the emotional and psychological aspects of recovery, acknowledging that setbacks can leave deep wounds that need healing. Lynnette understands that true transformation requires addressing the underlying beliefs, fears, and mindset that may have contributed to our struggles. By combining financial guidance with introspective exploration, she provides a holistic approach to bouncing back, ensuring that readers not only improve their financial situations but also find inner strength and resilience.

While *Bounce Back* is undoubtedly a timely resource, tailored specifically for those who have been impacted by the pandemic and its aftermath, its teachings are timeless. Setbacks can occur at any point in life, and the wisdom within this book will stand as a compass for anyone facing adversity. Whether you're striving to recover from job loss, business failure, medical expenses, or simply seeking a fresh start, Lynnette Khalfani-Cox's book will empower and equip you to rise above your circumstances.

In conclusion, *Bounce Back* is an essential resource for individuals and families searching for a way forward after experiencing setbacks. Lynnette Khalfani-Cox's honest, compassionate, and practical approach will guide you through the process of rebuilding your life, offering hope and inspiration every step of the way.

Let this book serve as your companion, your confidant, and your road map to a brighter future. Embrace its teachings, apply its principles, and discover the power within you to bounce back stronger than ever before.

DeForest B. Soaries, Jr.
President and CEO of Corporate Community Connections,
Inc., and founder of the dfree® Financial Freedom Movement

Introduction

"The greatest glory in living lies not in never falling, but in rising every time we fall."
—Nelson Mandela

Are you ready to transform your life and achieve financial security? Imagine a future where money matters are no longer a source of stress and worry but instead a gateway to stability and financial freedom. Picture yourself standing tall and resilient in the face of any setback that comes your way. Envision yourself thriving, not just surviving, in a world that often seems stacked against you. This is not a distant dream or an unattainable fantasy. It is within your reach, and I'd be honored to help guide you every step of the way. In the pages of *Bounce Back: The Ultimate Guide to Financial Resilience*, you are about to embark on an extraordinary journey of personal transformation and empowerment. Welcome to a world where your financial dreams finally become your reality, where setbacks are mere stepping stones to success and where resilience is your greatest asset.

Today, you stand at the threshold of a new beginning. Close your eyes for a moment and imagine a life free from the shackles of financial worries. Gone are the days of feeling overwhelmed by debt, living paycheck to paycheck, or being at the mercy of unexpected financial emergencies. I know this might be hard to picture, especially if you've gone through a recent life-altering event or you're feeling like your finances are a wreck. Even if things aren't a complete financial mess, you probably could stand to improve certain aspects of your personal finances because let's face it: the majority of Americans have one or more money problems. Serious money problems.

Consumer debt is widespread—including mortgages, credit card bills, auto loans, and student loans. Then there's the issue of most Americans having little to no savings: not any emergency cash cushion or much, if anything, in the way of retirement savings. Credit problems are yet another financial challenge affecting plenty of adults in the United States. More than 40% of Americans surveyed by Lending Tree said bad credit caused them to be denied financial products such as mortgages and credit cards. With a poor credit rating, your car insurance premiums could also be higher, you can get turned down for that apartment you want to rent, and you may even lose out on a new job or career promotion you're seeking.

Speaking of work, wages haven't kept pace with inflation: most folks haven't received sizeable cost-of-living adjustments, and most employers have not been generous in doling out merit-based pay raises.

Add it all up, and it's hard to make ends meet and to get ahead—especially since food, energy, education, and health care costs all continue to rise even when your paycheck doesn't.

In the middle of battling all these problems, you've probably been hit with a financial emergency or two, right? Maybe your car broke down recently, so you had to get a payday loan or whip out your Visa or MasterCard to get it fixed. Or perhaps somebody in your family has been sick, and now you've racked up huge medical bills. It's not just debt, of course, that might have put you in the hole. A slew of unexpected misfortunes or setbacks—from divorce to job loss—may have thrown your finances off-kilter.

Well, I'm here to tell you that you're not alone—and you can recover from these setbacks.

In fact, I'm living proof that you can overcome personal adversity, even if you've had a string of bad luck or made various poor financial or personal decisions in the past.

My Story of Overcoming Financial and Personal Problems

You see, back in 2001, I had $100,000 in credit card debt. Yes, you read that right: I had six figures worth of credit card debt alone! Fortunately, I paid it all off in three years, and I never missed a single payment. In late 2004, I wound up writing a book about how I got out of debt, and it became a *New York Times* bestseller. That book is called *Zero Debt: The Ultimate Guide to Financial Freedom*. In the two decades since then, I've gone from debt to wealth and have written more than 15 personal finance books, including the one you're reading right now, *Bounce Back: The Ultimate Guide to Financial Resilience*.

Over the years, as I've built a seven-figure net worth, I learned a lot about what it takes to recover from setbacks. Now I'm sharing my hard-earned wisdom with you within these pages.

Bounce Back will show you, step-by-step, exactly how to recover from any of the 10 most common setbacks and scenarios that can ruin your finances. I call these 10 setbacks the **"Dreaded Ds"**—because they can be quite dreadful (and sometimes embarrassing) when you first encounter them.

The 10 Dreaded Ds you may face are:

- **D**ownsizing from a job;
- **D**ivorce;
- **D**eath of a loved one;
- **D**isability;
- **D**isease;
- **D**isasters (natural or man-made);
- **D**ebt;
- **D**amaged credit;
- **D**ollar deficits (i.e. living check to check and lacking savings); and
- **D**iscrimination.

Chances are you, or someone you know, is in the throes of one of these challenges at this very moment. In fact, a majority of Americans struggle with these problems in any given year. According to research from Pew Charitable Trusts, 60% of US households face a "financial shock"—a large, unplanned expense or a reduction in income—in any given year. Some common sources of financial shocks include job loss, medical emergencies, major home maintenance costs, and more. These unexpected events can cause financial strain and lead to a cascade of other issues, such as accumulating debt, dipping into savings, or making difficult choices between essential expenses. The prevalence of financial shocks has become so bad that, in the wake of the COVID-19 pandemic, the US government recognized a need to establish a federal initiative aimed at helping Americans better recover from disasters and other economic shocks. In December 2021, President Joe Biden signed Executive Order 14058, Transforming Federal Customer Experience and Service Delivery to Rebuild Trust in Government.

That Executive Order led to the creation of nine "Life Experience" projects, providing a new model for how every agency of the federal government should better design and deliver benefits, services, and programs to Americans facing various life-altering events. (I'll explain more about this critical, ongoing initiative in Chapter 8, which focuses on disaster recovery.)

For now, understand that this is precisely where this book comes in handy. *Bounce Back* will be your trusty guide to navigate the rough waters of these financial setbacks and identify existing and emerging sources of support. I'll walk you through each of the Dreaded Ds, sharing practical advice, actionable strategies, resources, and inspiring stories from people who've been in your shoes. By the time you finish this book, you'll have a clear sense of how to regain control of your finances—and your emotions—and build a solid foundation for your future.

Discrimination Can Damage Your Finances Too

Maybe some of you were surprised to see discrimination listed as one of the Dreaded Ds. You might not always think about it, but discrimination can hit you hard in the wallet—and be an emotional blow, too. For instance, imagine you're job hunting, and you're overlooked because of your age, race, gender, or sexual orientation. It's disappointing to be passed over. But that's also a missed opportunity for a stable income and career growth. Or picture yourself trying to rent a place to live, but landlords have a bias against you. You'd probably feel frustrated about having limited housing options, and you may have to pay higher rent as well. Even when shopping, you could face price discrimination, where certain products are marked up based on who's buying.

For example, the so-called pink tax is a sneaky form of discrimination that takes a toll on women's finances. The pink tax refers to the extra amount women often pay for products and services that are pretty much the same as the ones men use—things such as razors, shampoo, or clothes. The only difference is these items are marketed to women, often in a lovely shade of pink. It might not seem like a big deal at first glance, but those extra dollars can add up fast. A New York City Department of Consumer Affairs study showed that women pay up to 13% more for personal care items and 8% more for clothing. Meanwhile, the California Senate Committee on Judiciary and Senate Select Committee on Women, Work & Families has found that Californian women pay an annual average of $2,381 more than men for the same goods and services. That works out to a pink tax of roughly $188,000 throughout a woman's life. Ouch! That's like a hidden tax just for being a woman. (Fortunately, lawmakers in both

California and New York have now passed laws banning discriminatory gender-based pricing in those states. However, there's still no federal law prohibiting the pink tax.)

Don't worry, though, there are ways to fight back against the pink tax and we'll tackle that in Chapter 12. But as you can see, discrimination isn't just about feelings; it can really affect your financial well-being. Too often, however, financial experts (myself included) have doled out well-intended advice designed to help people better manage their finances. But in nearly all cases, the ideas, strategies, and tips shared put the onus of improving squarely on the shoulders of the individual. Less frequently do we "experts" call out the systemic forces—including racism and various forms of discrimination—that make it hard for people to act, change, or put into practice the advice and solutions prescribed. *Bounce Back* addresses this reality.

Each chapter in *Bounce Back* focuses on one of the Dreaded Ds and reveals how you can financially, emotionally, and in some cases even physically recover from these situations—just like I have.

Would you believe that I've gone through nine of the 10 Dreaded Ds? It's true. I've been laid off from a good, high-paying job. I've had horrible credit. I've had negative balances in my bank accounts and have been so broke that I had a car repossessed. I've been through a ridiculously costly divorce. Besides those exorbitant credit card bills I mentioned, I also spent more than 15 years paying off $40,000 worth of student loans. Like all of you reading this book, I battled the fallout from the COVID-19 pandemic and natural disasters too. I've overcome obesity, high cholesterol, and being prediabetic. I've faced housing discrimination. Worst of all: I've endured the devastating loss of an older sister who passed away suddenly and way too soon.

Despite all these setbacks, I've managed to emerge stronger and thrive financially, emotionally, and physically too. So believe me when I say that I know—from both my personal experiences and my professional expertise—that a turnaround is always possible. It's not just me, of course, who has bounced back from adversity. Throughout *Bounce Back*, I'll tell you about plenty of people who have done so—including one woman who has experienced all 10 Dreaded Ds and yet is now thriving!

A Spiral of Success

I don't know what's going on in your life right now. But rather than feeling that you're in a downward economic spiral—kind of an unwanted financial freefall—wouldn't you love to turn things around too, and instead get into a staircase of recovery or a spiral of success? That's what happens when you create an environment in which you can layer good habits and solid financial practices one upon another. And when you change your past approach and mindset too.

But I recognize that change can sometimes be scary. It's also sometimes intimidating to put into practice even the best advice, especially when it may take you out of your comfort zone or what you've been accustomed to doing. Just take heart in knowing that you don't have to do everything I recommend all at once. Instead, if you'll just take it one day at a time and take action to build upon the positive, easy-to-follow steps I reveal, you'll immediately start to see a snowball of great economic results. With less financial stress, your emotional state will improve too.

Trust me: it can be done. I don't care if you've been struggling for months or years to get your finances on track. It doesn't matter if you've gone bankrupt, had a spouse that ruined your credit, or you've been sick and unable to work. Whatever troubles that have been ailing you, there are solutions and strategies to overcome your tribulations.

How to Use This Book: Faith, Finances, and Your Future

There are 12 chapters in *Bounce Back*. The first two chapters focus almost exclusively on your emotional well-being. Chapter 1 explains what resilience is—including financial resilience, emotional resilience, social resilience, and physical resilience. Chapter 2 highlights 10 core action steps you'll need to take to build your resilience and recover emotionally from any of the Dreaded Ds. I firmly believe that without the right emotional preparation and mindset, you won't be able to fully implement the financial steps needed to gain economic security. Chapters 1 and 2 of *Bounce Back* are also designed to help those of you who have picked up *The Bounce Back Workbook*, the companion to this book, to better customize my advice and put it into action based on your unique circumstances. *The Bounce Back Workbook* is chock full of exercises and activities that will allow you to reflect on your past and current money behaviors and beliefs and take action to bring about a more secure future.

In writing *Bounce Back* and *The Bounce Back Workbook*, ensuring your financial stability isn't my only goal. I also want to empower you, help you begin to heal from prior personal or financial traumas, and aid you in recognizing and breaking any unhealthy patterns you may have developed (consciously or unconsciously) that are associated with your personal finances.

That's a pretty tall order. So I'm not going to handle this task alone, based solely on my own experiences and knowledge. I'm also going to share with you the wisdom I've learned from a lot of different financial experts: including other money coaches, financial therapists, certified financial planners, psychologists, and others. Furthermore, within each topic or each Dreaded D, I've also tapped the expertise of specialists who work in those areas, as well as everyday people who've lived through these setbacks—and successfully overcome their challenges. Ultimately, you'll get the benefit of a range of professionals and lay people who offer tried-and-true advice—as well as some unique and little-known strategies—to get you on the road to recovery. By the time you're done, you'll see that *Bounce Back* and *The Bounce Back Workbook* are loaded with helpful advice, tips, nuts-and-bolts strategies, and practical activities that help you rebound economically and emotionally from each of the Dreaded Ds described.

After the two opening chapters, each successive chapter of *Bounce Back* covers one of the 10 Dreaded Ds in specific detail. Since Chapters 3 through 12 of *Bounce Back* are each devoted to a particular financial setback, once you read the first two chapters, you can jump right to the chapter describing the problem that has been plaguing you, if desired.

However, having coached so many people working their way out of financial jams, I know that money issues tend to be layered and interconnected. So regardless of your economic dilemma(s), I'd encourage you to also read this book from cover to cover. Furthermore, even if you aren't struggling with a particular Dreaded D right now, reading this information may help you assist someone you know who's facing that challenge. Above all: don't skip the final two chapters, which are devoted to stretching your dollars, saving money, and planning for emergencies—as well as battling the structural inequality and systemic forces that make it difficult for many people (especially women and people of color) to get ahead. The strategies I'll share in the final two chapters will also help you avoid or minimize the impact of any future Dreaded Ds you may experience. Believe me: this information can transform your financial life!

I should also say that, as a Christian, I've been blessed in so many ways: not just financially but also spiritually, emotionally, and personally with a wonderful marriage and great kids, not to mention an awesome career as well. You don't have to be a Christian, or a person of faith, as I am, to benefit from the lessons imparted in *Bounce Back*. But at the very least, you do need to have some faith in yourself. You should have faith that things can turn around, faith that tomorrow can be brighter, and faith that your future isn't hopeless—no matter what you've been through or been told.

Without hope, a positive outlook, and a belief in what's possible, you'll never be fully motivated to dig yourself out of the financial pit you might be in, and you'll never be sufficiently inspired to act. It's action, at the end of the day, that is necessary to launch your financial comeback. Nobody ever turned around his or her finances by wallowing in self-pity. And certainly, no one ever achieved economic comfort or security by pointing the finger and playing the blame game, or just living a life of regret and constantly stewing over this or that mistake.

Your setbacks or mistakes—whether personal, financial, career-based, or otherwise—are now in the past. There's no point in looking in the rearview mirror when what you really want to do is bounce back, go forward, and get on the road to financial freedom.

Listen, you survived the global COVID pandemic, and everything else life has thrown at you, right? So, from this moment forward, look ahead to your future and not back to the past. Be firm in your conviction that today is the start of your financial awakening. It's a new day and the start of a new financial life for you. Instead of living on the brink of an economic meltdown, you're about to bounce back: stronger, better, wiser, and yes, more financially and emotionally secure, than ever.

Let's get started!

Chapter 1
Resilience and Grit in the Face of Adversity, Transition, and Change

"Adversity will come, but the real test is in how you bounce back, and use the lessons learned to become even better."

—Serena Williams

Ever since I was a young kid, I've loved watching professional sports. From basketball, tennis, and gymnastics, to boxing, football, track, and more—I love seeing elite athletes compete. I'm the kind of fan who yells at the TV screen and jumps up and down when my team or favorite athlete wins or scores. But I know I can be a little over-the-top too. I've been known to startle other people or get a hoarse voice when the action gets good or something explosive happens on the field or court and I suddenly burst out screaming or cheering during a match. Admittedly, I sometimes drive my family (and even my dogs) crazy with my boisterous antics. But I just really connect with top performers putting it all on the line and going all out to do whatever it takes to get to victory.

I've realized, though, that I don't get hyped up just because I'm watching my favorite athletes get the "W," or the win. What I'm often drawn to is their determination—the way many high-performing sports figures are larger-than-life personalities who just won't quit. They fight against all odds and persevere even when they're down for the count and it looks as if they can't possibly win. I guess that's why, even as a kid, I loved the Rocky Balboa movies, starring Sylvester Stallone. I was just eight years old when the original Rocky film came out. Yet, I can still clearly see Rocky running through the streets of Philly and up the steps near the Philadelphia Museum, arms above his head after he triumphantly made it to the top. Later, when *Rocky II* came out, I raised my 10-year-old little fists to cheer Rocky again, as he hoisted the gold championship belt above his head and told his wife one of the most iconic lines in sports movie history: "Yo, Adrian . . . I did it!"

Those were movies, of course, but in real life, top athletes seem to always find a way to dig deep and pull off similar, memorable victories—they have the resilience to bounce back from incredible setbacks and adversity.

Maybe you've heard of pro surfer Bethany Hamilton. When she was just 13, Bethany was bitten by a 14-foot-long tiger shark, and it took her whole left arm. Luckily, she was with friends, who rescued her. But the shark attack still caused her to lose 60% of her body's blood by the time she made it to the hospital. After that kind of trauma, most people would've just quit surfing. Not Bethany. She was back on her surfboard only a month later! She taught herself how to surf one-armed, and eventually, she became a professional surfer. Bethany even went on to win national titles, and she's still crushing it on the waves today.

Or take Peyton Manning, the NFL legend. This guy was a megastar quarterback when he suffered a neck injury on the football field that required multiple surgeries, including procedures to repair herniated discs. Some folks were like, "That's it. He's done." But Manning showed them! He had already spent 14 seasons with the Indianapolis Colts. He sat out the 2011 season, rehabbed like a boss, and then made an epic comeback with the Denver Broncos (one of my former favorite teams, way back when John Elway was their quarterback). Because of his injuries, Manning literally had to learn how to throw the football again during his rehab. Nonetheless, Manning led the Broncos to two Super Bowls, winning one of them at age 37, and breaking a bunch of records along the way. Manning truly showed us that, with resilience, there's no challenge too big to overcome.

The Drive: A Famous Sports Comeback

And speaking of John Elway, I'm old enough to remember "The Drive"—which is often called one of the most famous comebacks in NFL history. The year was 1987, and it was the AFC Championship Game between the Cleveland Browns and the Denver Broncos. The stage was set at Cleveland's Municipal Stadium, and it was an intense, nail-biting game. With just five minutes and 32 seconds left on the clock, the Broncos were down 20-13, and things weren't looking too hot for them. But then, something magical happened. Elway, the Broncos quarterback, stepped up and led his team on a legendary 98-yard drive, starting from their own 2-yard line. The pressure was on, and the odds were stacked against them. The crowd of nearly 80,000 fans in Cleveland was deafening, and the weather was freezing. However, Elway didn't let that get to him.

He masterfully orchestrated a series of plays, completing crucial passes and even running the ball himself when needed. The Broncos moved methodically down the field, converting on key third downs, and keeping the drive alive. With just 37 seconds left, Elway threw a five-yard touchdown pass to Mark Jackson, tying the game at 20-20. You could feel the energy in the air—this was a comeback for the ages! The game went into overtime, and the Broncos were unstoppable. They marched down the field once more, setting up a game-winning field goal by Rich Karlis. The kick was good, and the Broncos won 23-20, securing their spot in Super Bowl XXI. Football fans still talk about "The Drive" to this day because it's such a great testament to Elway's grit, leadership, and never-say-die attitude.

It's also a powerful reminder that even when the odds are against you, with determination, skill, and resilience, nearly anything is possible. I realize, of course, that you're probably not an NFL player or a pro athlete. Nonetheless, when things look bleak, it's worth it to keep your head in the game and keep pushing forward. You never know when your own "Drive" moment might come—perhaps when you least expect a turnaround!

As you can see, each of the incredible athletes mentioned earlier battled adversity but managed to demonstrate incredible amounts of resilience and emerge victorious. Wouldn't you like to be able to have the same kind of resilience and grit? Let's start by examining how you perceive adversity—and particularly, transition and change.

Understanding the Value of Transition and Change

Some disruptions to our lives are downright awful and unnerving when they hit. Maybe you've just lost your job, experienced the death of a loved one, are going through a divorce, or trying to get out of a boatload of debt. Whatever situation you're facing, these adversities are undeniably hard to cope with, and it can feel as if your life has been upended. In the middle of your circumstance, perhaps you've been focused primarily on what's *changed* in your life. Especially what's different, what's missing, or what's difficult. If you've been dwelling on what's changed—in your language, your actions, and your thoughts—I honestly can't blame you. You're doing what nine out of 10 people in your shoes would probably do. Very few of us have been provided with the tools and perspectives to have an alternative view of hardship other than *this is horrible (or unfair, or stressful), and I want this mess to be over as soon as possible!*

So I want to first invite you to adopt a different mindset and reframe your thinking about life's challenges. You may not believe it at this point, but for now, just try to keep an open mind about the following assertion: bouncing back from any setback is far more manageable—and even life-enhancing—when we view the Dreaded Ds not just as harsh changes we have to deal with, but also as crucial transitions or periods of positive transformation in our lives.

This concept originated with William Bridges and his theory of transition and change, which he developed in 1979. According to Bridges, who was an expert on change and a business consultant, when change happens, people have to navigate personally and psychologically over three stages: ending, neutral zone, and new beginnings.

The first stage is the ending, which is where you may be right now. You've experienced a loss or a significant change, and you're likely feeling a sense of grief or loss over what you're leaving behind. This could be a job, a relationship, or even a cherished way of life. Letting go of things that we were accustomed to having is never easy. You may feel demoralized, dejected, or just flat-out disengaged from life at this stage, which is natural and to be expected.

Once you've acknowledged the loss and decided to let go, you move into the neutral zone. This is a period of exploration and learning. You might feel lost as you're preparing for something new, but you don't yet know what it is. It might feel like you're in a state of limbo, but this stage is crucial for your growth and transition. You're not only learning new things but also creating new processes as you head toward new beginnings.

Finally, there's the stage of new beginnings. As you explore new ways of being, you develop new understandings, personal values, relationships, and beliefs. You'll begin to see a different future for yourself, one that's infused with excitement, energy, optimism, and positivity about what's to come. This stage represents the rebuilding of your life, the reestablishing of your identity, and the reinvigoration of your morale and engagement.

The Bridges Model of Transition and Change is centered on the concept of *transition* rather than the idea of *change*. While these two terms may seem synonymous, they differ in one significant way: with the Bridges framework, change is an *external* event or situation—something that happens *to* you. Change occurs regardless of your acceptance or refusal of it. By contrast, transition is an *internal* process; it's something that happens *within* you. Transition is a psychological journey you undertake in *response* to change. Unlike change, which can be abrupt and swift, transition tends to be a more gradual process, taking place over a longer period of time, typically many months or even years. You have the ability to choose how long it takes. Think of transition as your way of processing, or coping with, change. Transition is your unique way and time spent internally coming to terms with an external change that's occurred.

The Bridges Model first made its appearance in Bridges's 1979 book, *Transitions: Making Sense of Life's Changes*. Over time, Bridges, along with his business partner and spouse, Susan Bridges, revised and republished the work several times. The 1991 publication, *Managing Transitions*, showcased how the model could be effectively utilized in the workplace and professional settings. After William's passing in 2013, Susan further expanded on the model's applications.

The Upside of Your Transition and Stress

Fast-forward to today, and financial experts have recognized the need for an additional stage: *planning* for transition. Most notably, the Sudden Money Institute was founded in June 2000 to help financial planning clients going through transition better handle the personal side of money. This think tank created the Certified Financial Transitionist® (CeFT®) designation, and a division for training and certification called the Financial Transitionist® Institute. Many financial planners who serve as financial transitionists say the Bridges transition model is foundational to understanding personal change. It provides a road map for navigating through the maze of emotions, confusion, and frustrations that often accompany significant life events or disruptions. Transitions are not easy, but they do always have an upside: they lead to new ways of doing or being, helping you to grow and adapt to your new circumstances. And that's not all. Susan Bradley, CEO and founder of Sudden Money Institute, created the *Sudden Money Institute Transitions Journal*, in which she notes: "Change almost always brings with it some level of stress, and there's the big danger: somewhere along the way, stress got a really bad name. But we don't believe stress is necessarily negative. Here are just three things stress has going for it:

- Stress helps you build resilience.
- Stress helps you identify what really matters in your life.
- Stress gives you an opportunity to turn a challenge into a positive personal transformation (Bradley, 2019, p. 4).

Stephanie Genkin, CFP®, the founder of My Financial Planner, LLC, and a Brooklyn-based fee-only registered investment advisor agrees. "The old model of thinking is that all stress is bad," she says. "But the new thinking says some stress is really positive: in that stress is also possibility." That's why Genkin, who is also a Certified Financial Transitionist, poses this question to people facing adversity: "Is life happening *to* you, or is life happening *for* you?"

"We tend to look at things like the Dreaded Ds as bad luck. But nobody goes through life without having some of these events happen," Genkin says. "About 25% of our lives will be spent in transition," Genkin adds. "So everybody should be preparing themselves to see what your capacity is for dealing with this."

Genkin speaks from both personal and professional experience. She lost both her parents within a relatively short time frame, with her mother passing last, in 2022. Both losses were devastating, but her mom's death really cut deep. Genkin was extremely close to her mother, speaking to her every night on the phone at 10 p.m., and visiting often with her. "The source of my confidence was my mom," Genkin says, citing many key moments in her life from childhood through adulthood when her mother told her she could do anything—including starting her financial planning business. "She was very invested in everything I did," Genkin recalls.

After her mom's death, Genkin went to therapy for eight straight weeks and also started attending group grief counseling. She got so involved that she's now running the grief counseling group. Additionally, she participates every Thursday afternoon in a Jewish positive psychology group. "This is grounding for me, to have a Jewish expression of my mourning," Genkin says. "I also get resources, books, guidance, and encouragement in just knowing that I'm not alone in this."

"We're all going to go through painful transitions," she adds.

Ultimately, Genkin says that successfully navigating the Dreaded Ds boils down to a few things: planning for various life phases and transitions, accepting and figuring out how to embrace even life's messiest or toughest events, and being willing to learn the positive lessons that change teaches you.

Perhaps that's why the Sudden Money Institute says of its mission: "We make financial transitions less stressful, more productive, and frequently enjoyable."

Even if you cannot (yet) fathom the idea of your transition being "enjoyable," take comfort in knowing that whether the change you experienced came about by choice or by chance, there's a distinct pattern for how we all internalize and respond to major life transitions. And while your timeline for going through each stage won't be the same as the next person's, the features and obstacles of the stages are quite consistent and predictable. Based on its practitioners' expertise in helping people get through life challenges, the Sudden Money Institute has defined four stages of transition: anticipation, ending, passage, and new normal. These echo Bridges's stages, with an added stage of anticipation or planning for major life events.

Stage 1: Anticipation. This is a period of foreseeing or looking ahead to a significant change or event. Note that not all change events are unhappy ones. For example, someone might be selling a business, receiving a financial windfall, or getting married. But it's the new, unknown aspect of the phase ahead that often sparks a mix of excitement, anxiety, and uncertainty.

Stage 2: Ending. This stage involves recognizing that a certain aspect of life—or perhaps a life itself, in the case of death—has ended. Other examples of endings include the termination of a relationship, career, or a lifestyle. The ending stage is definitive, and there's no going back.

Stage 3: Passage. During this stage, the initial shock of the change has worn off, and you start adapting to the new situation. This stage involves letting go of old ideas about life and exploring new ones. It's a transitional stage toward the new normal and tends to be the longest of the stages. But "passage is also the realm of possibility," Genkin notes. "Passage is also the point where you're starting to think about and hopefully reconstruct your narrative."

Stage 4: New Normal. At this stage, you have fully integrated the event that initiated the transition into your life. You have accepted the event as part of your personal history, but you talk about it in the past tense, and it doesn't singularly define you. This stage signifies that you have arrived at the best possible outcome, given the circumstances.

How typical is it for the average American to go through one of these transition stages? When I interviewed Genkin for *Bounce Back*, she told me that she decided to become a Certified Financial Transitionist after having an epiphany about the people she was helping. "I realized every single one of my clients was either coming out of a transition, preparing for one, or in the middle of one," she said.

Defining and Developing Resilience

Now that we understand how commonplace transitions are, let's turn our attention to helping you become more equipped to navigate any transition and bounce back from change. The subtitle of this book is *The Ultimate Guide to Financial Resilience*. But what exactly is resilience? More specifically, what is financial resilience? How do you know if you have it? And if you don't, how can you develop it? Additionally, how can other forms of resilience help us to become more financially resilient?

We can learn a lot about resilience based on what psychologists teach us about healthy ways to handle challenging circumstances.

Research by psychologists such as Angela Duckworth and others has shown that resilience and grit play crucial roles in determining your success and overall well-being.

Duckworth's research delves deep into the importance of resilience and grit in the pursuit of success and happiness. Resilience and grit, which are closely interrelated traits, are key to overcoming obstacles and maintaining a sense of balance throughout life's ups and downs.

Resilience, as defined by Duckworth and her peers, is not just the capacity to bounce back from setbacks; it also encompasses the flexibility and adaptability needed to navigate through difficult situations. This dynamic trait enables you to learn from your experiences and grow stronger as you face life's inevitable challenges.

Grit, on the other hand, is characterized by a steadfast dedication and unwavering determination to achieve your long-term objectives, even in the face of adversity. This quality fuels your drive to keep pushing forward, relentlessly pursuing your goals despite the obstacles and setbacks you encounter along the way.

Together, resilience and grit form a powerful combination that promotes personal growth, boosts self-esteem, and fosters a sense of purpose. By cultivating these qualities, you're better equipped to handle life's uncertainties and emerge from challenging situations with newfound strength and wisdom.

In summary: resilience is the ability to adapt, recover, and grow in the face of adversity. It is derived from a combination of personal qualities, learned skills, and environmental factors that contribute to our ability to bounce back from life's challenges.

You may or may not consider yourself resilient, based on the definition described earlier. Fortunately, research has shown that resilience can be cultivated and improved over time.

But think for a moment about whether you have *financial* resilience. Have you ever considered what it means to be able to readily spring back—in economic terms—when life didn't go according to plan? Let's consider what it means to have financial resilience, as well as social, emotional, and physical resilience too.

Financial Resilience

The Financial Resilience Institute is a Canadian-based nonprofit whose mission is to promote financial health and resilience to citizens across the globe. The Institute defines resilience as "your ability to get through financial hardship, stressors or shocks as a result of unplanned life events." Here's a simple way of thinking about this definition: you probably have a decent level of financial resilience if you can get hit with a big, unexpected bill—say, a $1,000 car repair or an emergency roof fix—and pay it with cash, with no problem.

The Institute also measures how financially resilient people are and classifies households into four categories: extremely vulnerable, financially vulnerable, approaching resilience, and financially resilient. According to the Institute, 78% of Canada's population is financially vulnerable and not financially resilient.

Meanwhile, the US-based Financial Health Network, a national nonprofit, reports that an estimated 70% of Americans are not financially healthy. The Financial Health Network has its own categories to define financial health and how it relates to financial resilience. It says financial health is "a person's ability to save, spend, borrow, and plan"—and there are eight indicators of financial health.

You're deemed to be financially healthy if you:

- Save
  - You have sufficient liquid savings; and
  - You have adequate long-term savings.
- Spend
  - You spend less than you earn; and
  - You pay all bills on time.
- Borrow
  - You have manageable debt; and
  - You have a prime credit score.
- Plan
  - You have appropriate insurance; and
  - You plan ahead financially.

How many of those eight areas ring true for you? Do any of them accurately describe your circumstances? If not, read on—because you may not be aware of how outside forces have impacted your ability to achieve financial health and resilience.

Structural Inequality and Systems

The Financial Health Network has found that financial health comes about when the daily systems around you—from your bank to your employer to your health care provider—"help you build resilience and pursue opportunity" over time. This is a key point: systems. No discussion about financial wellness and resilience would be complete if we gloss over the fact that your financial standing is often tied to structural issues in society and the ways in which systems operate to help or impede your financial health. And the truth is, throughout most of America, many systems have built-in barriers for large numbers of the population. This is true for our health care system, the educational system, the financial system, the workplace, the government, and more. In other words, your environment can be a benefit or a barrier when it comes to your resilience.

Case in point: if you struggle to balance your checkbook or find that you're always overdrafting your bank account, you may chalk that up to you running low on funds—or maybe you even blame yourself for allegedly being "bad" with managing your money. But what about the role of the financial institution with whom you're doing business? What if banks—either intentionally or inadvertently—made it harder for some people to avoid getting slapped with fees? As it turns out, that's not just a hypothetical question. It's a fact within the banking world.

Latinos and Black Americans pay more than twice as much in bank fees compared to their white counterparts, according to a recent Bankrate survey. These fees include overdraft charges, ATM fees, and monthly service charges, which can really add up and hurt your wallet. The survey found that the average annual fees for Latinos and Blacks were $190 and $180 respectively, while white customers paid just $78 on average.

Why is this? One reason is that banks in Black and Hispanic neighborhoods in the US often require higher account balances for customers to avoid service fees. The average minimum balance in white neighborhoods was $626, compared with $871 in Black neighborhoods, according to research from McKinsey & Co. In other words: to sidestep fees, you have to keep more money in your checking account if you bank in a Black neighborhood. It's a striking example of financial inequality in the banking system, which makes it even harder for communities of color to build wealth and achieve financial stability. Little wonder that McKinsey partners Shelley Stewart and Jason Wright said in the study: "Black families are being underserved and overcharged by institutions that can provide the best channels for saving."

Another example: assume you're a woman who earns 75 cents on the dollar for what a man makes at your job, and he's doing the same work. Pay inequity is baked into so much of the labor market that of course women with lower salaries find it harder to save than their male counterparts! We'll discuss discrimination more in Chapter 12. For now, however, I want you to think broadly about your own financial health and what systems have helped or hindered you. Reminder: the purpose here isn't to play the blame game. Rather, I want you to be mindful of both your own actions and those of the larger systems in which you operate because these systems have a direct, oftentimes significant impact on your financial health and resilience.

The Financial Health Network groups people into three categories: financially healthy, financially coping, and financially vulnerable. People who are financially healthy are able to manage their day-to-day expenses, absorb financial shocks, and progress toward meeting their long-term financial goals. Unfortunately, more than two-thirds of people in America are classified as financially coping (struggling with some aspects of their financial lives) or financially vulnerable (struggling with almost all aspects of their financial lives).

As you reflect for a moment, consider what has caused you to be in your present circumstances. Would you currently classify yourself as financially healthy, financially coping, or financially vulnerable? Was there a point in your life when you had better financial health than you currently have? Oftentimes, if we can pinpoint when our financial troubles began, it helps us better understand ourselves, including the things we may have done—or failed to do—that led to or compounded our circumstances. None of this is to pass judgment or make you feel guilty. As you read *Bounce Back*, I want you to feel supported and shame-free, even as I help you achieve financial clarity in order to move forward honestly and directly.

No matter which one of the Dreaded Ds you've encountered, some crucial steps will be required to help you build resilience and better cope. In the following chapter, I will focus on 10 core strategies vital to emotional resilience and recovery. But for now, let me give you a quick preview of these core strategies. They include:

1. **Practicing mindfulness:** Practicing mindfulness helps reduce stress, improve emotional regulation, and increase self-awareness, all of which contribute to resilience.
2. **Cultivating gratitude:** Cultivating gratitude can help shift your focus from the negative aspects of your life to the positive, promoting resilience and well-being.

3. **Journaling:** Reflective writing can help process emotions, gain perspective, and identify patterns of thoughts and behaviors, all of which build resilience.
4. **Being patient with yourself:** Developing resilience is a process that takes time and effort. Remember that setbacks are normal and that progress may not always be linear.
5. **Practicing self-compassion:** Treat yourself with kindness and understanding, especially during difficult times. Acknowledge your emotions and allow yourself the space to experience them without judgment.
6. **Seeking professional help:** Sometimes, we need the guidance of a therapist, counselor, financial expert, or professional advisor to help us navigate through challenging situations. Don't hesitate to seek help if you feel overwhelmed or unable to cope.
7. **Staying connected:** Surround yourself with a supportive network of people who can provide encouragement, empathy, and practical assistance when needed. Remember that you are not alone in facing life's challenges.
8. **Focusing on self-care:** Prioritize your physical, mental, and emotional well-being. Engage in activities that bring you joy, relaxation, and a sense of purpose. Regular self-care can help boost your resilience and overall well-being.
9. **Establishing a new money game plan:** Conquer your Dreaded Ds and update your financial life to reflect the reality of your current circumstances.
10. **Creating a financial plan B:** Address a variety of potential what-if scenarios and Dreaded Ds that could affect your finances. Evaluate how you'd tackle each scenario. Also, strategize for the long term to give yourself more economic security and control.

Look closely at these 10 strategies, and you'll notice that only two of them—the final two—are specifically financial in nature. Now, why would a money coach who's trying to tell you how to bounce back financially from various misfortunes only highlight two financial strategies in the recovery journey?

It's because I know that money management is typically only about 20% tied to practical, or the how-to, aspects of personal finances, whereas 80% of it is emotional. Some experts say our emotions account for even more of our financial decisions, habits, and practices.

For example, Nobel Prize–winning psychologist Daniel Kahneman showed in one study that people make financial decisions based 90% on emotions, and just 10% based on logic.

Understanding this aspect of behavioral economics means that I would be doing you a major disservice if I only rattled off a bunch of money-management how-to steps without first addressing the elephant in the room: your mindset and emotional state. Likewise, I would be remiss if I didn't tackle the impact of structural inequality and the numerous ways it impacts your financial well-being. So, throughout this book, I'm going to address the things within your control that you can do personally or emotionally in order to position you to best cope, act, and thrive financially, even in the face of adversity or injustice.

Many Forms of Resilience

As previously mentioned, there's not just one type of resilience. I want to help you develop financial resilience, naturally. But there are actually many forms of resilience, including emotional resilience, social resilience, and physical resilience. And you'll likely need to develop these before developing financial resilience—or at the very least, in conjunction with financial resilience.

Building Emotional Resilience

Emotional resilience is the ability to effectively manage and cope with difficult emotions, such as stress, anxiety, and sadness. Developing emotional resilience is essential for bouncing back from setbacks and maintaining your overall mental well-being. Techniques for managing emotions during adversity include practicing mindfulness, self-compassion, and emotional regulation strategies, such as deep breathing exercises.

Try this out now by doing a powerful exercise: create a self-compassion letter.

Write a Letter to Yourself from the Perspective of a Compassionate Friend

Address your feelings and struggles, and offer support, understanding, and encouragement for your predicament. This exercise helps you acknowledge your emotions, foster self-compassion during challenging times, and offer support and encouragement from the perspective of a compassionate friend.

Here's a step-by-step guide on how to write a self-compassion letter:

Find a Quiet, Comfortable Place to Write

Set aside some time and find a space where you can write without distractions.

Begin with a Friendly Salutation

Address the letter as you would to a close friend, using a warm and caring tone. For example, "Dear [Your Name],"

Acknowledge Your Feelings and Struggles

Describe the difficult situation or emotions you're currently facing. Be honest and specific about what you're going through. For example, "I know you're feeling overwhelmed and stressed because of (insert whatever you're going through)."

Express Understanding and Empathy

Show that you understand the difficulty of the situation and validate your emotions. For example, if you've recently been terminated, you might write: "It's completely normal to feel this way. Losing a job is a significant life event, and it's natural to feel scared and uncertain about the future."

Offer Support and Encouragement

Remind yourself of your strengths and past successes, and express confidence in your ability to overcome this challenge. For example, "You've faced tough situations before, and you've always managed to come out stronger. I believe in your resilience and your ability to get through this difficult time."

Share Practical Advice or Coping Strategies

Suggest concrete steps you can take to cope with the situation or improve your emotional well-being. For example, if you were laid off, you might say: "Consider reaching out to your support network, updating your résumé, and exploring new job opportunities. Also, don't forget to practice self-care and engage in activities that bring you joy and relaxation."

Close the Letter with Kindness and Affirmation

End the letter by reiterating your support and offering a kind, uplifting message. For example, "Remember that you are not alone and you have the inner strength to overcome this challenge. Take care of yourself and be gentle with your heart."

Once you've finished writing the self-compassion letter, read it aloud to yourself or save it to revisit when you need a boost of self-compassion and emotional support. This exercise can be a great tool for building emotional resilience and settling your emotions during unsettling times.

Fostering Social Resilience

Social resilience is the ability to draw on the support and resources of others during difficult times. A strong support network is crucial for overcoming setbacks and maintaining emotional well-being. Building and maintaining a support network requires effort and communication, but the benefits are immeasurable.

Do the following exercise to jumpstart your ability to connect with others and share your experiences. Make a list of at least three trusted people in your life who can provide support during challenging times. Now write down a time and date (no more than a week away) when you will reach out to each person and just be honest about your experiences, feelings, and any specific support you may need. Don't have three people? Even if you have one person, do it.

If you don't have a single family member or friend you can contact, just do an online search for a free support line and talk to the individual on the other end of the phone in an honest, direct manner. You can even use Artificial Intelligence tools such as Replika, which bills itself as the AI app "for anyone who wants a friend with no judgment, drama, or social anxiety involved." Don't scoff at the prospect of engaging AI—and don't balk at using whatever method works for you, whether that's in person, online, by video, phone, or text. Experts such as psychologist and social resilience researcher Michael Ungar emphasize the importance of social support in overcoming adversity. He suggests that strong connections with others can help people access resources and develop skills that promote resilience.

Enhancing Physical Resilience

Maintaining physical health is crucial for developing resilience and coping with adversity. Recall that two of the Dreaded Ds relate specifically to health: disability and disease. But the other Dreaded Ds—for example, debt or divorce—can wind up impacting your health too, in negative ways. A healthy body can better withstand stress and recover from setbacks. So incorporating exercise and relaxation techniques into your daily routine can help you maintain your physical resilience.

Even simple things such as counting your breaths for 30 to 60 seconds can help. Try this exercise now: Find a comfortable sitting position, close your eyes, and take a few deep breaths. Now, inhale slowly through your nose for a count of four, hold your breath for a count of four, and exhale slowly through your mouth for a count of four. Repeat this process for 30 seconds to a full minute, or longer if desired.

In addition to breathing exercises, aim to engage in regular physical activity that you enjoy, such as walking, jogging, yoga, or dancing. Exercise has been shown to reduce stress, improve mood, and increase overall well-being. Moreover, prioritize getting adequate sleep and maintaining a balanced diet, as both play essential roles in supporting physical resilience. Another key aspect of physical resilience is knowing when to seek medical care and following through with recommended treatments. By proactively addressing health issues and taking care of your body, you can better equip yourself to handle life's challenges and bounce back from adversity.

Eventually, you want to develop a daily self-care routine that includes physical activity, relaxation techniques, and adequate sleep. Commit to following this routine for at least one week and observe any changes in your physical or emotional state. Creating a self-care routine for physical resilience can have an enormous impact on your overall outlook and well-being.

Research by Kenneth Ginsburg, a pediatrician and human development specialist, emphasizes the importance of physical resilience in overall well-being. He suggests that a healthy body can better cope with stress and recover from setbacks, promoting resilience in other areas of life.

Recognizing and Embracing Your Strengths

As you can see, a lot of developing resilience is about your perspective in life—your mindset and emotional outlook, as well as your physical status. Admittedly though, your outlook might be far from rosy right now—especially if you've recently grappled with hardship. But here's the thing: no matter what you've been through, you're still alive and kicking. That's an accomplishment in itself because, despite anything you've faced, you somehow managed to get through it! Recognize the power in that. Survival alone means you've had some level of perseverance. So tap into that inner grit and resilience. Even if it means taking two steps forward and one step back.

No one can guarantee that life will always be smooth sailing. In fact, even if you rebound from a major setback or somehow vanquish a huge problem you've been facing, you may still have to use every ounce of grit and tenacity that you can draw upon to soldier on. That's what happened to my former favorite quarterback, John Elway.

Remember that famous comeback story I told you about? After an unforgettable performance and "The Drive" during the 1986 AFC Championship Game, Elway and the Denver Broncos advanced to Super Bowl XXI, held on January 25, 1987. They faced off against the New York Giants, who were led by their quarterback, Phil Simms. Unfortunately, things didn't go as planned for Elway and his Broncos teammates. They started off strong, taking a 10-7 lead in the first half. However, the Giants took control of the game in the second half, with a dominant performance both offensively and defensively. The Giants scored 30 unanswered points, with their defense proving too much for the Broncos's offense to handle.

In the end, the New York Giants won Super Bowl XXI with a decisive 39-20 victory. Phil Simms was named the game's Most Valuable Player (MVP), as he completed 22 of 25 passes for 268 yards and three touchdowns.

Though the outcome definitely wasn't what Elway and the Broncos had hoped for, Elway's career was far from over. Elway was naturally disappointed but remained optimistic about the future. During a post-game interview, he said: "We just couldn't get it going. We had our chances early and didn't take advantage of them. The Giants just played a great game. But we're a young team, and we'll be back."

Elway's comments showed that despite the crushing loss, he recognized the talent and potential of his team. And sure enough, his forward-looking attitude highlighted his leadership and resilience, qualities that would ultimately help him immensely in later years. Elway would go on to lead the Broncos to five Super Bowl appearances in total, eventually winning back-to-back championships in his final seasons, in 1997 and 1998, during Super Bowl XXXII and XXXIII. Those victories solidified Elway's status as an NFL legend.

To his credit, Elway never gave up. If you refuse to give up also, maybe you'll have a powerful testimony to share with someone—making you a legend among your own circle of friends, family, and people in your sphere of influence. Can you picture overcoming adversity and having your own comeback story? That would definitely be something to cheer about.

Resources for Resilience and Grit

1. **American Psychological Association** – Professional organization representing psychologists that promotes resilience through research, education, and practice.
2. **International Resilience Project** – Nonprofit providing resilience training programs for youth, families, and communities.
3. **The Positivity Project** – Provides curriculum and training to build resilience, positive relationships, and emotional skills.
4. **The Resilience Institute** – Offers resilience programs, coaching, and consulting for organizations and leaders.
5. **ACE Interface** – Works to prevent and mitigate adverse childhood experiences (ACEs) by building resilience.
6. **Financial Psychology Institute** – Coaching and resources on the psychology of money and financial resilience.
7. **The Sudden Money Institute** – Coaching for those undergoing financial transitions.
8. **Financial Transitionist Institute** – Training on guiding clients through financial change.
9. **The Financial Resilience Institute** – Canadian organization focused on financial resilience.
10. **The Financial Health Network** – US authority on financial health and resilience.

Chapter 2
Building Your Resilience

"When one door closes, another opens; but we often look so long and so regretfully upon the closed door that we do not see the one which has opened for us."
—Alexander Graham Bell

Now that you have an idea of the various forms of resilience, let's take an even closer look at how you can develop resilience. Specifically, let's explore in detail how you can bounce back from any of the Dreaded Ds using the 10 core strategies I mentioned in Chapter 1.

Strategy 1: Practicing Mindfulness

Mindfulness involves being present in the moment, focusing on your thoughts, emotions, and physical sensations without judgment. This practice can help you become more aware of your reactions to stressors and allow you to respond more effectively. By developing a nonjudgmental awareness of your inner experiences, you can cultivate emotional resilience and better navigate challenging situations.

To start practicing mindfulness, try setting aside a few minutes each day to focus on your breath, observe your thoughts, and engage in grounding exercises. Grounding exercises can include techniques such as body scanning, where you pay attention to each part of your body in a sequential manner, or the 5-4-3-2-1 technique, which involves identifying five things you can see, four things you can touch, three things you can hear, two things you can smell, and one thing you can taste.

You can also explore resources such as guided meditations, apps, or mindfulness courses to deepen your practice. Many people find that joining a mindfulness group or participating in a structured course provides additional support and motivation.

In addition to formal mindfulness practices, try incorporating mindfulness into your daily life by simply paying attention to everyday tasks, such as eating, walking, or washing the dishes. This can help you stay grounded in the present moment and develop a greater appreciation for the simple pleasures in life.

As you cultivate mindfulness, you'll likely notice an increased ability to regulate your emotions, recognize negative thought patterns, and respond to challenges with greater resilience. Over time, these skills will empower you to bounce back from adversity and setbacks, leading to a more fulfilling and emotionally balanced life.

Strategy 2: Cultivating Gratitude

Gratitude can help shift your focus from what's going wrong in your life to what's going right. By acknowledging the positive aspects of your life, you can foster resilience and well-being. Embracing an attitude of gratitude allows you to maintain a balanced perspective during times of adversity and can contribute to improved mental health and overall happiness.

One way to cultivate gratitude is to keep a daily gratitude journal where you write down at least three things you're grateful for each day. This practice helps you intentionally focus on the positive aspects of your life, training your mind to notice and appreciate the good things that often go unnoticed. As you continue to journal, you'll likely find that even small acts of kindness or simple pleasures can become sources of gratitude and happiness.

You can also share your gratitude with others by expressing appreciation for their actions, presence, or support. Not only does this help you cultivate your own sense of gratitude, but it also strengthens your relationships and can create a positive ripple effect. When you express gratitude toward others, they may feel more inclined to do the same, fostering an environment of mutual appreciation and support.

Practicing gratitude meditations is another effective way to develop an attitude of gratitude. During these meditations, you can focus on specific aspects of your life for which you're grateful, or simply bring to mind people, experiences, or objects that bring you joy. As you do this, allow yourself to feel the warmth and happiness that arises from acknowledging the positive aspects of your life.

By cultivating gratitude through journaling, sharing with others, and practicing meditations, you'll be better equipped to handle life's challenges and setbacks. Your increased ability to focus on the positive will help you maintain a sense of perspective, fostering emotional resilience and promoting overall well-being.

Strategy 3: Journaling

Journaling is a powerful tool for processing emotions, gaining perspective, and identifying patterns of thoughts and behaviors that may be holding you back. By expressing your thoughts and feelings on paper, you can gain a deeper understanding of your emotions, develop self-awareness, and track your personal growth. This practice can ultimately contribute to your emotional resilience by allowing you to work through challenging experiences and better understand your reactions to them. Organizational psychologist Benjamin Hardy, who wrote *The Gap and the Gain*, explains in his book that journaling can be a way to help your future self become a better version of who you are today.

To incorporate journaling into your routine, set aside time each day or week to write about your experiences, emotions, and insights. I find that journaling right before bed or right when you wake up in the morning is super helpful to stimulate your writing. But anytime that works for you is fine. Establishing a regular writing practice can help you build emotional resilience over time, as you become more adept at reflecting on and learning from your experiences. Creating a comfortable and quiet space where you can write without distractions may also encourage deeper reflection and make the process more enjoyable.

You can also use journaling prompts to guide your writing and explore different aspects of your emotions or experiences. Prompts might include questions such as, "What did I learn from a recent setback?" or "How can I reframe a negative situation into a positive one?" These prompts can help you delve into specific topics and uncover new insights about yourself and your emotions.

Exploring different writing styles, such as stream-of-consciousness writing or reflective writing, can also enhance your journaling practice. Stream-of-consciousness writing involves putting down your thoughts as they come to you, without worrying about grammar or structure. This method can help you freely express your emotions and uncover deeper feelings that may not be immediately apparent. Reflective writing, on the other hand, involves a more structured approach, where you analyze and draw meaning from your experiences. By trying different writing styles, you can discover the method that resonates with you the most and supports your emotional resilience.

Through consistent journaling, you'll develop a greater understanding of your emotions, thoughts, and reactions to challenges. This self-awareness can help you navigate adversity more effectively, build emotional resilience, and ultimately lead to personal growth and increased well-being.

Strategy 4: Being Patient with Yourself

Developing resilience is a process that takes time and effort, and it's essential to be patient with yourself as you work through setbacks and obstacles. Recognizing that growth and progress don't happen overnight can help you maintain realistic expectations and avoid becoming discouraged by temporary setbacks. Embracing self-compassion and understanding that everyone faces challenges can also support your resilience-building journey.

Remember that progress may not always be linear, and setbacks are normal. Life is filled with ups and downs, and it's crucial to accept that there will be moments when you might struggle or feel overwhelmed. Instead of being harsh or critical of yourself during these times, remind yourself that overcoming adversity is a learning process, and it's natural to experience setbacks along the way.

Give yourself grace and celebrate small victories as you build resilience. Acknowledging and celebrating your achievements, no matter how minor they may seem, can help reinforce your efforts and boost your confidence. By focusing on your progress and the positive steps you've taken, you'll be better equipped to navigate future challenges with greater resilience and a more optimistic mindset.

Strategy 5: Practicing Self-compassion

Self-compassion involves treating yourself with kindness and understanding, especially during difficult times. It's about recognizing your own humanity and being gentle with yourself when you face setbacks, make mistakes, or encounter hardships. Practicing self-compassion can help you develop emotional resilience, as it encourages you to accept and learn from your experiences without becoming overwhelmed by negative emotions.

One part of self-compassion is simply acknowledging your true emotions (not faking it) and allowing yourself the right to feel whatever you feel without judging yourself. It's essential to be honest with yourself about how you're feeling and to understand that experiencing a range of emotions, including negative ones, is a natural part of life. Instead of suppressing or denying your emotions, allow yourself to feel and process them. Recognizing and validating your emotions can help you better understand your needs and develop healthier coping strategies.

Practice self-compassion by speaking kindly to yourself. Just as you would offer words of encouragement or support to a friend or loved one, it's important to be gentle with yourself when you're struggling. Be mindful of your inner dialogue and try to replace negative self-talk with more compassionate and understanding language. Remind yourself that nobody is perfect and it's normal to face challenges and make mistakes. Embracing self-compassion will not only help you better cope with adversity but also support your overall well-being and personal growth.

What if you find it nearly impossible to get rid of that critical voice in your head? The one that tells you something like "I messed up again" or "My life is never going to get better."

Take a few pointers and draw from the insights of Saundra Davis, one of the financial coaching industry's premier authorities. Davis has been practicing mindfulness and self-compassion for 30 years, and for two decades she's headed Sage Financial Solutions, where she's trained more than 2,500 other financial professionals to become certified financial coaches. Among other things, Davis is an Accredited Personal Finance Coach, an International Coaching Federation Master Certified Coach, a financial behavior specialist, and a certified mindfulness teacher. She also holds a master's degree in financial planning and is the former president of the Financial Therapy Association. Based on her wisdom gleaned over many years and her helping countless individuals, I took to heart the advice she shared with me.

For many people, "It can be difficult to start with self-compassion," Davis says, due to the numerous and complex ways we often criticize ourselves, often without even realizing it. "Most of us don't even know when we're being harsh with ourselves," she notes. Davis says we're often "hard on ourselves" because we mistakenly think that being tough on ourselves is how we perform best or get optimal outcomes. In truth, that's not the case. Being overly tough on yourself comes at a cost, she says, and that price is often your mental health. Her solution: start by extending compassion to others first, and practice doing so regularly. That will lay the groundwork for you to better understand what compassion looks like and hopefully eventually treat yourself in a like manner. "The journey to self-compassion often starts with being compassionate to someone else before you work your way back to yourself," says Davis. We'll explore self-compassion throughout *Bounce Back* as we address the Dreaded Ds. Additionally, every chapter of *The Bounce Back Workbook* provides further opportunities for you to engage in specific activities, exercises, and reflections that will support your efforts to become more self-compassionate. Remember, this will help you build emotional and financial resilience.

Strategy 6: Seeking Professional Help

If you feel overwhelmed or unable to cope, don't hesitate to seek the guidance of a therapist, counselor, or financial coach. There is no shame in asking for help, and reaching out to professionals can be an essential step in developing emotional resilience. These experts can provide support, tools, and strategies to help you navigate through challenging situations, process your emotions, and develop coping mechanisms to overcome adversity. Some tips to get started:

Identify the Right Professional for Your Needs

Depending on your specific circumstances and concerns, you may benefit from the guidance of different types of professionals. For example, therapists and counselors can help you address emotional and mental health challenges, while financial coaches or advisors can assist with navigating financial difficulties. Take the time to research and find a professional who specializes in the areas where you need support.

Consider Different Therapy Styles and Techniques

There are various therapeutic approaches that can help you build emotional resilience, including cognitive behavioral therapy (CBT), dialectical behavior therapy (DBT), or acceptance and commitment therapy (ACT). Familiarize yourself with these different methods and discuss them with a potential therapist to determine which approach may be most beneficial for your needs.

Leverage Online Resources and Support Groups

In addition to one-on-one sessions with a professional, you may find it helpful to join online forums and support groups or attend workshops related to your specific concerns. Connecting with others who share similar experiences can offer valuable insight, encouragement, and a sense of community as you work through challenges.

Keep an Open Mind and Be Patient

Developing emotional resilience is an ongoing process, and it's essential to be patient and open to growth. As you work with a professional, you may uncover new insights or be asked to try new strategies that may feel uncomfortable at first. Trust the process and be willing to adapt and grow as you gain a deeper understanding of your emotions and thought patterns.

By seeking professional help when needed, you can access valuable resources and support to build emotional resilience and better navigate life's challenges. Remember that asking for help is not a sign of weakness but rather a proactive step in taking control and reclaiming your life.

Strategy 7: Staying Connected

Surround yourself with a supportive network of people who can provide encouragement, empathy, and practical assistance when needed. Building and maintaining strong social connections is crucial in fostering emotional resilience and helping you navigate life's challenges more effectively.

Here are some ways to stay connected and create a supportive community:

Reach Out to Friends and Family

Make a concerted effort to maintain regular contact with your loved ones, whether through phone calls, text messages, or in-person visits. Share your experiences, listen to their stories, and offer mutual support in times of need. Your friends and family can be valuable sources of advice, encouragement, and understanding.

Join Support Groups or Clubs

Seek out organizations, clubs, or support groups in your area that align with your interests or needs. These groups can offer camaraderie, shared experiences, and valuable advice from others who have faced similar challenges. Participating in group activities can also help you build new friendships and connections.

Engage in Community Activities

Get involved in your local community by volunteering, attending events, or joining social clubs. Not only will this help you build connections with others, but it can also provide a sense of purpose and accomplishment.

Create a Support Network

Identify key individuals in your life who can be part of your support network. These might include friends, family members, colleagues, or neighbors whom you can rely on for emotional support or practical assistance. Make a conscious effort to nurture these relationships, and be there for each other during challenging times.

Maintaining strong connections with others can provide the support and resources you need to bounce back from adversity. Staying connected is a vital component in developing emotional resilience and overall well-being.

Strategy 8: Focusing on Self-care

Prioritize your physical, mental, and emotional well-being. Engage in activities that bring you joy, relaxation, and a sense of purpose. Regular self-care can help boost your resilience and overall well-being. Schedule time for exercise, hobbies, and relaxation to ensure you're maintaining a healthy balance in your life.

Putting a premium on self-care is essential for building resilience and maintaining overall well-being. By focusing on your physical, mental, and emotional needs, you can better navigate adversity and maintain a sense of balance.

Here are 10 tips for incorporating self-care into your daily routine:

Maintain a Balanced Diet

Aim for a diet rich in fruits, vegetables, whole grains, lean proteins, and healthy fats. Proper nutrition fuels your body and supports overall health. Additionally, maintaining a balanced diet can improve your mood, energy levels, and mental acuity. This nutritional balance helps build a resilient body that can weather stress and challenges more effectively.

Stay Hydrated

A lot of people don't drink enough water—even though we all know we should! In fact, nearly half of all Americans (47%) admit they don't take in the recommended amount of H_20, according to a poll by CivicScience. How much is enough? Health experts typically recommend anywhere from 8 to 12 glasses of water each day to avoid dehydration and help prevent problems such as headaches, fatigue, a weakened immune system, and dry skin. Therefore, drink plenty of water throughout the day to keep your body functioning optimally. Adequate hydration also supports digestion, mood, and energy levels. Remember that staying hydrated not only supports physical wellness but also cognitive function, helping you think clearly and make wise decisions. Regular hydration also aids in detoxifying the body and maintaining skin health, contributing to overall wellness.

Get Regular Checkups

Schedule routine medical, dental, and vision checkups to stay on top of your health and address any concerns early. Regular checkups ensure you can catch potential issues before they become serious, providing peace of mind that bolsters emotional resilience. Moreover, it signals to yourself that you're a priority, enhancing your sense of self-worth and well-being.

Stretch and Move

Take breaks throughout the day to stretch, stand up, or walk around, especially if you have a sedentary job or lifestyle. This helps improve circulation, prevent muscle stiffness, and reduce the risk of injury. Regular movement also stimulates the production of endorphins, the body's natural mood enhancers. Plus, these mini-breaks offer mental reprieve, helping you to return to your tasks with renewed focus and energy.

Prioritize Personal Hygiene

Establish a daily routine that includes showering, brushing your teeth, and grooming to maintain cleanliness and overall health. In addition to the physical benefits, a solid personal hygiene routine can enhance your self-esteem and sense of control. These practices not only uphold physical health but also contribute to your overall sense of well-being, affirming your self-worth every day.

Limit Screen Time

Prolonged exposure to screens can lead to eye strain, sleep disruption, and physical discomfort. Set boundaries around screen time and take regular breaks to rest your eyes and move your body. Remember that creating these boundaries contributes to maintaining a healthier life balance and preserving your mental health. Additionally, less screen time encourages more opportunities for meaningful connections and experiences.

Manage Stress

Engage in activities that help you relieve stress, such as yoga, tai chi, or walking in nature. Managing stress can help prevent the development of stress-related physical ailments. Mind-body activities like these not only reduce stress but also build emotional resilience by enhancing mindfulness and present-moment awareness. These practices can further increase feelings of peace and satisfaction, contributing to a sense of purpose and contentment.

Exercise Regularly

Physical activity is crucial for maintaining both physical and mental health. Find an exercise routine that you enjoy and can commit to, whether it's walking, yoga, swimming, or strength training. Regular exercise can stimulate a positive mood, boost your energy levels, and help you maintain a healthy weight. By finding joy in your exercise routine, you're more likely to stick with it, and it becomes an act of self-love rather than a chore.

Get Plenty of Sleep

Having adequate rest is essential for you to function well physically and to have mental clarity too. Develop healthy sleep habits, such as sticking to a consistent sleep schedule and creating a relaxing bedtime routine to improve the quality of your sleep. Optimize your sleep environment by keeping your bedroom cool, dark, and quiet. Limit exposure to screens and stimulants such as caffeine and alcohol close to bedtime. Remember, sufficient sleep allows for the restoration and repair of your body and mind, supporting your resilience. Moreover, it enhances cognitive function, decision-making, and emotional regulation, essential aspects of overall wellness.

Listen to Your Body

Pay attention to any pain, discomfort, or unusual symptoms, and seek medical advice when needed. Be proactive in addressing any physical concerns that arise.

Recognizing and addressing these concerns promptly is not only vital for your physical health but also demonstrates self-respect and responsibility. Tuning into your body's needs and signals fosters a more profound mind-body connection, ultimately aiding in emotional resilience too.

By focusing on these physical self-care tips, you can support your overall well-being and strengthen your capacity for resilience. Remember that taking care of your physical health is an essential aspect of a balanced self-care routine. With consistency, these practices can lead to improved self-confidence and a renewed sense of empowerment, which are critical components of resilience. Keep in mind that every step you take toward self-care is a step toward a stronger, more resilient you.

Strategy 9: Establishing a New Money Game Plan

Recovering from financial setbacks or life-changing events, such as downsizing, divorce, or the death of a family member, requires a proactive approach to managing your finances. Establishing a new money game plan can help you regain control and build a stronger financial future. The tactics you'll need to use will be outlined more explicitly in subsequent chapters, but broadly speaking you'll have to do the following:

Assess Your Current Financial Situation

Begin by reviewing your income, expenses, assets, and liabilities. Gather all relevant financial documents, such as bank statements, credit card bills, and investment accounts, to have a clear understanding of your financial picture. This comprehensive view allows you to make informed decisions and instills a sense of control over your finances. Furthermore, it serves as a strong foundation for any financial rebuilding, empowering you to take proactive steps toward financial resilience.

Create a Monthly Budget

Based on your assessment, develop a realistic monthly budget that accounts for all of your income and expenses. Be sure to include essential expenses, such as housing, utilities, and groceries, as well as discretionary spending, such as entertainment or a gym membership. Adjust your spending habits as necessary to meet your financial goals. A well-managed budget can help prevent financial strain, foster peace of mind, and encourage a sense of responsibility. It also facilitates financial discipline, which is crucial for maintaining long-term financial stability.

Set Financial Goals

Determine both short-term and long-term financial goals that reflect your new circumstances. These might include paying off debt, building an emergency fund, saving for retirement, or investing in your future. Write down your goals and create a plan to achieve them. Having clear financial goals can provide motivation, instill a sense of purpose, and enhance your confidence in managing finances. They also give you a sense of direction, which is crucial during periods of financial uncertainty.

Regularly Check Your Net Worth

Calculate your net worth by subtracting your liabilities from your assets. Monitor your net worth regularly to track your progress and tweak your financial plan as needed. Regularly assessing your net worth helps ensure you're moving in the right direction financially and enables you to respond quickly to any changes. It also provides a tangible measure of your financial growth, fostering a sense of accomplishment and resilience.

Seek Professional Guidance

If needed, consult with a financial advisor, accountant, or attorney to help you navigate complex financial decisions or legal matters. These professionals can provide valuable advice and help you create a tailored financial plan that aligns with your goals. Their expertise can provide reassurance, mitigate potential financial risks, and offer personalized strategies to optimize your financial health. This step emphasizes the importance of leaning on others' expertise when necessary, reinforcing that financial resilience is often a team effort.

Stay Proactive and Adaptable

Recognize that your financial situation will likely change over time, so be prepared to adjust your plan accordingly. Stay informed about financial trends and opportunities, keeping yourself open to making changes to your financial strategy as necessary. A proactive and adaptable approach keeps you prepared for unexpected financial challenges and positions you to seize new opportunities. It also cultivates financial agility, a key aspect of financial resilience.

Maintain Open Communication with Loved Ones

If you share finances with a partner or family members, communicate openly about your financial goals and expectations. Work together to create a shared financial plan that addresses the needs and priorities of everyone involved. Open communication builds trust and understanding, fostering a supportive environment for financial recovery. Additionally, it aligns your collective financial efforts, promoting a sense of unity and shared responsibility.

By having a clear financial plan in place, you can better navigate the ups and downs of your financial journey and bounce back from adversity more effectively. Likewise, staying adaptable and committed to your financial goals empowers you to build a more resilient financial future.

Strategy 10: Creating a Financial Plan B

Building a contingency plan for potential setbacks or unforeseen events is crucial for maintaining financial resilience. By considering various what-if scenarios and formulating strategies to address them, you can better manage financial challenges and minimize their impact on your life. Chapter 11 discusses long-term planning in more detail. But as a preview, here are the overall steps to take to ensure you've created a comprehensive financial plan B:

Identify Potential Risks and Setbacks

Start by listing the possible events that could adversely affect your financial situation, such as job loss, loss of a partner through death, divorce, or separation, illness or disability that leaves you unable to work, or natural disasters such as fires or hurricanes. By acknowledging potential threats, you develop a realistic perspective on what *could* impact your finances. This conscious acknowledgment allows you to devise tailored strategies, fostering a sense of preparedness and diminishing anxiety around unforeseen events. The goal isn't to engage in fearmongering. Rather, you just want to have a healthy assessment of potential risks you may encounter.

Evaluate Your Emergency Fund

An emergency fund is a vital safety net that can help you manage unexpected expenses or loss of income. Aim to save at least three to six months' worth of living expenses in a readily accessible account, such as a high-yield savings account. An emergency fund provides immediate financial relief in crisis situations, preventing the need to incur debt or sell assets. It also adds a layer of security and peace of mind, knowing you're prepared for life's surprises. (Don't let this guidance overwhelm you right now. If you currently have little to no savings, I realize that the prospect of amassing three to six months' worth of your bills may seem daunting, or perhaps impossible. No worries: we'll get to a lack of savings, or dollar deficits—another Dreaded D—in Chapter 11).

Review Your Insurance Coverage

Make sure you have adequate insurance coverage for your needs, including health, life, disability, and property insurance. Regularly assess your policies to ensure they provide sufficient protection and update them as needed. Insurance serves as a critical financial cushion against unexpected losses, protecting your long-term financial well-being. Regular reviews ensure you remain sufficiently protected as your circumstances evolve.

Diversify Your Income Streams

Explore ways to create multiple income sources to reduce reliance on a single job or investment. This could include taking on freelance work, starting a side business, investing in rental properties, or pursuing passive income opportunities. Diversification promotes financial stability and reduces risk. Moreover, it fosters self-reliance and entrepreneurial spirit, key aspects of financial resilience.

Create a Plan for Each Scenario

For each potential setback, devise a plan to address the financial implications. This could include cutting expenses, tapping into your emergency fund, relying on insurance benefits, or leveraging your diversified income sources. Having a prepared response lessens the emotional strain during tough times and speeds up financial recovery. It emphasizes the value of proactive planning, reinforcing your ability to navigate challenging circumstances.

Maintain a Flexible Budget

Build flexibility into your budget to accommodate unexpected changes in income or expenses. This might involve creating separate budget categories for discretionary spending, savings, or debt repayment that can be adjusted as needed. A flexible budget allows you to adapt to financial fluctuations with ease, promoting a more stable financial environment. It also underscores the importance of financial adaptability, a cornerstone of resilience.

Keep your Skills Up to Date

Invest in your personal and professional development to remain competitive in the job market. Stay informed about industry trends, acquire new skills, and maintain a strong professional network. Continuous learning enhances your employability and income potential, creating more avenues for financial stability. It also empowers you to be proactive about your career trajectory, instilling a sense of control over your financial future.

Review and Update Your Plan Regularly

As your financial situation and priorities change, revisit and update your plan B accordingly. This will help ensure that your contingency plan remains relevant and effective. Regular reviews of your plan B help you remain aligned with your evolving financial goals while staying prepared for any potential setbacks. It also encourages an ongoing commitment to financial mindfulness and resilience.

By having a well-thought-out financial plan B in place, you can feel more confident and steadier when faced with financial challenges. Strategize for the long term to give yourself greater economic security and control over your financial future. It's important to remember that this planning not only provides a safety net but also fosters a sense of empowerment, enabling you to approach future challenges with greater assurance.

By implementing these 10 core strategies, you'll be well on your way to developing the resilience needed to bounce back from financial or personal setbacks or mistakes. Remember that the journey to financial resilience is not a one-time event but a lifelong process that requires self-aware reflection, adaptability, and persistence.

This journey teaches you to trust in your ability to overcome financial obstacles, enhancing your self-confidence and promoting a more positive outlook on your financial capabilities. Keep working on these strategies, and you'll find yourself better equipped to handle whatever life throws your way. Your ongoing dedication to these strategies demonstrates a commitment to your financial well-being, reinforcing the value of patience and consistent effort in achieving financial resilience. Ultimately, your willingness to persist through adversity is what will truly prepare you for whatever comes next, allowing you to face the future with confidence.

Resources for Building Resilience

1. **American Institute of Stress** – A leading organization providing resources and education on managing stress and building resilience.
2. **Mental Health America** – Advocacy group dedicated to promoting mental health and resilience through education, support groups, and other programs.
3. **Mindfulness Society** – Nonprofit organization providing mindfulness-based resilience training.
4. **Positive Psychology Institute** – Conducts research and offers services related to positive psychology, gratitude, resilience, and well-being.
5. **National Alliance on Mental Illness (NAMI)** – Grassroots mental health organization with support groups and programs focused on resilience.
6. **Psychology Today** – Magazine and online platform of mental health resources including resilience-related content.
7. **Happify** – Provides activities and games based on positive psychology to reduce stress and build resilience.
8. **Headspace** – Offers guided meditation and mindfulness exercises to boost resilience.
9. **Financial Therapy Association** – Organization of professionals helping clients develop emotional resilience around money.
10. **Financial Psychology Institute** – Coaching on the psychology of money, financial resilience, and well-being.

Chapter 3
Downsized from a Job

"In the middle of difficulty lies opportunity."

—*Albert Einstein*

I'll never forget the day I lost my high-profile job as a television reporter. I had been working as a *Wall Street Journal* reporter for CNBC and I was thriving as a financial journalist. I was doing stellar on-air work. I got along great with my bosses and colleagues, and I loved my career. CNBC's TV audience loved me too.

So what happened? In three words: *money and mischief.*

Dow Jones & Co. was the parent company of the *Wall Street Journal*, and the company had a partnership with CNBC. Under the terms of the deal, Dow Jones sent some of its print reporters (people like me) to work on television and translate financial stories for a TV audience. It was fun stuff. I got to interview all kinds of people: from stockbrokers and analysts to Fortune 100 CEOs and small business owners. But back then, in 2003, Dow Jones was also facing a downturn in advertising. With fewer companies forking over advertising dollars, Dow Jones simply couldn't afford as many employees.

It started with a hiring freeze. Then that hiring freeze extended to a round of layoffs: 200 people were let go in one fell swoop, and I was one of them.

The shocking thing, at least for me, was that I thought I was safe. I had just negotiated a "handshake" deal with my TV boss at CNBC. As part of the deal, I got a bump up in pay, and I received the right to work four days a week—taking off on Fridays to write my first book, called *Investing Success*. Everything was going well for a few weeks until the folks on the TV side wouldn't sign off—in writing—on the verbal deal I struck with my boss. She assured me, though, that the written contract would be forthcoming and that it was merely a formality. But week after week passed, and no contract materialized.

The Handwriting on the Wall

In retrospect, of course, I should've seen the handwriting on the wall. Even more important, I should have never agreed to a verbal deal and failed to immediately get everything in writing. That was a tough lesson. But you can imagine my surprise when, a few months after negotiating the terms of our deal, my boss called me into her office to deliver the bad news.

She was blunt about it, saying: "I'm very sorry to tell you this, Lynnette, but you know we've been under a hiring freeze." I nodded my head yes and remained silent. I wanted to see where she was going with this conversation. In my mind, I was thinking, "Okaaaay. But what does that hiring freeze have to do with me?"

Then she proceeded to tell me that not only was the hiring freeze remaining in force, but the company had to reduce headcount to cut costs, and unfortunately, my job was among the positions being eliminated. This was the *money* aspect of my termination.

I was completely taken aback. Worst-case scenario, I had thought that she might try to back out of our deal and say the higher-ups wouldn't sign off on our deal and we'd have to revert back to my previous pay and normal work schedule. To be honest, the thought of a layoff didn't remotely cross my mind. In my shock, I'm sure I was less than my normal eloquent self. But I managed to stammer out: "But, but what about our deal? That came before the hiring freeze."

Never in a million years did I think she would say what came next.

My boss looked me dead in the eyes, and she uttered two words that sent a chill down my spine: "What deal?" she asked.

I was completely floored. I paused to gather my wits. Then I reminded her of the "handshake" agreement she and I had reached, how I had been getting higher pay and taking off on Fridays—so, clearly, we had a deal.

She just looked at me like I had three heads—as if she didn't know what I was talking about. But she knew. And she knew that I knew! At that moment, however, it became 100% clear what was happening: I was getting nothing because I had nothing in writing. And without a written contract, she definitely wasn't going to go to bat for me—let alone fall on her sword—and tell her bosses that she'd *already* reached a deal with me. She was wrong, but she wasn't willing to right that wrong by advising the company to honor the prior agreement she made with me. This was the *mischief* aspect of my firing.

So in the end, I was out of a job—and quite unceremoniously too, considering the decade-long work I'd done at Dow Jones. It was a bitter pill to swallow.

Now, in all candor, I should say a few things about my situation. First, all the other bosses I had at the company served as great role models and fantastic mentors, and they treated me with the utmost professionalism. Unfortunately, at the tail end of my tenure there, I just had to deal with someone who was less than scrupulous amid a bad economic time for the company in general.

It's also worth noting that I didn't just get the boot immediately; none of us did. Dow Jones gave us a couple of months' notice and a decent severance package too. None of that, however, took away the sting of getting fired.

Downsizing and Layoffs Are Painful—and Widespread—in America

Regardless of whether or not you saw the handwriting on the wall, or got completely blindsided like I did, going through a layoff is not fun. In fact, it's one of the most stressful things you'll probably ever endure. It can shake your confidence and rattle your self-esteem. It can provoke feelings of bitterness or anger. And—as I learned all too well—losing a job can certainly wreak havoc on your finances.

Sadly, though, downsizing is a fact of life in modern America: 40% of Americans say they've been laid off at some point in their careers. Even in the best of times, millions of people get laid off each year in the United States as is evidenced by statistics from the US Bureau of Labor Statistics. According to the BLS, for nearly two decades, from 2002 to 2019, layoffs and discharges topped 20 million every single year. In 2020, the year the COVID pandemic struck, layoffs peaked at 40.8 million. By 2021 and 2022, amid the recovery and pent-up demand for workers, layoffs fell to record lows of 17 million and 15 million, respectively.

The Rise of AI Will Lead to More Job Loss

Unfortunately, layoffs are climbing again, especially as AI rapidly displaces many job functions. No one has a crystal ball. And experts don't agree on exactly how much job loss will occur due to machines replacing humans in the work world.

But one thing is clear: with the rise of large language models such as ChatGPT and other AI tools, the vast majority of industries and jobs stand to be impacted by artificial intelligence.

In its 2023 Future of Jobs report, the World Economic Forum reported that 75% of employers across all sectors plan to adopt and use artificial intelligence in the workplace. As a result, the WEF estimated that 42% of all business tasks will be automated by the year 2027 (up from the current level of 34%). The jobs most at risk, according to the WEF, are clerical or secretarial roles, with bank tellers and related clerks, Postal Service clerks, cashiers, ticket clerks, and data entry clerks expected to be most disrupted by this technology. Workers in these categories alone are projected by the WEF to lose 26 million jobs by 2027. Meanwhile, a 2023 report by the investment bank Goldman Sachs predicted that artificial intelligence could replace the equivalent of 300 million jobs overall globally by the year 2030, including 25% of work tasks in the US and Europe. Additionally, at the Goldman Sachs 2023 Disruptive Technology Symposium in London, the rise of generative AI (e.g. Chat GPT) was touted as a game-changer in AI usage and adoption—a phenomenon more disruptive than the COVID-19 pandemic.

Whether you get downsized due to technology or just terrible luck, losing a job is one of the most severe financial blows you can ever face. The economic impact of getting a pink slip isn't just that you've suddenly lost a steady paycheck. You probably also lost a host of workplace benefits too—anything from health care and dental coverage to commissions, annual bonuses, stock options, or retirement contributions from your employer. As a result of these financial shortfalls, downsizing can often lead to a string of other personal problems, such as big medical bills or credit card debt that you run up while you try to get by with little to no cash flow. As if the financial consequences of being laid off weren't bad enough, you must also confront two other hurdles: you need to cope with the emotional sting of being let go, and you need to find new employment. In the face of such adversity, it's understandable that your finances have taken a hit in the wake of downsizing. Fortunately, you can engineer an emotional, financial, and career comeback after losing a job.

In this chapter, you will learn:

- How to deal with shock, anger, or other emotions tied to getting fired;
- Healthy habits to diminish negative emotions and focus on proactive solutions;
- Three crucial financial steps you must take in the wake of job loss;
- Interim economic moves to make to surviving a downsizing;

- The best career reentry strategies to find new employment;
- Whether or not you should quit looking for a job—and opt for entrepreneurship.

The Emotional Aspects of Job Loss

For those of us who have been downsized, it's crucial to first face the emotional side of a layoff. Recruiters, outplacement specialists, and career coaches say one of the biggest mistakes many professionals make after being downsized is to try to immediately leap back into the job market without addressing the emotional blow they've just experienced. When people automatically start looking for work again, "They see job descriptions and they start looking at all the ways that they're not a fit for certain positions. Then the negative cascade starts flowing," says Maggie Mistal, a life purpose and career coach of 20 years and a speaker on career-related topics.

In the early phase of job loss, it's natural to feel a range of emotions—anything from grief, betrayal, or shock to anger, sadness, and anxiety. So give yourself permission to feel these emotions without judgment, as acknowledging them is a crucial step in processing and moving forward. Facing your emotions and processing them is far better for you—in the short and long run—than glossing over the emotional hit from a job loss or just ignoring how you truly feel. Without taking the time to assess your emotions you may inadvertently amplify the blow of being downsized—and even hurt your chances of gaining a satisfying new position. Read on to discover why.

The Psychological Contract

Although I was pretty salty about how I was treated by my last boss, the truth is: even if I had a written contract, it's possible I still could have been let go from my job. Plenty of people have had contracts in black-and-white and been terminated, nonetheless.

And when employees face abrupt departures, they often find it hard to wrap their heads around things because not only was a potential written contract broken, but a psychological contract has been shredded too.

The psychological contract refers to the unwritten set of expectations, beliefs, and obligations that exist between an employer and an employee. It goes beyond the formal, written employment contract and encompasses the more implicit understanding of what each party expects from the other in the employment relationship.

The psychological contract can include aspects such as job security, career development opportunities, work-life balance, fair treatment, trust, and respect. It plays a significant role in employee engagement, job satisfaction, commitment, and loyalty to the organization.

When the psychological contract is perceived to be fulfilled or exceeded, employees are more likely to be motivated, engaged, and committed to their organization. Conversely, if the psychological contract is seen as broken or unfulfilled, it can lead to feelings of betrayal, mistrust, and overall dissatisfaction.

The concept of the psychological contract was first introduced in the 1960s by organizational psychologist and behavioral scientist Chris Argyris, who was a professor at various universities throughout his career, including Yale University and Harvard Business School. However, the psychological contract theory was later popularized and further developed by Denise Rousseau in the 1980s and 1990s. Rousseau is now a professor at Carnegie Mellon. Her work on the psychological contract has been extremely influential in shaping our understanding of the complex relationship between employees and employers.

Obviously, when you get laid off, the psychological contract between you and your employer is totally disrupted. This often leads to a host of negative feelings, since your expectations about job security, fair treatment, and support from the organization are no longer met. The implications and effects that you experience as a result of a broken psychological contract can be quite profound, including:

Betrayal: You may have believed that your hard work, dedication, and loyalty to the company would be rewarded with job security and a long-term career. When a layoff occurs, it can feel like your employer didn't hold up their end of the bargain, leading to a deep sense of betrayal.

Mistrust: Trust is an essential component of the psychological contract, as employees rely on their employers to provide a stable work environment and treat them fairly. When a layoff occurs, you may question the company's motives, honesty, and transparency, leading to a lingering sense of mistrust that can affect your future employment relationships.

Disappointment: Employees often have expectations for career growth, opportunities for professional development, and a supportive work environment. When you're laid off, these expectations are shattered, often (but not always) leaving you feeling disappointed and disillusioned with the organization you once trusted.

Loss of identity: For many people, their job is closely tied to their identity and sense of self-worth. A layoff can lead to a loss of identity, as you're forced to reevaluate your professional standing and career trajectory.

Emotional turmoil: The impact of the broken psychological contract is not limited to feelings of betrayal, mistrust, and disappointment. It can also trigger a range of other emotions, including anger, sadness, fear, and anxiety, as you grapple with the uncertainty of your future and the implications of the layoff on your personal and financial well-being.

Impaired future relationships: The experience of a broken psychological contract can have lasting effects on your approach to future employment relationships. You may become more cautious and skeptical, less likely to trust employers, and more vigilant in seeking out formal contractual agreements to protect yourself from potential future disappointments.

Coping Strategies to Help

To cope with the emotional ramifications of job loss, this is where the core strategies explained in Chapter 2 can be of enormous value. Here's how to put some of those ideas into practice as you process the sting of being let go by an employer.

Being Patient with Yourself

After losing a job, it's essential to acknowledge that finding a new position or adjusting to a new career path may take time. Be patient with the process and give yourself space and permission to explore new opportunities without rushing into decisions. During this process, set realistic expectations too. Recognize that even if you get interviews or job offers, they may not be your ideal positions; your dream job may take time and effort. So be patient with yourself and stay focused on your job search goals, even if progress seems slow.

Practicing Self-compassion

Remind yourself that job loss is a common experience, and it doesn't define your worth or abilities. Treat yourself with kindness and understanding, just as you would a friend in a similar situation. Tell yourself that your value as a person is not solely determined by your employment status because you truly are more than a job or title. Try to avoid harsh self-criticism that lacks empathy; that just feeds into a negative cycle of thinking or counterproductive actions. It can also help to reframe your thoughts. Replace negative thoughts with more balanced, constructive ones. For example, instead of thinking, "I'll never find another job," remind yourself that job loss is a temporary setback and many people have successfully rebounded from similar situations.

Seeking Professional Help

After losing a job, consider seeking the assistance of a career counselor or job coach to help with résumé building, interview skills, and identifying new job opportunities. You might also consult a financial advisor to help you reassess your financial situation and plan for the future.

Staying Connected to Others

Contact former colleagues, friends, and family for emotional support, job leads, or networking opportunities. Joining professional associations, attending industry events, or participating in job search groups can also help you stay connected and expand your professional network. At the same time, stay connected with those close to you outside of the job world. Share your feelings with caring friends, family, or even a mental health professional who can provide emotional support, understanding, and guidance. Talking about your experience can help you process your emotions and gain perspective on your situation.

Prioritizing Self-care

Although you may just want to curl up under the covers and stay in your pajamas all day, fight the urge to do that once you've processed your emotions around being downsized. A better strategy is to look after yourself emotionally and physically. Maintaining a daily routine can provide a sense of stability and control in uncertain times. As you develop a self-care routine, engage in activities that help you manage stress and promote emotional well-being, such as regular exercise, meditation, or spending time on hobbies you enjoy. Try to partake in activities that bring you joy or that are calming too, such as taking in free comedy shows or spending time outdoors in nature. Prioritize rest and a balanced diet to support your physical well-being too.

By following these suggestions, you can learn to cope with the shock, anger, and other emotions tied to job loss and start building resilience to overcome this setback.

Three Crucial Financial Steps in the Wake of Job Loss

As you're assessing your career standing and dealing honestly with your emotions, you may be naturally experiencing stress or anxiety over financial matters. You don't have to wait to address some money-related issues. In fact, it's wise to tackle a few important chores as soon as possible when you get notice of a layoff. Here are three crucial financial steps to take in the wake of job loss to help you regain stability and better prepare for the future.

Review and Adjust Your Budget

Examine your current financial situation and create a revised budget based on your new circumstances. Identify areas where you can reduce spending and prioritize essential expenses, such as housing, utilities, and food. Cut back on nonessential expenses such as dining out, entertainment, or luxury items to conserve resources during this transitional period. As you review and adjust your financial priorities, prioritize paying off debt that may be sapping your cash flow. Above all: don't make the mistake of continuing your prior regular spending patterns based on the idea that you'll quickly land a new job. The sooner you make the necessary adjustments to your monthly spending, the stronger you'll be financially—even if a good-paying position comes along relatively quickly. A revised budget will also help you maintain financial control and make informed decisions amid economic uncertainty.

Apply for Unemployment Benefits

As soon as possible after losing your job, file for unemployment benefits to help provide a temporary source of income while you search for new employment. There's no federal unemployment program. You'll need to apply through your state. Eligibility and benefit amounts vary by state, so visit your state's unemployment agency website or contact their office to learn more about the application process and requirements. Generally, most states require that you've worked and earned at least a specified minimum during the past 12 to 24 months and that you are now actively looking for a new job.

Build or Maintain an Emergency Fund

If you don't already have one, work toward building an emergency fund to cover at least three months' worth of living expenses. This fund will provide a financial safety net during your job search and help you avoid taking on additional debt. Don't know where to begin? To come up with some quick cash, start by selling stuff you no longer want, need, or use: electronics, household furniture, clothes, and so on. Get rid of things in your basement, attic, garage, or elsewhere, and use the money raised to put into a savings account. If you already have an emergency fund, reassess the amount to ensure that it's adequate for your current situation and adjust your budget to maintain or grow the fund as needed.

By focusing on these crucial first financial steps, you'll better manage your finances, minimize the impact of job loss, and diminish economic stress once you begin your search for new employment opportunities.

Interim Economic Moves to Survive a Downsizing

In any labor market, it can sometimes be difficult to find the best-fit job. So if you find that your job search drags on for longer than anticipated, you should also be prepared to adopt additional money moves to shore up your finances and keep you and your family afloat. Here are some suggestions for interim economic moves you can make to survive a downsizing until finding new employment.

Explore Freelance or Gig Work

Depending on your skill set and industry, consider taking on freelance projects or gig work to generate income while searching for a full-time job. This can also help you build connections and expand your professional network.

Consider Temporary or Part-time Employment

While it may not be your ideal job, taking on a temporary or part-time position can provide financial stability and fill the gap until you find full-time employment.

Investigate Government Assistance Programs

Depending on your situation, you may qualify for programs such as the Supplemental Nutrition Assistance Program (SNAP) or Medicaid, which can help cover essential expenses while you're out of work. Based on the cost of living, the US Department of Agriculture Food and Nutrition Service adjusts SNAP benefits at the beginning of every fiscal year, which starts October 1.

For 2024, here are the maximum SNAP benefits allotted to a family of four, according to the USDA website:

- 48 states and DC: $973
- Alaska: $1,248 to $1,937
- Hawaii: $1,759
- Guam: $1,434
- US Virgin Islands: $1,251

SNAP benefits won't cover all your food costs, but they can ensure you and your family won't go hungry in the wake of job loss. Don't be too proud to apply or inquire to see if you qualify.

Consider Refinancing or Consolidating Debt

If you have high-interest debt, such as credit card balances or student loans, explore refinancing or consolidating options to lower your monthly payments and interest rates.

Tap into Savings Cautiously

If necessary, use your savings to cover essential expenses, but be cautious not to deplete your emergency fund or long-term savings completely.

Negotiate with Creditors

If you're struggling to make payments on loans or credit cards, contact your creditors to discuss options for temporary relief, such as reduced payments or forbearance.

Seek Professional Financial Guidance

Consult with a financial advisor, credit counselor, or career coach for personalized advice on managing your finances and job search strategy during this challenging time.

Again, you may or may not need to take any of these steps while you're in between jobs. But if you even remotely think that you'll need extra financial support or resources, don't hesitate to implement whatever actions are necessary to better navigate the financial challenges associated with downsizing.

Job Hunting the Right Way

With the emotional matters addressed and the financial considerations tended to, now you can reasonably move forward with job hunting the right way.

Based on her two decades of experience working with job hunters and employees of all kinds, Mistal, the career coach, recommends a strategy that boils down to three facets: soul search first, research next, and then job search. Using this framework, Mistal authored a book entitled *Are You Ready to Love Your Job: Making a Great Living through Soul Search, Research and Job Search*.

Here's what it means to do soul search, research, and job search, according to Mistal:

Soul search: Ask yourself: if you could wave a magic wand and get what you wanted, what would that look like? Don't be beholden to anything. Take the best of your past experiences forward. But if anything wasn't the best, don't bring it with you in your next job or career. While soul searching, take a multifaceted view of what you want in a career. "Sure, people want to consider salary, their commute, and title," Mistal says. "But also think of things like the skills you love to use; having purpose, meaning or impact; and the creativity involved in a job." From the lofty to the practical, Mistal encourages people to write out their ideal job description—even if it's ever been done before.

Research: The goal here is to find people in the space you want to work. "If you've been in accounting but always had an interest in technology, go do an information interview with someone in tech. The info interview is one of my favorite tools and it really works," Mistal says. They let you really see what a job or career path looks like, allowing you to "look before you leap," she adds.

Job search: As mentioned earlier, resist the urge to immediately job hunt after a layoff. When you're ready, have an action plan that includes your own narrative about why you're a fit for specific positions. Most of all, Mistal suggests using the best channels for getting hired.

"Job postings are 'the front door.' If you're knocking on the front door and you're not getting any answers, don't assume they don't want you in the house. Just knock on the back door—and the info interview is a good back door," she notes.

You're more likely to create an advantage for yourself if you can get someone in the job or industry to give you feedback during an informational interview—which may entail everything from what it's like to work at a given place to them walking your résumé to the right hiring manager. "A lot of jobs are still landed by referral. That hasn't changed. If your résumé is getting lost, change your approach," Mistal advises.

10 Best Career Reentry Strategies to Find New Employment

When seeking new employment after a job loss, it's important to use effective career reentry strategies that can increase your chances of success. Career coach Rob Barnett, the author of *Next Job, Best Job*, says that after a layoff, "You've got to reassess, re-position, and redefine who you are." Your ability to clearly demonstrate your uniqueness, and stand out among other applicants, will be key in landing the next position, according to Barnett.

Dawid (David) Wiacek, an executive coach, career coach, and résumé writer who runs Career Fixer LLC, agrees. But he also says to be prepared to *not* get a job you might desperately want, because that's part of the process and you may not have been best suited for the role. To deal with this reality, Wiacek recommends the following process: reflect, analyze, improve.

Reflect, Analyze, and Improve Your Way to a New Job

According to Wiacek, there's a chance that you didn't land the job because, contrary to your self-assessment, your performance during the interview process was less than ideal, or perhaps just not quite as strong as the selected candidate's. So give yourself some time to reflect on your interview experience and identify areas where you can enhance your skills. Also, be sure to analyze the details of the interview and how you came across. Did you confidently and smoothly respond to behavioral questions? Were you able to provide ample, solid examples of relevant abilities? Did you engage the interviewer(s) with numerous insightful queries? Did you maintain enthusiasm and professionalism throughout the entire process?

If you built a good connection with your interviewers and plan to send a thank-you email (which you should), Wiacek recommends asking them for one piece of feedback, such as what stood out most about your application, or where should you concentrate your efforts to refine your interview techniques for future opportunities. While you might not always receive a direct response, it could be enlightening if you do. Analyze closely any feedback and take it to heart because it reflects how others see you and provides a chance for further self-analysis or growth. If you're a true professional, Wiacek says, you possess the ability to recognize your own limitations and actively strive to overcome them. Each interview should serve as an opportunity to refine and improve how you communicate your value to a potential employer.

Nicknamed "A Ted Lasso for your career," Wiacek is a tough-but-kind executive coach who says that if you do land an offer right away, it may not be the one you should take.

"Decision-making suffers if you're in desperate mode, so give yourself as much time as you reasonably can to find a good fit," he recommends. "Jumping back into the first company that gives you an offer is akin to a rebound in dating—chances are it might not last. Spend time carefully plotting out what you want and need in your next job, and weigh carefully whether the job offer meets those needs," he says.

On the other hand, Wiacek notes that if you've been out of the workforce for too long and a mediocre offer lands in your lap, "don't be afraid to say yes and think of it as a temporary solution. If you need to pay the bills/rent and you're actually desperate for a job, sometimes taking a non-ideal job for the short term can help allay your financial worries so that you can reset and refocus on finding a better job."

Besides, he adds, there is some truth to the fact that you are more employable or desirable to recruiters when you're currently employed. Just know that if you end up taking a temporary job and it becomes all-consuming, it can actually backfire "because you won't have enough time or energy to look for other jobs," Wiacek cautions.

In addition to these tips, here are the 10 best strategies Barnett, Wiacek, and other career experts suggest for those looking to reenter the job market:

Update Your Résumé and LinkedIn Profile

Ensure your résumé and LinkedIn profile are up-to-date, highlighting your most recent experience, skills, and accomplishments. Tailor your résumé for each job application to align with the specific requirements and keywords of the job posting. "Define yourself clearly at the top of your LinkedIn and at the top of your resume," Barnett says, and cut out everything else unrelated to the positions you're seeking. Don't make the mistake, he warns, of including information about a "survival job" you took on just to make ends meet while you were job hunting. If part-time work or a temporary position you assumed isn't relevant to the job or career you're aiming for, omit it from your résumé.

Network the Right Way

Reach out to friends, family, former colleagues, and professional associations to let them know you're in the job market. Networking can uncover job opportunities that may not be publicly advertised and can lead to referrals or job interviews. Remember, your network of friends, former colleagues, or professional associates can be great resources for potential job leads or desirable contract-based work. A word of caution about tact, however: "Don't hound people, don't pester them, don't constantly ask for job leads and help," Wiacek says. It's important to give of yourself, not just take. You can "donate" your ear, you can listen, mentor, or volunteer. "Catch up with old friends and colleagues, keep the relationship warm throughout your life—don't just reach out when you need something (like a job), because people will sense that, and they might resent you because it feels very transactional," Wiacek notes. So always cultivate relationships, even when you're happily employed.

Enhance Your Skills

Identify gaps in your skill set and pursue relevant courses, certifications, or workshops to make yourself a more attractive candidate. This demonstrates your commitment to continuous learning and staying current in your field.

"If you lack a college degree, don't let that stop you," Wiacek says. He recommends taking free or low-cost courses online, whether they be self-led or instructor-led. "Learn a new piece of software or two. And add those certifications or courses to your resume as Continuing Education or Professional Development."

Practice Your Interview Skills

Prepare for job interviews by researching common interview questions, practicing your responses, and refining your communication skills. Be ready to discuss your job loss in a positive and professional manner if asked.

Set Daily Job Search Goals

Establish specific, measurable goals for your job search, such as the number of applications to submit or networking connections to make each day. This will help you maintain focus and momentum.

Create a Job Search Plan

Develop a structured plan for your job search that includes researching target companies, setting application deadlines, and following up on applications and networking leads.

Use Job Search Engines and Online Resources

Take advantage of online job search engines, company career pages, and industry-specific job boards to identify job openings in your field.

Attend Job Fairs and Networking Events

Participate in job fairs, industry conferences, and networking events to meet potential employers, expand your professional network, and learn about job opportunities. "Practice your networking, listening, and small-talk skills. Get your head back in the game," Wiacek advises.

Leverage Social Media

Use social media platforms such as LinkedIn, Twitter, and Facebook to research companies, connect with professionals in your industry, and stay informed about job openings and industry trends.

Stay Persistent and Positive

Job hunting can be challenging, so maintain a positive attitude, stay persistent, and remain open to new opportunities. Remember that setbacks are a natural part of the job search process, and resilience is key to success. One way to stay positive is to focus on what you can control: Although you can't change the fact that you were downsized, you can control how you respond to the situation. Focus on actions that can improve your prospects, such as updating your résumé, networking, and acquiring new skills.

By incorporating these career reentry strategies, you'll boost your chances of finding new employment and successfully transitioning to a new position.

Should You Look for Another Job at All?

For some of you, however, you may not want to find another job at all. Perhaps you've always wanted to start a business or run your own company. Maybe you even dreamed of operating an enterprise that's totally outside your previous line of work—or that's in a different industry but that allows you to fully leverage your past work experience.

That's what worked for Dawn Kelly, who successfully transitioned to entrepreneurship after a long career in public relations. Dawn was living a very comfortable life working at Prudential in Newark, New Jersey, making more than $300,000 a year. But in September 2015, after 16 years at Prudential, her world came crashing down. During her normal commute from her Queens, New York, residence to New Jersey, Dawn received an early-morning message that she should report first thing to her new boss on the company's sixth floor. "I knew immediately what that meant," Dawn recalls. "I did PR for the company. Whenever Pru let somebody high-level go, they always sent them to the 6th floor."

After being terminated, Dawn was left reeling with feelings of failure and despair. She couldn't help but ask herself, "Why me? What did I do wrong?" She had always had excellent performance reviews. In fact, she was an award-winning PR executive. Nonetheless, after a recent change in management, her new boss was getting rid of people like her, who'd been hired by the previous boss. The following months were filled with pain as she questioned her self-worth and struggled to find her footing. Dawn was in a dark place, feeling like a failure not only professionally but also personally. She worried that her family was laughing at her and judging her for losing her job. She fell into a deep depression, barely able to get out of bed or face the world. She began to withdraw from her loved ones, consumed by her own self-pity and doubt.

"It was horrific," Dawn says, adding that the layoff "hit me like a ton of bricks."

"I had no indication it was coming. I was doing my job well, traveling for the company. They were paying for professional memberships for me and everything," she continues. "After being fired, I just couldn't get out of my bed. I think I stayed in my bed for about two months. I was just so sad."

A Pivotal Turning Point

One day, Dawn's daughter, who was then 26 years old and seeing her mother's downward spiral, decided it was time to intervene. "My daughter came into my room, and she said to me very point-blank: 'You're not going to like what I have to say,'" Dawn remembers. "She then said: 'If you can find my mother, can you ask her to contact me, because I don't know who you are. My mother is a fighter, and I just don't know who you are."

That conversation became a pivotal turning point in Dawn's journey, fueling her to channel her energy into something productive and life-changing. She realized that she had the power to change her circumstances and that she owed it to herself and her family to do so. She became determined to pick herself up and fight to regain her emotional happiness, financial security, and career bliss.

After doing some serious reflecting about what she really wanted in life, Dawn decided she never wanted to have a boss again, and that she wanted to open a juice bar in her neighborhood. She'd always loved fruits and vegetables and tried to be healthy her whole life. And she knew nothing like what she envisioned was available in her urban community.

"To be honest, everybody thought I was crazy, and people told me that it wasn't going to work," Dawn says.

Despite having no experience running a company, Dawn signed up for business classes and started learning everything she could about entrepreneurship. In 2017, with the knowledge and confidence she had gained, Dawn opened The Nourish Spot, a healthy juice, smoothie, salad, soup, and yogurt parfait bar in Queens, New York. Coincidentally, Dawn officially opened the doors to her new business on Sept. 9, 2017—two years to the day after her firing from Prudential.

"I did not plan it at all," she says. "It actually hit me that morning when all my friends were outside at The Nourish Spot, and we were about to do the ribbon cutting. They were telling me to come out. I looked at the date and I was like, 'Oh my God,'" because she realized her newfound start in business coincided with the fateful day she was let go by her former employer.

The Nourish Spot has since become a thriving business, expanding to include concessions at the US Open and Citi Field, the baseball stadium that is home to Major League Baseball's New York Mets team. With each step, Dawn's confidence and accomplishments have grown. In 2022, she was seated as one of the first members of the Mayor of New York City's Small Business Advisory Commission. The commission helps make things better for entrepreneurs and small business owners throughout New York City and is a way for Dawn to pay it forward to others. Dawn also recently enhanced her skills further by being selected for and completing the Goldman Sachs 10K Small Business program. She calls it "one of the best things that ever happened to me" as it helped her further clarify her business goals and objectives. In 2024 and beyond, she now has ambitious plans to grow The Nourish Spot brand further by bottling their signature dressings and juices, as well as franchising and opening locations in airports.

Through it all, Dawn has found strength and purpose. She says the three most rewarding aspects of her new business are that she gets to work with her adult children at The Nourish Spot; she employs young people in her community; and, not coincidentally, she taps into her vast knowledge as a former PR executive to build awareness of a company she owns and loves.

"I get to utilize my over 30 years of PR and marketing experience to push my brand forward," Dawn says with a smile. "Who knew that all those years of publicizing things—for Prudential, and at my previous employers, AARP and York College—that I would end up using those same skills to make the world know what we're doing at The Nourish Spot? I'm really proud that I've come full circle."

Today, she is a symbol of resilience, perseverance, and triumph, having overcome her personal and professional challenges. Dawn's story serves as an inspiring example for anyone facing a challenging setback. "I've been through the fire," she says. But she never let fear hold her back. "Everything I've done, I did it afraid," she says.

"Do it afraid," she advises those who have been downsized or are considering starting their own businesses. "Now it's time to get paid to do what you love."

Is Entrepreneurship Right for You?

Although many people say they'd love to become their own boss, the truth is that not everyone is cut out for entrepreneurship. No one path is the right solution for all of us. But if you're weighing the prospect of making the leap from employee to entrepreneur, here are five factors to consider in evaluating whether or not you should quit looking for a job—and choose to become a small business owner instead:

1. **Passion for your idea or industry:** If you have a strong passion for a particular business idea or industry, entrepreneurship might be a better fit. This passion can drive your motivation, creativity, and commitment to overcome the challenges of starting and running a business.

2. **A desire for autonomy and control:** If you value having greater control over your work, decision-making, and professional growth, entrepreneurship could be the right path. As a small business owner, you have more autonomy to shape your company's direction, culture, and priorities.
3. **Willingness to take risks:** Starting a business involves taking financial and personal risks. If you're comfortable with uncertainty and have the resilience to bounce back from setbacks, entrepreneurship might be a better option for you than traditional employment.
4. **Strong problem-solving and decision-making skills:** Entrepreneurs often face unexpected challenges and need to make tough decisions quickly. If you have strong problem-solving and decision-making skills and can adapt to changing circumstances, you may thrive as a small business owner.
5. **Financial readiness:** Before embarking on entrepreneurship, assess your financial situation and determine if you have the necessary resources or access to capital to support your business idea. If you're in a position to invest in your business and can manage financial risks, entrepreneurship might be a viable option.

If some of these factors resonate with you, it's worth considering entrepreneurship as an alternative to traditional employment. However, be sure to conduct thorough research, assess your overall readiness, and seek advice from experienced entrepreneurs or professionals before making this decision.

Whether you'd like to secure a new job or pursue entrepreneurship after being downsized, *The Bounce Back Workbook* can help you regain your career footing. Be sure to utilize the *Workbook* for a host of personalized reflections, checklists, and additional insights that will help you work-wise and emotionally. The *Workbook* can also aid you no matter what stage you're in since it has customized activities for you to perform that cover three phases: "Understanding and Processing Job Loss," "Preparing for the Job Search," and "Initiating a Job Search."

Like Dawn, I've found entrepreneurship to be incredibly satisfying, and I've never looked back. Did I miss my old job at CNBC? Yes, somewhat, initially. But I've had the good fortune to go back on CNBC and other TV networks, not as an employee, but as a business owner and personal finance expert many times since then. In fact, I also had a full-circle moment when two decades after my 2003 departure, I was invited to come on CNBC as a guest expert and explain to their audience how I had achieved a perfect 850 FICO credit score—a feat accomplished by only 1% of Americans each year.

Things like that don't surprise Maggie Mistal, the career coach. "A layoff pushes people in new directions, and it winds up being something you never expect in terms of growth and progress," she says. "It's very hard at first," she notes. "But in the big picture, you're going to look back later and be grateful for this moment. This job loss really is a blessing in disguise. I've seen it over and over again."

Downsized from a Job Resources

1. **AARP** – Provides resources for older adults facing job loss, career shifts, and retirement.
2. **Alzheimer's Association** – Support for caregivers leaving jobs due to responsibilities.
3. **American Jobs Centers** – Free federal job search assistance, training referrals, and career counseling.
4. **CareerOneStop** – US Department of Labor program for job seekers.
5. **CareerPivot** – Company providing outplacement services after job loss.
6. **Institute for Career Transitions** – Nonprofit helping with job changes and transitions.
7. **Jobs for the Future** – Organization focused on skills and credentials development.
8. **National Career Development Association** – Connects job seekers with career counselors and coaches unions.
9. **SCORE** – Provides free mentoring and business advice to aspiring entrepreneurs.
10. **State workforce development agencies** – Help for dislocated workers in every state.

Chapter 4
Divorce

"Life is full of bumps and bruises, but it's how you bounce back that matters most."
—*Dolly Parton*

The first time I got married, I was barely 24 years old. I thought I knew what I was getting into. But boy was I wrong! Looking back now, I call my early 20s my "young and dumb" phase. I really didn't have a clue what was required to have a healthy marriage, nor, in my opinion, did my ex-husband. Nonetheless, we got married completely convinced that our marriage would last forever. Some 13 years later, we were sitting in divorce court trying to undo what clearly wasn't working. In the interim, a host of problems had emerged: everything from communication issues, philosophical quarrels, and religious differences to emotional distance, sex problems, and money woes.

The bottom line is we weren't compatible and probably never really were. But the rose-colored glasses and the "in love" feelings we initially experienced made us think that would be enough. Obviously, it wasn't. With each passing year, we seemed to grow apart, with me diving into work and him focusing on pursuing a graduate degree. We became more like roommates than spouses, and even two rounds of marriage counseling didn't help.

One big challenge emerged early on and grew more intense over time: my former spouse is named Akil, and he was and is very Afrocentric, meaning he has a perspective and outlook that emphasizes the importance of African culture, history, and values—often as a means to promote self-awareness, cultural pride, and empowerment among people of African descent. This approach seeks to center African experiences as kind of a counterbalance to mainstream white or Eurocentric perspectives. At the time, that was part of what drew a wedge between us. A year after we got married, Akil got accepted to the University of Pennsylvania, where he planned to earn a PhD in sociology, with an emphasis in race relations and social stratification. He would later spend a semester studying in South Africa (where I joined him too) at the University of Pretoria, and that further cemented his ideas about the role of racism and its harmful impact on virtually every aspect of life, globally, but especially in the United States.

I share this information because my ex's Afrocentric philosophy often became a sticking point for us. I felt that he saw the world purely in racial terms, in Black and white, and I didn't view the world that way. We'd occasionally have arguments where I would say: "Why do you think race is a factor in *everything*?" and he'd reply, "Because it *is*." Ironically, with some distance and maturity, I now mostly agree with him—especially in the wake of the racial reckoning that emerged in America, and worldwide, following the brutal police killing of George Floyd. But certainly, at the time when we were married, Akil's outlook irked me tremendously, in part because of how his views played out in our relationship.

For example, my ex wanted me to change a slew of things I wasn't willing to change—everything from my clothes and my hair to my name and my career. Specifically, he wanted me to wear traditional African attire and to sport braids or locks, as opposed to wearing my hair in a straightened "European style." He also urged me to adopt a traditional African first name and to switch careers, because he thought that teaching people about money wasn't Afrocentric enough. He told me once in couples' therapy: "I always pictured you'd have a career that helped Black people more." Dumbfounded, I replied that Black people—of all people—needed to learn about money and personal financial management, given the state of economic affairs for most of us. So I contended that my career actually did help Black people. While I was quite secure in my identity and goals, when these kinds of episodes emerged, I felt as if he thought I wasn't "Black enough."

In any case, by early 2004, I wanted out of the relationship and told him that. Akil didn't want to end the marriage, but I was emotionally done and no longer vested in the marriage at all. In all honesty, I had held on for years mainly to be a dutiful, supportive wife while he earned his PhD. What was supposed to be a five-year joint master's-PhD program turned into 11 long years of study. During those years, hefty doses of community activism on his part slowed his progress, in my opinion. Additionally, during that time, he didn't work (except occasionally as a TA), and I was the sole breadwinner in the family. Along the way, I kept thinking: "I can't just bail because he needs my help and support to complete graduate school." All of this led to a reversal in terms of traditional gender roles, and that didn't help matters either. Nonetheless, in 2004, he finally finished his studies, earning his PhD from Penn. At a party at our home to celebrate his accomplishment, he publicly thanked a host of people—but not me. A close friend later asked me: "Lynnette, were your feelings hurt that Akil didn't even mention you and thank you?" She felt he had slighted me, given my many years of emotional, financial, and even academic support of his efforts. But as it turns out, I was so mentally exhausted by it all that I hadn't even noticed the omission. So I didn't even see his thank-you speech as a slight, although apparently, other people did. By January 2005, I moved out and officially started the divorce process, retaining a mediator—as opposed to us hiring two separate lawyers—in an effort to avoid unnecessary conflict. When we separated, we had a written agreement that covered financial matters and that stated we were each free to live our lives as single, independent people who would be divorcing.

The Financial Cost of My Divorce

I wanted so desperately to get out of what was for me a stressful and emotionally unfulfilling marriage that I was willing to pay whatever it took. I remember telling him: "I know you don't have a job yet, so I'll pay for everything." And that meant, quite literally, everything: car notes, mortgage, our two young kids' private school tuition, food, utilities, the works.

In the beginning, and for years after our divorce was finalized, I paid a boatload of money in alimony and child support. Even though we had joint custody of our children—with the kids living with each of us 50-50—I was forking over big sums to my ex-husband, month after month.

At the peak, in the first seven months after we split up, I shelled out $6,670 per month in child support and alimony. My obligations then stepped down over a five-year period, varying from a high of $4,000 a month to a low of $1,200 per month.

Ultimately, my ex and I both remarried—coincidentally, within a week of each other in 2007. Fortunately, we apparently both got it right the second time around. Akil got married on June 30, 2007, to a woman named Sia, who I believe suits him very well. As for me, I married my soulmate, Earl, right before my 39th birthday. Earl and I considered ourselves so lucky to have found each other that we decided to get married on a lucky date: 7/7/2007. Thankfully, we've been happily married ever since. I am truly grateful to have bounced back from divorce.

If you're anything like me, and you've been through the breakup of a marriage, I'm sure you didn't expect things to end that way. No one walks down the aisle thinking that his or her union will end in divorce. However, divorce is all too common in American society.

About 50% of first marriages wind up in divorce court, Census Bureau data show. And the divorce rate is even higher for those in subsequent marriages: 67% of second marriages, and 74% of third marriages fail. For most couples, significant financial stress results from the breakup of a household. Whatever income was available must now support two households, instead of one. People who were previously deep in love can get deeply vindictive during divorce, causing some individuals to purposely sabotage their or their soon-to-be ex's finances. Plus, the dissolution of a marriage—at least in the eyes of state law— often requires financial payments from one spouse to the other, in the form of alimony or child support. Ultimately, when a married couple decides to go their separate ways, there are a host of financial decisions to be made, negotiations to be worked out, and agreements to be reached. A bad divorce deal or a protracted legal dispute can be a long-term financial setback, haunting you for many years to come.

Women Pay Alimony and Child Support Too

I'm proof positive of that last point. I've already shared that I was the one who paid my ex-husband alimony and child support—not the other way around as is most common. (Women are overwhelmingly recipients of alimony or child support, but a growing number of women are payers, according to a survey from the American Academy of Matrimonial Lawyers.) But my financial issues with my first husband didn't come to an end when my support obligations ended.

In my case, when I left the home I previously shared with my ex-husband, I only took three things: my car, my clothes, and my computer. I made a point to *not* ask him for anything—except one thing: I requested that when our kids went to college, we should both support them and split their higher education expenses. He readily agreed and we put this in writing in our divorce agreement. (At the time of our divorce, our kids were about eight and six years old.)

But guess what happened when our children went off to college. As you might have suspected, this became a major point of contention. We battled in court over and over again, with me insisting that he had to abide by the terms of our agreement. In fact, I was furious that after all the money I'd paid to Akil, he would even think of reneging on this point. After initially having an attorney, I fired her, and I represented myself—meaning I was a "pro se" litigant, in legal lingo. I went up against three different attorneys hired by my ex over the years. And I won every time. Ultimately, I obtained, not one or two—but five different court orders from two different judges compelling my ex to adhere to the terms of our divorce agreement. I should also mention that Akil is a professor at a community college and earns a six-figure salary, so he was gainfully employed in the same job from 2005 until now. But my former spouse objected to the out-of-state public colleges my children selected, and he claimed he couldn't afford to pay. Nonetheless, after years of legal disputes, and delays due to the pandemic causing court closures, I finally secured something called a QDRO— a Qualified Domestic Relations Order—giving me the right to tap his retirement accounts in order to fulfill his child support obligation to pay for half of their college expenses.

Because Akil didn't pay what he was supposed to, my husband, Earl, and I bore those college costs. It wasn't until 2022—three and half years after our oldest daughter finished college and while our son was a senior in college—that I finally received the last money Akil owed for college: approximately $36,000. Again, we divorced in 2006, but this matter didn't get resolved until 16 years later! Let this be a lesson to you: have an airtight divorce agreement and document everything; it will help tremendously in the event of a dispute down the road with an ex. But that's not all you need to do to bounce back from divorce.

In this chapter, you will learn:

- How to properly disentangle economically from a previous spouse;
- How to protect or build your credit rating during and after a divorce;
- Why long-term planning amid divorce proceedings is far more important than short-term wins;
- Common financial mistakes to avoid during and in the aftermath of divorce;
- Post-divorce stories of emotional recovery.

Casting Off Your Ex-spouse Financially

Just like it can be an emotional ordeal to go through a breakup, recovering from a divorce and disentangling economically from a previous spouse can also be quite a complex process. There are, however, five key steps you can take to properly separate your finances after divorce and begin rebuilding your own life.

Step 1. Close Joint Accounts

Begin by making a list of all joint bank accounts, credit cards, loans, and other financial accounts that you share with your former spouse. This includes checking, savings, and investment accounts, as well as mortgages and car loans. If possible, you'll want to communicate with your former spouse or soon-to-be ex in order to minimize surprises and avoid unnecessary headaches and drama. If you can't discuss the timing and process of closing and dividing joint accounts with your ex, have a mediator or your attorney handle it. Either way, clear communication is essential to avoid misunderstandings and potential disputes. You should ultimately reach an agreement on how to split the assets and liabilities according to your divorce settlement, court order, or any preliminary agreement the two of you put in writing.

Before proceeding with any account closures, consult your divorce attorney to ensure you are following legal requirements in your state and protecting your interests. They can guide you through the proper steps and ensure that all necessary paperwork is completed.

Your next step is to contact the relevant financial institutions. Get in touch with each financial institution holding your joint accounts to inform them of the divorce and your intention to close or separate the accounts. They can provide you with the necessary forms and instructions. Based on the agreement reached with your former spouse, divide and/or transfer the assets in the joint accounts. This may involve transferring funds or investments to individual accounts, selling assets and splitting the proceeds, or refinancing loans in one person's name.

Once the assets and liabilities are divided, either close the joint accounts or remove the name of the person who is no longer responsible for the account. Make sure to obtain written confirmation from each financial institution verifying that the accounts have been closed or names have been removed.

After closing joint accounts, open new individual bank accounts, credit cards, and investment accounts in your name only. This will help you establish your financial independence and rebuild your credit history.

Step 2. Update Beneficiaries and Estate Planning Documents

It is crucial to update beneficiaries and estate planning documents after a divorce to ensure that your assets are distributed according to your current wishes. Here are more details on the process and the documents you should review.

Retirement accounts: Retirement accounts, such as 401(k)s, IRAs, and pensions, typically require you to designate a beneficiary who will inherit the account upon your death. After a divorce, you may want to change your beneficiary from your former spouse to someone else, such as your children, a new spouse, or another family member. Contact your retirement plan administrator to obtain the necessary forms to update your beneficiary designation.

Insurance policies: Life insurance policies, annuities, and other insurance products also require beneficiary designations. To update these, contact your insurance company or agent and request the appropriate forms. Ensure that the new beneficiary information is accurately recorded by the insurance company to avoid future complications.

Other financial accounts: Financial accounts such as payable-on-death bank accounts or transfer-on-death brokerage accounts should also be reviewed and updated. Contact your bank or brokerage firm to revise the beneficiary designations on these accounts.

Last will and testament: Your will is a legal document that outlines how you want your property and assets distributed upon your death. After a divorce, review your will and revise it as necessary to remove your former spouse as a beneficiary or executor, and to reallocate assets to other beneficiaries. Consult with an estate planning attorney to ensure the changes are properly made and comply with applicable laws.

Trust: If you have a revocable living trust, you should review and update it after your divorce. You may need to remove your former spouse as a trustee, beneficiary, or both. Depending on the complexity of your trust, you may want to work with an estate planning attorney to make the appropriate revisions.

Power of attorney: A power of attorney document grants someone the authority to make financial and legal decisions on your behalf. After a divorce, review your power of attorney documents (both financial and health care) to ensure that your former spouse is no longer designated as your agent. If necessary, appoint a new trusted individual to act on your behalf.

Advance health care directive: An advance health care directive, also known as a living will, outlines your medical treatment preferences in case you become incapacitated. Review this document and update it to remove your former spouse as your health care proxy or decision-maker, and designate a new trusted person.

Updating beneficiaries and estate planning documents after a divorce is an essential step to ensure that your assets and personal decisions are managed in alignment with your current wishes. At any point where you need help, don't take shortcuts. Consult with an estate planning attorney or financial advisor to help you navigate this process and make the necessary changes.

Step 3. Change Your Name If Applicable and If Desired

Following a divorce, many women consider whether they should go back to their maiden name and drop their married last name. This is an entirely personal decision, and you may take into consideration a host of factors, including your career, kids, and even just whether you like one name better than the other. There's no right or wrong answer here. After being married for more than two decades, my best friend LaTrice and her husband, Jimmy, divorced in 2018. LaTrice kept her married last name until 2023. That year, as soon as the last of their four children graduated from high school and was set to go to college, LaTrice officially applied to change her last name. "I didn't want to be that mother with a different last name than her kids," she said, explaining it was important to her to convey that all her kids have the same father and that she'd been a married woman.

In my case, after my divorce and subsequent second marriage to my hubby, Earl Cox—whom I lovingly call "my forever husband"—I intended to change my name, to Lynnette Cox, and drop the Khalfani part from my first marriage. But it was actually Earl, who is also my agent and business manager, who advised me to not do so. "You have a brand and books, and an audience who knows you as Lynnette Khalfani," Earl said. "So just keep that name for a while, and hyphenate your name. Then, after a couple of years of transition and using Khalfani-Cox, you can drop Khalfani." So much for best-laid plans! Earl and I laugh now at how we're in our second decade of marriage, yet I'm still using Khalfani-Cox. And I keep saying, "One day I really am going to just have a simple name: Lynnette Cox." Ha!

Again, the choice is yours. But if you decide to change your name after a divorce, it is important to update your identification documents, financial accounts, and legal records to ensure a smooth transition. Here is a step-by-step guide to help you navigate this process:

1. **Obtain legal documentation:** First, obtain a certified copy of your divorce decree or court order that states your name change. This will serve as legal proof of your name change and will be required by various institutions when updating your records.

2. **Update Social Security records:** Contact the Social Security Administration (SSA) to update your name on your Social Security card. You will need to fill out an application (Form SS-5) and provide proof of your name change, such as the certified copy of your divorce decree, along with proof of your identity and US citizenship or lawful immigration status. Once your application is processed, you will receive a new Social Security card with your updated name.
3. **Update identification documents:** Next, update your identification documents, such as your driver's license, state ID card, and passport. Visit your local Department of Motor Vehicles (DMV) office to update your driver's license or state ID card, and bring the necessary documents, including the certified copy of your divorce decree and your current ID. For your passport, follow the US Department of State's guidelines on updating your name, which may involve applying for a new passport or submitting a renewal application with the name change.
4. **Update financial accounts:** Inform your bank, credit card companies, mortgage lender, and other financial institutions about your name change. You may need to provide them with a certified copy of your divorce decree or court order, along with any other required documents. Update your name on your checking, savings, and investment accounts, as well as your credit cards, loans, and other financial products.
5. **Update legal records:** Update your name on any legal documents, such as your will, trust, power of attorney, and advance health care directive. Consult with an attorney to ensure that your legal documents are properly revised and comply with applicable laws.
6. **Notify other institutions and service providers:** Inform other relevant institutions and service providers about your name change. This may include your employer, utility companies, insurance providers, health care providers, schools, professional associations, and any other organizations with which you have a relationship.
7. **Update your online presence:** Don't forget to update your name on your email accounts, social media profiles, and any online memberships or subscriptions. This will help maintain consistency in your personal and professional online presence.

By taking these steps, you can ensure a smooth transition to your new name after a divorce. Keep in mind that the process may take some time and effort, but updating your records is essential to avoid potential complications and confusion in the future.

Step 4. Establish a New Budget

In the wake of divorce, you'll need to create a new budget, one that reflects only your income, and perhaps the impact of alimony and/or child support. This will vary based on whether you're receiving support or paying it. Either way, it's vital to assess your post-divorce financial situation and develop a new budget that is consistent with your income, expenses, and financial goals. Here's an easy-to-follow system for how to create a new budget after divorce.

Assess your financial situation: Take stock of your post-divorce financial situation by considering factors such as your income, alimony or child support payments to be paid or received, and any changes in your living expenses.

List your income sources: Identify all your sources of income, including salary, freelance work, rental income, investments, and any alimony or child support payments you may receive.

Identify and categorize expenses: List all your expenses and categorize them into fixed costs (e.g. mortgage, rent, utilities, loan payments) and variable expenses (e.g. groceries, entertainment, clothing) expenses. Don't forget to account for any new expenses that may arise due to your changed circumstances, such as additional childcare costs or separate housing expenses.

Set financial goals: Establish short-term and long-term financial goals, such as building an emergency fund, saving for retirement, or paying off debt. Incorporate these goals into your budget, allocating funds toward achieving them.

Adjust your budget: Based on your new financial situation, adjust your budget to reflect your current income and expenses. This may involve cutting back on discretionary spending, increasing savings, or finding additional sources of income.

Monitor and revise: Regularly review your budget to ensure it continues to meet your financial needs and goals. Adjust it as necessary to accommodate changes in your income, expenses, or financial objectives.

Most people hate the word "budget." But proper budgeting will help you better manage your cash flow, maintain control of your finances, and plan for the future.

Step 5: Reevaluate Your Insurance Needs

As a final step in establishing financial independence during a divorce, you must assess your insurance needs, including health, auto, home, and life insurance, to ensure you have adequate coverage and update the policies as needed. Here are the main insurance areas to review.

Health insurance: If you were previously covered under your spouse's health insurance plan, you may need to obtain your own coverage. Explore options through your employer, the Health Insurance Marketplace, or private insurers. Ensure that you have adequate coverage based on your health care needs and budget.

Auto insurance: Update your auto insurance policy to remove your former spouse, and adjust coverage levels as needed. This may include updating the names insured, listed drivers, and coverage amounts for both liability and comprehensive coverage.

Home insurance: If you have moved to a new home or remained in the marital home, update your home insurance policy to reflect any changes in ownership, coverage needs, or mortgage information. This may include adjusting the policy limits, adding or removing coverage endorsements, or obtaining coverage for new assets or possessions.

Life insurance: Reassess your life insurance needs to ensure you have adequate coverage for your new financial situation. This may involve updating the policy's face value, beneficiaries, or premium payments. If you are paying or receiving alimony or child support, consider whether additional life insurance coverage is necessary to protect those payments in the event of your death.

By reviewing and adjusting your insurance coverage after divorce, you'll be proactively managing your finances and protecting yourself and your loved ones. Even though it may be the last chore you want to tackle, handling these aspects of your financial life will help you stay on track and have great peace of mind too.

Once you implement each of the five recommended steps, you'll be well on your way to properly disentangling economically from a previous spouse, regaining control over your finances, and setting the foundation for a stable financial future after divorce.

Protecting Your Credit During Divorce

I can't tell you the number of people I've encountered who told me that an ex-spouse ruined their credit before, during, or even after a divorce. Sometimes, a spurned husband or wife will spend money maliciously, charging up debts and leaving the other party on the hook to pay the bills. At other times, one spouse will simply stop paying certain bills they agreed to pay—such as car notes or mortgages.

When my husband, Earl, was married in his early 20s and later in the middle of a divorce, that's exactly what happened to him. Even though he and his ex-wife agreed to pay their credit card obligations and jointly maintain the home they'd bought together, one day he came home from work to find that she'd moved out of the house. She took the stuff she wanted and never paid another house payment again. Under the weight of trying to pay for everything, Earl's credit was ruined, and his finances were left in shambles. Thankfully, that was decades ago, and he's since established a stellar credit rating. But like many people, he learned some hard lessons about the importance of safeguarding and protecting your credit rating during and after a divorce.

Here are some steps to help you minimize the impact that divorce can have on your credit health.

Monitor your credit report: Obtain your credit report from each of the three major credit bureaus (Equifax, Experian, and TransUnion) and review them for accuracy. Dispute any errors you find, and ensure that all joint accounts have been properly separated or closed.

Pay bills on time: Consistently making on-time payments is one of the most critical factors in maintaining and improving your credit score. Set up payment reminders or automatic payments to help you stay on track.

Maintain low credit card balances: Keep your credit card balances low relative to your credit limits. A lower credit utilization ratio (the percentage of your available credit that you're using) can positively impact your credit score.

Separate joint accounts: As previously mentioned, as soon as possible, close or separate joint accounts shared with your former spouse. This will prevent your credit from being negatively affected by your ex-spouse's financial behavior. This won't, however, prevent a sneaky spouse from doing underhanded things such as opening new credit in your name. That's why it's important to monitor your credit and be alerted to any new accounts established under your Social Security number.

Establish new credit in your name: If you don't have credit in your name, open a new credit card account, or consider a secured credit card to establish a positive credit history. Use the credit responsibly, and pay off the balance in full each month.

Don't close old accounts: Unless there's a compelling reason, such as high fees or a joint account, avoid closing old credit card accounts. Keeping them open can help maintain your credit history's length, which is a factor in your credit score.

Avoid applying for too much credit: Even though you may have a need to establish one or two credit cards or lines of credit, limit the number of credit applications you submit in a short period. Multiple hard inquiries can negatively impact your credit score.

Seek professional advice: Consult with a financial advisor, credit counselor, or attorney to help you navigate the financial aspects of divorce and develop a plan to protect and improve your credit rating.

Be patient: Rebuilding credit takes time and consistent effort. Continue to monitor your credit, make timely payments, and practice responsible financial habits to gradually improve your credit score.

By diligently following these steps, you can protect and build your credit rating during and after a divorce and sidestep the credit woes that trip up so many others going through a breakup.

Long-term Planning During Divorce

In the heat of divorce, some people insist on getting short-term wins—such as claiming certain furniture or snagging the house. In some instances, this may not be financially prudent, especially if, for example, you can't afford the house in the long run. So be careful not to make petty or vengeful financial decisions, perhaps to spite an ex-spouse. Instead, consider how thoughtful, long-term planning amid divorce proceedings is far more important than knee-jerk reactions or short-term wins. After all, making decisions based on spite or immediate gratification can lead to financial strain and a host of negative consequences in the long run.

On the other hand, if you focus on long-term planning, that benefits you and everyone involved in many ways. For starters, you'll have a more sustainable financial future: thoughtful planning helps ensure that you can maintain a stable and viable lifestyle after the divorce. Although you may really want that house or car, careful planning means looking realistically at the overall affordability of those items, including long-term expenses such as maintenance and taxes.

By prioritizing long-term planning, you also minimize debt and financial stress because you avoid taking on unnecessary obligations or excessive commitments that may result from prioritizing short-term wins. Another benefit of long-term planning during divorce is that you better protect your retirement and savings goals. No matter how much you may want to stick it to your ex, who cares if they get the China plates you've been arguing over for months on end? Spend your energy instead negotiating for a higher percentage of their 401(k) assets or a bigger cut of that pension they have coming. The latter assets will do way more for you than those plates—which are probably just going to stay in the cabinets 95% of the time anyway! In other words, focus on the stuff that really matters.

Additionally, smart long-term planning helps ensure a fair and equitable division of assets, which is in the best interest of both parties. Focusing on short-term wins can lead to an unbalanced division of assets, which may create resentment, opening the door to future legal issues and squabbles. Whenever possible, you want to avoid drawn-out, costly legal battles. As much as you may detest the idea of it, cooperation and compromise during the divorce process can save you and your ex-spouse time and money.

If your first thought was: "I don't want to *save* my ex anything! I want them to *pay*!" that alone is a sign that you're harboring a high level of resentment and may be acting out in ways that ultimately don't serve your best interests.

Admittedly, maintaining a healthy emotional state in the throes of a divorce isn't always easy. Your former spouse probably knows exactly how to push your buttons. Still, I've learned that making decisions based on spite or anger will only exacerbate the stress and negativity around the divorce process. By focusing on long-term planning, you can approach the divorce process with a clearer and more rational mindset, which will benefit both you and your ex-spouse.

Finally, and perhaps most important, if you have kids, long-term planning often helps prioritize the well-being of your children: all parents should want to ensure their offspring's happiness and financial stability. This includes considering the costs of childcare, education, and other expenses that will impact their lives as they grow up.

Common Financial Mistakes to Avoid During Divorce

In the throes of divorce, there are many emotional and financial landmines you need to avoid. Sometimes, when situations pop up, you may want to throw your hands up in frustration or yell, "How come no one told me about this?!" Such frustrations are natural. That's why it's important to be aware of and to try to prepare yourself for an array of potential hazards or mistakes to avoid. Here are some common pitfalls to avoid:

Not Understanding Your Financial Situation

Failing to have a clear understanding of your assets, debts, income, and expenses can lead to poor financial decisions during the divorce process. Take the time to review and understand your financial situation, so you can make informed choices.

Overlooking Tax Implications

Divorce can have significant tax implications. Make sure you understand the tax consequences of dividing assets, retirement accounts, and other financial matters to avoid unexpected tax liabilities.

Failing to Update Your Estate Plan

Many people forget to update their wills, trusts, and other estate planning documents after a divorce. This can lead to unintended consequences and conflicts among your heirs. Update your estate plan to reflect your new circumstances.

Keeping the Family Home Without Considering the Costs

Holding on to the family home may have emotional appeal, but it can be a financial burden in the long run. Consider property taxes, maintenance, and other ongoing expenses before deciding to keep the house.

Not Considering the Long-term Impact of Asset Division

When dividing assets, consider the long-term growth potential and risks associated with each. For example, compare the long-term value of retirement accounts to more volatile investments or assets with ongoing costs.

Ignoring Insurance Needs

Review your insurance policies, including life, health, and disability insurance, to ensure you have adequate coverage after the divorce. You may need to adjust your policies or obtain new coverage based on your new circumstances.

Not Securing Spousal and Child Support Payments

If you're entitled to spousal or child support, make sure these payments are secured through legal means, such as wage garnishments or liens on your former spouse's property. Relying solely on an ex-spouse's goodwill may lead to missed payments and financial strain.

Failing to Establish Individual Credit

After a divorce, it's important to establish and maintain your credit. Make sure to open individual accounts in your name and maintain a good payment history to build your credit score.

Making Emotional Decisions

Avoid making financial decisions based on emotions or spite. Instead, focus on long-term financial goals and make rational choices that will benefit your future.

Not Seeking Professional Help

Divorce can be a complicated and emotionally charged process. Seek the advice of financial professionals, attorneys, and therapists to help you navigate the financial aspects of divorce and make well-informed decisions.

By steering clear of these common financial mistakes, you'll be able to bounce back faster and with more confidence and certainty after a divorce.

Post-divorce Stories of Emotional Recovery

For many people who go through the breakup of a marriage, getting the financial issues worked out can sometimes pale in comparison to working through the emotional baggage that gets dredged up during a divorce.

Pamela Zapata, a diversity and equity executive at a biotech firm, knows exactly what that's like.

Zapata married in 2004 and would have marked her 20th wedding anniversary in 2024. Instead, it's the year she and her spouse will likely be finalizing their divorce, after being separated for more than four years.

Things started falling apart after the couple had to terminate a pregnancy. She was 25 weeks pregnant, and her doctors recommended ending the pregnancy because the child had severe medical issues, only a 20% chance of surviving, and the baby's growth started impeding Pamela's own health. "I had to take the blame for killing my child," Pamela says, adding that, in her grief, she started to mask her unhappiness in various ways. "My way of dealing with death was shopping. I hid behind work. I hid behind the shopping. I wasn't even paying attention to basic things in life, and I paid the price for it."

She now realizes that she was, for a very long time, in a "zombie state" and had abdicated so many money matters to her spouse, with whom she shares two children, a 15-year-old son, and a 13-year-old daughter. "I let my ex-husband take care of all the finances. I was taking care of the house and kids and anything that had to do with cooking, cleaning, clothing, and making the family stay well. But the trade-off was, I was allowed to be stupid when it came to finances."

Pamela says she worked and put money into accounts, but the tacit agreement she had with her spouse basically amounted to him saying: "Don't worry about paying the bills or the credit cards. They'll get paid. And don't worry about your investments. I'll keep an eye on those."

Now, she says, she talks to legal and financial professionals who ask her questions such as "How much do you pay per year for various expenses?" When she says she doesn't know, they look at her like she's crazy.

"I'm just now understanding how to read my investment statements," she admits. "But I'm talking to people who are looking at me like: 'How on earth can you not know this?'"

"But no one asks him: 'What size are your kids' clothes? What are their grades like? Or have they had their vaccinations?"

When Zapata struggled financially after her spouse left, she says she tried to hide her financial woes from countless people. "It was like this big secret that I didn't want to let anyone know about," she recalls.

Interestingly, in anything in life where we harbor secrets, that activity holds us back and harms our mental health. Perhaps that is why, in Alcoholics Anonymous, there's a saying that goes, "You're only as sick as your secrets."

For Pamela, it wasn't until a girlfriend told her point-blank that when she divorced, she was "financially ruined." This friend apologized for not going out socially more with Pamela but said she just couldn't afford it. That honesty and openness led to a frank conversation with Pamela sharing her own truth and the two women started swapping stories. Soon, a third friend joined in with a similar tale of economic struggles.

At that point, Pamela realized she wasn't alone in going through her tough times.

Her advice now to others in the middle of a divorce: "Talk to other people. You think that no one else could possibly be feeling as shameful or as embarrassed as you are. But the truth is that others are going through it too. And it really does help to know that you're not alone."

Adds Pamela: "My grandmother always said: 'God never gives you more than you could handle.' I felt she was wrong at that time, but now I understand."

My Sister's Divorce Story

My oldest sister, Cheryl, got married in 1996 at age 32, after dating her husband, William, ever since she was 19 years old. Unfortunately, their union didn't last, and they got divorced seven years later, in 2003. Today, more than 20 years after their split, they are good friends who talk on the phone regularly, support one another emotionally, and successfully co-parent their daughter, Nina, who is now earning a PhD in genetics from Northwestern University

This might sound like a kumbaya family tale—or perhaps something akin to actress Gwyneth Paltrow's "conscious uncoupling" from singer Chris Martin. But it wasn't easy getting to a place of harmony and true friendship for Cheryl and William, not by any stretch of the imagination. In fact, their divorce was quite nasty at first. Cheryl thought William cheated on her—an accusation he vehemently denied. Whatever the case, Cheryl says she was totally blindsided when William came home one day and told her out of the blue that he wanted a divorce.

At the time, Nina was 18 months old. Cheryl was laying down, nursing her daughter, when, she says, "William simply handed me a white packet of paperwork. He said, 'These are divorce papers. You can have anything you want or change anything you want in here.'"

Although she was shocked—"We'd never even said the word divorce," Cheryl says—she also later recognized how deeply unhappy William was. In retrospect, Cheryl acknowledges, "He wasn't fulfilled in the marriage. I didn't treat him right. I was neglectful from an emotional standpoint. I was more into Nina and my work."

The court awarded Cheryl about $3,000 a month in alimony and child support for a period of about six months. But, she says, William was so angry about having to pay that money that he quit his job and lived off his 401(k) retirement savings for a year.

Before the divorce filing, he had her unwittingly sign paperwork giving her full authority over his retirement assets, according to Cheryl. William also locked the doors on the home to kick Cheryl out of the house, and she says he and his family took Nina for 32 days out of Georgia, where they resided in a hotel and in William's parents' house in Virginia. So it got really ugly.

Although Cheryl had been a stay-at-home mom, she had also worked in the health care industry and had a master's of arts degree in public health. She opened her own health care business, Achieve Home Nursing Services, and then worked like crazy.

In her very first year of business, her company grossed more than $1 million.

Going through the divorce was, she says, the kick in the pants she needed to prove that she could make it on her own.

"I never wanted to go on welfare or get food stamps and part of my upbringing of seeing [our mother] rely on public assistance, I really didn't want to do that. I saw it as a curse, and I was determined to do everything in my power to be self-sufficient. I also realized that I had placed so much of my trust in William, but I learned to transition that trust to God," Cheryl says.

There was one other major turning point in Cheryl's relationship with William—when the two of them had been at each other's throats.

"When Nina was in middle school, she came to me crying and said: 'Mommy, I need you and Daddy to love me more than you hate each other,'" Cheryl told me. "That totally changed my whole strategy and approach."

With therapy, communication, and cooperation, William and Cheryl have now evolved tremendously. From the outside, you'd probably never even suspect any of the previous bad blood. Cheryl credits God and their willingness to put Nina's interests first as to how she and William have both been able to bounce back from their divorce.

Divorce Resources

1. **American Bar Association** – Organization of divorce and family law attorneys.
2. **American Academy of Matrimonial Lawyers** – Leading divorce attorneys group.
3. **Association of Divorce Financial Planners** – Financial advisors who specialize in divorce.
4. **Children and Divorce** – Nonprofit providing coaching for kids experiencing divorce.
5. **Divorce Magazine** – Publication and divorce resource hub.
6. **Family Equality** – Advocacy group supporting LGBTQ+ families.

7. **First Wives World** – Support community equipping women with divorce resources.
8. **Institute for Divorce Financial Analysts** – Financial experts assisting divorcing couples.
9. **National Network to End Domestic Violence** – Specialized services for domestic abuse victims.
10. **Office of Child Support Services** – Federal agency that oversees the national child support program.

Chapter 5
Death of a Loved One

"When life throws you a curveball, it's not about how hard it hits; it's about how well you can bounce back and keep moving forward."

—Tom Hanks

Verlaina Warner Brown never expected to become a widow at age 53. But life threw her a major curveball when her husband, Cecil, passed away suddenly during the height of the COVID-19 pandemic.

Cecil, a 61-year-old book buyer for a college bookstore, had been living with prostate cancer, which he was managing well with medication. However, in late 2020, after changing his medication, he developed a fever. The couple went to Kaiser Hospital in Rancho Cucamonga, California, expecting a simple switch back to his previous prescription. As a precaution, doctors admitted Cecil to the hospital, and Verlaina told her husband she'd pick him up the next day.

The following day, though, Cecil developed breathing problems. "Two days later he could barely talk, and three days later, he was on a ventilator," Verlaina says.

Just 11 days after entering the hospital, Cecil died from COVID-19 on Christmas Eve 2020. To this day, Verlaina does not know how or where he contracted the disease.

The shock and the fallout of losing Cecil devastated Verlaina and completely shattered the life she knew. Initially, Verlaina says, she couldn't function at all.

"The first two weeks, I stayed in bed and didn't eat a thing. I just had water," she recalls.

She had always loved her job working as a patient access coordinator at UCLA Hospital and thought returning to work would help, but it didn't.

"When I was at work, I was like a zombie," she says. "My head wasn't clear," so she found herself going to the bathroom six or seven times a day, just to break down in tears privately. Not only was she dealing with the emotional blow of losing her partner, but there were also worries over a major loss of income—and all that entailed.

Lives Forever Changed

When Verlaina met Cecil, she was a single mom trying her best to make ends meet. After dating and falling in love, they married in 2008, becoming a blended family and parents to four children.

From the very beginning, Verlaina says Cecil took over the household finances, paying for nearly everything. "Not only was he kind and generous to me and my children, but he was also kind with his money," she says, adding: "The whole time we were married, I never paid rent or mortgage. He was responsible for that."

Cecil's death abruptly upended that dynamic. Thankfully, Cecil had amassed enough savings for Verlaina to live on for six months. Nonetheless, Verlaina quickly had to face the fact that she no longer had a two-person household and, thus, had to contend with a steep drop in income: Verlaina went from enjoying a combined household income of $170,000 a year—because Cecil was earning $100,000—to having only $70,000 a year, Verlaina's hospital salary.

In retrospect, Verlaina says she was overly dependent on her spouse, which made her transition particularly difficult. "When he died, a part of me died. It was the part that enjoyed being cared for by a man," she notes.

By the time Cecil passed, the kids were grown, but that didn't diminish the emotional and financial burdens. In fact, in some ways, Verlaina felt more responsibility for the children given Cecil's absence. But she finally had to admit that without his income, her previous standard of living—and the things she did for their children—had to come to an end.

"I had to explain to my children: 'I can't pay your cell phone bill anymore. I can't pay your car payment anymore. I'm on my own now.' It was very hard because I had done it for so long," Verlaina says. "They understood. But it was still hard for me to say it because I was in denial, mistakenly thinking I could somehow manage it."

Beyond those prior family obligations, there were other bills to pay as well, of course. The funeral cost $14,000, eating up the majority of the $20,000 in life insurance Cecil had. There was $9,000 in credit card bills, and later, $10,000 worth of tax debt that Verlaina would put on a payment plan. She's still paying off the IRS, to the tune of $200 a month.

Navigating these obligations hasn't been easy, but now, roughly three years later, Verlaina says she's finally faring much better—emotionally and financially.

The Road to Recovery

For Verlaina, the biggest challenge was coming to terms with her grief and finding the strength to move forward in constructive ways. For so long, she didn't want to talk to others, but she kept insisting she was OK. She also couldn't bring herself to fully accept the loss of Cecil, and her difficulties adjusting to her new reality played out in different ways.

For example, Verlaina went back and forth about letting go of some of her deceased husband's personal belongings that were in storage. She found herself paying $250 a month for a storage locker filled with Cecil's possessions, unable to bring herself to clear it out. For months, she would drive to the storage facility, punch in the code, and then leave without removing any items. Eventually, she mustered up the courage to face the painful task of sorting through Cecil's belongings, reminding herself: "As much as this hurts, you can't let this be the end of you."

Even with routine tasks, such as shopping for food, Verlaina had to reframe her thinking and her actions. "It took me six months to stop overbuying groceries" she admits. "I finally said to myself: 'Why are you buying all this food for two people, not cooking it, and letting it go to waste?'"

But the single most important step in her recovery was seeking professional help to cope with her grief. Verlaina enrolled in grief counseling for a year, and she credits it as a crucial decision. "That was the best thing I ever did," she says. "It was a place I didn't have to pretend. I was allowed to be raw, to cry, or just say and feel what I wanted." The counseling provided her with a safe space where she could express her emotions and begin the healing process.

Over time, she started having epiphanies about what she truly wanted—and didn't want.

She realized that she had been mourning so much in the wake of her spouse's death that her grief had become overwhelming and all-consuming, robbing her of any joy and sapping the very life out of her. "I finally came to realize I'm part of the living, and I didn't want to die," Verlaina says. "For me to sink into all that sadness, and wear it like a cloak, it would've killed me."

So, as she puts it, "I just put one foot in front of the other"—literally and figuratively. She began doing Pilates, stretching, and walking to maintain her physical health. She also faced many financial and other tasks she'd put off doing—everything from canceling Cecil's coverage on her health insurance policy to terminating Cecil's subscriptions and prescriptions, all of which saved money that she desperately needed.

Some potential sources of funding, however, didn't pan out. For example, Verlaina says many well-intentioned people advised her to collect Social Security survivor benefits after Cecil passed—not realizing she was not eligible for those benefits. She didn't qualify because she was not the required 60 years of age, nor was she disabled. (The Sudden Money Institute says it's common for family or friends to mistakenly give such wrong advice when they're trying to help.)

Despite the heartbreaking loss and financial setback she experienced, Verlaina has now managed to bounce back and find her footing again. She's even dating again and is in a committed relationship.

One of Verlaina's most important pieces of advice for others is to secure life insurance while you're healthy. "When people get married, everybody talks about the wedding, or the honeymoon. It may not be romantic, but they should be talking about life insurance," she suggests.

Verlaina's journey doesn't just embody love, loss, and recovery. In many ways, her story is a testament to the incredible strength and resilience of the human spirit. If you ever need a powerful reminder that even in the face of adversity and heartbreak, we all have the capacity to overcome and find our way back to ourselves, perhaps you'll remember Verlaina Warner Brown.

Bouncing Back Amid the Pain

As Verlaina's story also illustrates, the passing of a loved one isn't just a devastating emotional situation. Very often, the death of a main breadwinner or close relative also sparks a major financial crisis for those left behind. Sadly, far too many Americans struggle economically in the wake of a family member's death. Funeral expenses, which can cost many thousands of dollars, pose an immediate financial squeeze. The loss of a deceased person's income is an equally serious, longer-term fiscal challenge. And very often, someone who has died may have owed a mortgage, auto loan, credit card debt, or other bills and obligations that must now be paid or settled in some fashion. Yet, if you've been weathering a financial storm due to a death in the family, there is hope—and a future worth living despite any fresh grief or lingering sadness.

In this chapter, you will learn:

- Coping strategies to deal with grief;
- Six transition truths;
- How to understand your "ancillary" losses;
- The five crucial first steps to take;
- How to handle special circumstances;
- How to find missing money; and
- How to handle financial grief.

Coping Strategies to Deal with Grief

Preston D. Cherry, a certified financial planner and president of Concurrent Financial Planning, LLC, recommends journaling and "self-audits" where you take some alone time to think through what's happened as a way to deal honestly with grief.

One of the most important things to recognize, according to Cherry and other experts, is that there's no set timetable for grief. It can last a year or a lifetime. It comes and goes in waves. It may diminish over time, or it may simply take different forms as you grow, change, mature, or develop different coping skills and perspectives. Grief also manifests itself in different ways for different people, so there's no magic blueprint for how to deal with every circumstance. There are, however, some strategies and tools you can utilize at various points, including when things get tough and when you want to do whatever you humanly can to recover emotionally and financially from unimaginable loss.

In addition to journaling and taking time for self-reflection, there are other coping strategies that can be helpful when dealing with grief. One important strategy is to seek support from others, whether it's through talking with friends and family or joining a support group. This can help you feel less alone in your grief and provide a space to process your emotions.

Another helpful coping strategy is to take care of yourself physically. This includes eating well, getting enough sleep, and engaging in regular exercise. While it can be difficult to focus on physical health during times of grief, it's an important aspect of self-care that can help improve mood and reduce stress.

Engaging in creative activities such as painting, music, or writing can also be a helpful way to process emotions and find meaning in the loss. Additionally, seeking professional help from a therapist or counselor can provide support and guidance in navigating the complex emotions that come with grief.

Ultimately, it's important to find coping strategies that work for you and your unique situation. While there's no one-size-fits-all approach to dealing with grief, finding healthy ways to process emotions and taking care of yourself can help you navigate the difficult journey of grieving and eventually find healing.

The Six Transition Truths

When dealing with a life-altering event such as the loss of a loved one, it's bound to make you question all sorts of things: your relationships, your financial standing, and maybe even your desire to go on. Know that these are all natural thoughts and feelings during a time of major transition. The Sudden Money Institute has outlined what it calls "Six Transition Truths" that are commonplace when you undergo a life transition. These are especially helpful to keep in mind when you're dealing with a major loss such as the death of someone you cared about deeply.

Transition Truth No. 1

You'll navigate your transition with greater calm if you resist the urge to DO.

Simply put, this means you don't have to rush to do anything. In fact, you're better off doing nothing rather than imposing artificial deadlines to perform tasks or making decisions under pressure when you're not clear-headed. Remember: transitions take months or years to process.

Transition Truth No. 2

You have a say in the matter.

The narratives you create about your life and its events shape every decision you make. When these stories begin to spiral out of control, they can easily become overwhelming and impact the course of your entire life. So pay close attention to your thoughts regarding your relationships, future, and even your perspective on money. Whenever you find yourself caught up in repeated internal dialogues or a lot of negative talk, consider asking yourself the following questions:

- Is the version of my story genuinely true, or have I simply repeated it so often that I've come to accept it as truth?
- Am I treating myself kindly in this narrative? If not, what changes can I make to cultivate a more compassionate version of my story?

- What evidence do I have to support my envisioned outcome? Is it possible that I'm prematurely assuming the conclusion of my story, disregarding the various ways in which things could unfold differently?

Transition Truths 3–6

Every transition alters a person's identity.
Every transition involves letting go.
Every transition is aided by defining what's vitally important to your life and should be protected at all costs.
Every transition allows for new possibilities.

When you look at these "transition truths," it helps you realize that even amid awful circumstances such as death, you can discover meaning, find new purpose, and move forward.

The Trauma of Losing My Sister

I mentioned in the introduction to *Bounce Back* that I, too, have experienced the death of a loved one—in my case, it was my older sister, Debby, who passed away on December 30, 2014.

Debby was just 49 years old when she died and had an 11-year-old daughter. She had been in good health, so her death came as a huge surprise to our family, and it affected me profoundly.

Like Verlaina, after my sister's death, I was curled up in bed and unable to function. For two months, my husband, Earl, had to run our business by himself and hire others to do the work I was supposed to do—such as writing articles or creating financial content. Earl canceled my speaking engagements because I just didn't have it in me to get in front of crowds. Making matters worse, it took a very long time for authorities to even determine the cause of her death. Debby was found alone, fully clothed and wearing boots, on the floor of her bathroom in her residence in Dallas, Texas. An autopsy and toxicology reports ruled out drugs and alcohol. She had no apparent physical ailments. Her heart and liver were in perfect condition. In fact, she'd just run a marathon the month before her death. So my family was at a total loss as to what could have happened.

It didn't help when the medical examiner told us the cause of death was "inconclusive." That led our family to hire a private pathologist, who conducted her own autopsy. Same results: "inconclusive." Finally, the private pathologist also examined Debby's other organs and found the presence of oxalate crystals—which indicated ethylene glycol poisoning.

We still don't know exactly what poisoned Debby and caused her death. A police investigation found no substances in her home, car, garage, or anywhere to account for it. I suspect vaping could have been a possible source because we did find vape pens and vaping liquid in her home. And back then, there was absolutely no regulation, and vape companies marketed vaping as "safe" and "nicotine free." My sister was an early adopter, always trying out the next "cool" thing. So although I was surprised to learn that she vaped, it wasn't entirely out of character. But the painful reality is that my parents, sisters, and I have had to live ever since then without knowing precisely how or under what circumstances my sister died.

Many people say that losing a spouse or a child is the worst emotional pain a person can feel. I'm a mother of three and a happily married wife. Based on the devastating trauma I felt upon learning of my sister's death—I started screaming, shaking, and sobbing uncontrollably—I can't even imagine the reaction I'd have if I were to lose my husband or any of my children.

What I can say, however, is that I'm now at a point of peace about my sister. I can speak of her now and not cry. I wouldn't have thought this was even possible in the year or two after her death. But when I think of her, it's all good memories—not like how I was in the beginning, when I was wracked by grief and thoughts of how terribly unfair it all was. I miss Debby, to be sure. I have photos of her throughout my house, and I smile just looking at them. My sisters and I speak of Debby often, honoring her memory and all the amazing things she did and put into the world. However, I feel like my grief over Debby's death has transitioned into serenity, acceptance, and even fond appreciation for the many great qualities she possessed that I'm more acutely aware of now. I also firmly believe that I will see her again one day in heaven, and that gives me great comfort.

Understanding Your Ancillary Losses

Like Verlaina, I did go through a lengthy period of grief counseling and then personal counseling, both of which helped me immensely. One of the things I learned in counseling—and that helped me bounce back from Debby's death—is that when a loved one dies, it's not just about the loss of the person, it's also about all of the "ancillary losses" that those of us left behind suffer.

Ancillary losses refer to the secondary or indirect losses that family members and close friends may experience after the death of a loved one. These losses are often related to various aspects of our lives, such as emotional, social, financial, and practical matters. While the primary loss is the absence of the deceased person, ancillary losses can compound grief and affect the overall well-being of the bereaved.

If you've lost a loved one, examples of secondary or ancillary losses you face may include the following.

Emotional Support

The deceased might have been a significant source of emotional support for you or your family members. The loss of this support can leave you feeling isolated and overwhelmed.

Financial Stability

The death of a breadwinner can lead to a significant decline in your financial situation, creating additional stress and potentially causing you or your family to adjust your lifestyle or living conditions. And even if a loved one's death doesn't directly diminish your financial well-being, it can still affect you. Case in point: in my family, Debby was instrumental in supporting my mom, who is retired. Since Debby's passing, my husband and I and my sister, Cheryl, have picked up the slack to provide financial assistance to my mother.

Roles and Responsibilities

You or your relatives may have relied on the deceased for various roles and responsibilities, such as parenting, caregiving, or household management. The surviving family members may need to take on these tasks or delegate them to others, leading to additional stress and potential identity shifts.

Social Connections

The deceased may have been a central figure in your family's social circle. Their death can lead to changes in relationships with friends, neighbors, and extended family, potentially resulting in a loss of social connections and support. In our family, for example, Debby was a main point of connection, a person who planned holiday gatherings and more.

Shared Dreams and Plans

You or other grieving family members might have had shared dreams and plans with the deceased for their future, such as retirement, travel, or starting a family. The death of a loved one can lead to the loss of these anticipated experiences.

Sense of Self

Perhaps you or other family members defined yourselves in relation to the deceased, such as being a spouse, parent, or sibling. As a result, the passing of a loved one can result in an identity crisis and require the bereaved to redefine their sense of self. In fact, the Sudden Money Institute says transitions such as dealing with death—and all transitions—alter a person's identity.

Familiar Routines

Daily routines and rituals that involved the deceased can be disrupted, leading to a sense of disorientation and loss of structure in the lives of you and your surviving family members.

Overall, ancillary losses can significantly impact the grieving process and contribute to the complexity of bereavement. Therefore, it's essential for you to acknowledge and address these secondary losses to facilitate healing and better position yourself to bounce back from the death of a loved one. If you've never heard of or fully processed your ancillary losses, be sure to see *The Bounce Back Workbook* for some key exercises and further insights that will help you on your recovery journey.

Taking the First Crucial Five Steps

While no amount of planning or preparation can ever replace the person you've lost, taking steps to regain financial stability can help to alleviate some of the stress that comes with such a significant loss. So let's start with an overview of the first five steps you need to take to financially recover and bounce back after the death of a loved one.

Step 1: Give Yourself Time to Grieve

First and foremost, allow yourself the space and time to grieve. (Remember Transition Truth No. 1?) While it's essential to address urgent financial matters, it's equally important to prioritize your emotional well-being. Understand that your grief may ebb and flow, and be patient with yourself as you process your emotions. It's OK to feel overwhelmed or unsure of how to proceed. Reach out to friends, family, and support groups to share your feelings and seek comfort. Taking care of your mental and emotional health will help you to better manage the financial recovery process.

Kimberly Foss, a certified financial planner, and founder of Empyrion Wealth Management in Roseville, California, has more than 30 years of experience managing clients' assets. Much of her work focuses on helping women in transition (including widows) manage their financial lives, including retirement planning, estate planning, and investment accounts.

She strongly emphasizes the importance of doing nothing in the immediate aftermath of a loved one's death. "Don't do anything major in the first year. Period," says Foss. "I've had clients say, 'I think I need to move.' But moving may involve selling a home, et cetera, and you're just not in your right mind when you've lost someone."

"When emotions prevail—fear, fight, or flight—you're simply not making good decisions," Foss adds.

CFP Kathleen M. Rehl, the author of *Moving Forward on Your Own: A Financial Guidebook for Widows*, agrees. She counsels that the period immediately following the death of a spouse should often be a "decision-free zone."

Step 2: Locate and Organize Important Documents

In the aftermath of a loved one's passing, at the appropriate time, you'll need to locate and organize important documents related to their estate, finances, and personal affairs. These documents may include:

- Wills and trust documents;
- Life insurance policies;
- Bank and investment account statements;
- Real estate deeds and mortgage documents;
- Vehicle titles and registration;
- Tax returns and financial records;
- Funeral and burial arrangements.

As you gather these documents, create a system to keep them organized and easily accessible. This will help streamline the financial recovery process and ensure that you have all the necessary information at your fingertips when it's time to make important decisions.

Finding and organizing important documents after the loss of a loved one can seem like a daunting task, especially when you're in the midst of grieving. However, taking the time to locate these documents and keeping them organized will make the financial recovery process smoother and less stressful. Here are some helpful tips and advice to guide you through Step 2.

Start with the Obvious Places

Begin your search for important documents in your loved one's home, office, or other places where they kept personal belongings. Look in filing cabinets, drawers, desks, and storage boxes. Don't forget to check safety deposit boxes and any secure storage facilities they may have used. It's also a good idea to search their computer and email for digital records and files.

Reach Out to Professionals

If your loved one worked with a lawyer, financial advisor, accountant, or other professionals, they might have copies of essential documents or know where they are stored. Reach out to these professionals and ask for their assistance in locating the necessary paperwork. They may also be able to provide you with valuable guidance and advice as you navigate the financial recovery process.

Request Duplicates If Needed

In some cases, you might not be able to locate certain documents, or they may be damaged or outdated. Don't get discouraged. Just contact the relevant institutions, such as banks, insurance companies, and government agencies, to request duplicate copies. Keep in mind that you may need to provide proof of your loved one's death, such as a death certificate, and your relationship to the deceased to obtain these documents. And speaking of death certificates, get plenty of them—at least 10, because chances are you'll need to supply originals to a host of organizations. (More on death certificates later.)

Create a Filing System

Once you've gathered all the important documents, it's crucial to create a filing system to keep them organized and easily accessible. This can be as simple as using a filing cabinet with labeled folders or as sophisticated as scanning the documents and storing them digitally on a secure cloud storage platform. Choose a method that works best for you and ensures the safety and confidentiality of the documents.

Keep a Master List

As you organize the documents, create a master list detailing the location and contents of each file or folder. This will help you quickly find the information you need as you work through the financial recovery process. Share this list with a trusted family member or friend so they can assist you if needed.

Update Your Records Regularly

As you work through the financial recovery process, you may receive updated or additional documents. Make sure to incorporate these into your filing system and update your master list accordingly. Regularly reviewing and updating your records will ensure that you always have the most current and accurate information at your fingertips.

By following these tips, you can effectively manage this task and ensure you have all the necessary information to make informed decisions and move forward in your journey toward financial stability. Remember, too, that it's OK to ask for help from friends, family, and professionals during this process. They can provide valuable support and guidance as you navigate this challenging time.

Step 3: Inform Relevant Parties and Institutions

After locating important documents, the next step is to notify relevant parties and institutions of your loved one's passing. This may include:

- Banks and financial institutions;
- Life insurance companies;
- Creditors and loan providers;
- Social Security Administration (if applicable);
- Employers and pension plan administrators;
- Utility providers and other services.

Informing these institutions in a timely manner will help prevent any potential issues with accounts, benefits, or services. Additionally, it can help protect against identity theft and fraud that could occur if someone tries to use your loved one's personal information. If you need to go in person to any institution, Foss recommends getting a trusted friend or family member, perhaps two of them, to help you reach out to financial professionals. The idea is to have someone you trust to go alongside you when you're ready and need to talk to investment advisors, insurance representatives, and other financial professionals.

This not only makes economic sense, but it's also common sense. Losing a loved one is a heart-wrenching experience that brings with it a whirlwind of emotions. In the midst of your grief, it's easy to overlook certain practical or financial aspects of life that need to be addressed or to forget questions you meant to ask. Financial professionals may also tell you things that simply go over your head, or you may not be able to think clearly or recall information from meetings; so that second person will serve as another set of eyes and ears.

To make the process of notifying relevant organizations about your loved one's passing go more smoothly, try using the following tips.

Obtain Multiple Copies of the Death Certificate

Before you start contacting organizations, obtain plenty of certified copies of your loved one's death certificate. Many institutions will require a copy as proof of death before they can process your request or provide you with information. You can usually obtain death certificates from the funeral home, the county or city vital records office, or the state Department of Health.

Make a List of Organizations to Contact

Take the time to create a comprehensive list of organizations you need to notify about your loved one's passing. This may include banks, credit card companies, insurance providers, mortgage lenders, utility providers, and government agencies, among others. Don't forget to include any memberships, subscriptions, or online accounts your loved one may have had.

Prioritize Your Notifications

It's important to prioritize which organizations you contact first. Start with those that have the most significant impact on your financial situation or legal responsibilities, such as banks, insurance companies, and the Social Security Administration. Then, move on to less urgent notifications, such as utility providers and subscriptions.

Keep Track of Your Communications

As you contact each organization, document the date of your communication, the name of the representative you spoke with, and any relevant reference or confirmation numbers. This information will be useful in case you need to follow up on any requests or disputes.

Be Prepared to Provide the Necessary Information

When notifying organizations, be prepared to provide your loved one's full name, Social Security number, date of birth, and date of death. Additionally, you may need to provide your relationship to the deceased, your contact information, and, in some cases, proof of your authority to act on their behalf, such as a copy of the will or a letter of administration from the probate court.

Seek Professional Assistance If Needed

If you're unsure how to handle certain notifications or if you encounter complications, don't hesitate to consult with a professional, such as an attorney, financial advisor, or tax professional. They can provide you with guidance and support to ensure that you're properly managing your loved one's affairs and handling everything correctly.

Step 4: Assess Your Financial Situation

Once you have notified relevant parties and gathered essential documents, it's time to assess your current financial picture. You'll need to take stock of your loved one's assets, debts, and ongoing expenses—and make a list of all sources of income, including insurance payouts, Social Security benefits, and any other inheritances or financial support you may receive. This information will be crucial as you begin to create a budget (that's Step 5) and make financial decisions moving forward.

But I understand that tackling money matters is probably the very last thing you really want to do at this point. Unfortunately, at some point, you can't avoid it. Assessing your financial situation after a loved one's death can be a challenging and emotional task. Verlaina recalls that looking at everything in black and white was the "scariest, most ferocious part" of the financial process for her. But she also knew that understanding her true financial circumstances was essential to making informed decisions and creating a plan for the future.

Here are some helpful tips and advice for tackling Step 4.

Make an Inventory of Assets

Begin by making a comprehensive inventory of your loved one's assets. This may include bank accounts, investment accounts, real estate, vehicles, personal property, and valuable collections. Take note of the estimated value of each asset, as well as any related debts, such as mortgages or loans. This inventory will provide a clearer picture of your loved one's net worth and help you understand how their assets can be used to cover debts and ongoing expenses.

Identify Debts and Ongoing Expenses

Next, create a list of your loved one's debts and ongoing expenses. Debts can include credit card balances, loans, mortgages, car notes, medical bills, and more. Ongoing expenses may consist of utility bills, property taxes, insurance premiums, and any other recurring payments. Understanding the full scope of your loved one's financial obligations will help you create a plan to address them.

Determine Sources of Income and Financial Support

Once you have a clear understanding of your loved one's assets and obligations, identify any sources of income and financial support that may be available to you. This can include life insurance payouts, Social Security survivor benefits, pension benefits, and inheritances. Be sure to research the eligibility requirements and application processes for any benefits you may be entitled to receive.

Consult with Professionals

Navigating the financial complexities after a loved one's death can be challenging, particularly when it comes to determining your rights and responsibilities. Consequently, it's wise to consult with financial advisors, estate attorneys, and tax professionals who can help you understand your obligations and the best course of action for addressing your loved one's financial affairs.

Understand Your Legal Responsibilities

As a survivor, it's essential to know which debts you are legally responsible for paying and which you are not. In general, you are not responsible for your loved one's individual debts, such as credit card balances or personal loans, unless you are a cosigner or joint account holder. However, if you are a spouse or joint property owner, you may be responsible for certain shared debts, such as mortgages or car loans.

Debts that are not your legal responsibility will typically be settled through your loved one's estate during the probate process. Creditors may file claims against the estate for payment, and any remaining assets may be used to cover these debts. If the estate doesn't have sufficient assets to cover all debts, some may go unpaid, and creditors will generally have no legal recourse to collect from surviving family members. But it's important to note that laws regarding debt and inheritance can vary by state, so consult with an estate attorney or financial professional to understand your specific legal obligations.

Finally, as you assess your financial situation, it's essential to also keep in mind any potential tax implications that may arise from your loved one's death. This can include estate taxes, income taxes on inherited assets, and taxes on retirement accounts. Again, if anything is unclear to you, consult with a financial advisor or tax professional to ensure you are aware of your tax obligations and can plan accordingly.

Step 5: Create a New Budget and Financial Plan

With a clear understanding of your financial situation, you can now create a new budget and financial plan that reflects your current circumstances. This may involve adjusting your living expenses, reevaluating your savings goals, and determining how to allocate any insurance payouts or inheritance you receive. As you create your budget, consider the following:

- Prioritize paying off high-interest debts and loans;
- Establish an emergency fund to cover unexpected expenses;
- Reassess your retirement and savings goals to ensure they align with your new financial situation;
- Review your insurance needs, such as life, health, and property insurance, and make any necessary adjustments;
- Allocate funds for ongoing expenses related to the estate, such as property maintenance, taxes, and legal fees.

While creating a new budget and financial plan may feel daunting, doing so will provide you with a sense of control and direction as you navigate what likely feels like a shaky period—or a time of downright upheaval. Remember to be realistic about your financial situation and to adjust as needed. Keep in mind, too, that creating a new budget after the loss of a loved one is an essential step toward your financial recovery and stability. It may require some sacrifices and lifestyle adjustments, but taking control of your finances will provide you with a much-needed sense of security and direction. Here are some more detailed tips and advice for tackling Step 5.

Determine Your New Income and Expenses

Start by identifying your new or current sources of income, which may include your salary, insurance payouts, Social Security benefits, or other financial support. Next, make a list of your ongoing expenses, taking into account any changes resulting from your loved one's passing. This might include additional childcare costs, reduced utility bills, or new expenses related to managing their estate.

Create a Detailed Budget

Once you have a clear understanding of your income and expenses, create a detailed budget that outlines your monthly spending plan. Start by prioritizing essential expenses, such as housing, utilities, groceries, and debt payments. Then, allocate funds for discretionary spending, such as entertainment, dining out, and hobbies. Be realistic about your financial situation, and adjust your spending habits accordingly.

Make Necessary Adjustments

In some cases, you may find that your new financial situation requires making sacrifices or lifestyle changes to accommodate a reduced cash flow. This could involve cutting back on nonessential expenses, such as dining out, subscription services, or vacations. It might also mean downsizing your home, selling a vehicle, or finding ways to increase your income through part-time work or freelance opportunities. Be open to making these changes, and focus on the long-term benefits of adapting to your new financial reality.

Build an Emergency Fund

If you haven't already, now is the time to start building an emergency fund. Aim to save at least three to six months' worth of living expenses in an easily accessible account. This financial cushion can provide peace of mind and help you avoid going into debt if unexpected expenses arise. (Chapter 11 will give you more ideas about how to jump-start your emergency nest egg and how to build an emergency fund over time.)

Reevaluate Your Financial Goals

The loss of a loved one can significantly impact your financial goals, such as retirement planning, home ownership, or education savings. Take the time to reevaluate these goals and adjust your savings and investment strategies accordingly. You may need to consider alternative options, such as delaying retirement or seeking financial aid for education, to accommodate your new financial situation.

Seek Professional Guidance

Creating a new budget and adjusting to your new financial reality can be daunting, particularly if you haven't been accustomed to handling the finances. Don't hesitate to seek professional guidance from a financial planner, advisor, money coach, or credit counselor. They can help you develop a customized budget and financial plan that considers your unique circumstances and goals.

In summary, creating a new budget after a loved one's death is a crucial step toward regaining control over your finances and building a stable future. By following these tips and advice, you can develop a realistic and achievable financial plan that helps you navigate this difficult period. Instead of dwelling on what you may have lost financially, or what you have to give up, embrace the changes and sacrifices necessary for your financial well-being, and focus on the long-term benefits of taking control of your financial future.

At every point of this initial phase, don't hesitate to seek advice from an expert if you're unsure of how to proceed. If you need to slow things down or take a break from financial tasks, that's perfectly fine too. As you work through these first five steps, it's essential to remember that recovering financially after the loss of a loved one is a process that takes time and patience. Be gentle with yourself and allow yourself the space to grieve and adjust to your new reality. Lean on your support network and get professional guidance when needed. While the road to financial recovery may be challenging, taking these initial steps can help you regain stability and build a brighter future for yourself and your family.

Handling Special Circumstances

Although everyone's circumstances are different, here are some common financial challenges you may face when a loved one passes—and potential solutions to help you overcome them:

Loss of Household Income

Challenge: If your spouse was still working, you may experience a significant reduction in your household income, making it difficult to cover your expenses. **Solution:** Consider finding part-time work, exploring freelance opportunities, or seeking assistance from government programs, such as unemployment benefits or Social Security survivor benefits, to help supplement your income during this transition.

Reduction in Social Security Benefits

Challenge: If you and your spouse were both retired, your household may lose one Social Security benefit, resulting in a reduced income.
Solution: Contact the Social Security Administration to discuss your options for receiving survivor benefits. In some cases, you may be eligible for a higher benefit based on your spouse's work history.

Change in Tax Status

Challenge: Your tax rate may increase as you transition from filing jointly to filing as a single individual.
Solution: Consult with a tax professional to determine your new tax liability and discuss potential deductions or credits that may help reduce your tax burden.

Loss of Access to Credit Cards

Challenge: You may lose access to credit cards that were established under your spouse's name. That can be a major problem if you were counting on being able to use those lines of credit.

Solution: Review your credit report to identify which accounts are in your name and consider applying for new credit cards, if necessary. Be cautious about taking on additional debt during this time.

Delayed or Blocked Access to Savings and Investments

Challenge: You may experience delays or difficulties accessing savings, retirement accounts, and investments if beneficiary information was not properly completed.
Solution: Contact the financial institutions holding these accounts and provide them with a copy of the death certificate and any required documentation to expedite the process. Seek legal advice if you encounter significant obstacles.

Inheritance Complications in Second Marriages

Challenge: If you're widowed from a second marriage, your spouse's assets may go to first-marriage children instead of you. Verlaina found out, for instance, that two of the accounts owned by her husband Cecil named his children as beneficiaries. She didn't mind, but the point is to be aware of these possibilities. "Don't take it for granted that you're the beneficiary on every account," Verlaina cautions.
Solution: Consult with an estate attorney to understand your legal rights and potential claims to your spouse's estate. Review your spouse's will, beneficiary designations, and any prenuptial agreements to ensure your interests are protected.

Finding Missing Money

Finding and accessing insurance, assets, or missing money belonging to a deceased relative can also help you bounce back financially. However, this can sometimes be a frustrating endeavor. So you'll need to approach it with patience and diligence. Here are some steps to guide you through the process.

Gather Important Documents

Begin by collecting any important documents, such as wills, insurance policies, bank statements, and investment account records. These documents can provide valuable information about your relative's assets and insurance policies, as well as any potential sources of missing money.

Contact Insurance Companies

If you've located insurance policies, contact the respective insurance companies to inquire about the claims process. Provide them with a copy of the death certificate and any required documentation to initiate the claim. If you're unsure about the existence of any insurance policies, you can also check with your relative's employer, professional associations, or financial advisors.

Search for Bank and Investment Accounts

Review your relative's bank statements and investment account records to identify any accounts that may hold assets. Contact the financial institutions to notify them of your relative's passing and provide them with the necessary documentation, such as the death certificate and proof of your authority to access the accounts (e.g. executorship or legal representation).

Investigate Unclaimed Property

Each state maintains a database of unclaimed property, which may include bank accounts, safe deposit box contents, and uncashed checks. Visit the National Association of Unclaimed Property Administrators (NAUPA) website at `unclaimed.org` and search for your relative's name in the relevant state databases.

Check for Retirement Accounts and Pension Benefits

If your relative was employed or a member of a union, they may have retirement accounts or pension benefits. Contact their former employers or union representatives to inquire about any potential retirement assets or benefits. Additionally, you can search the Pension Benefit Guaranty Corporation (PBGC) website at `PBGC.gov` for unclaimed pension benefits.

Review Tax Records

Examine your relative's tax records for any indications of assets, such as interest or dividend income, which may help you identify additional accounts or investments.

Consult with Professionals

If you're struggling to locate or access your relative's assets, consider consulting with an estate attorney, financial advisor, or professional genealogist. These professionals can provide valuable guidance and assistance in your search.

Making It Past the Initial Phase

Now, what if you're past the phase where you had to tackle paperwork, deal with creditors, handle probate issues, or track down assets—but you still find yourself struggling to bounce back?

There may be practical financial issues at play, such as the loss of income. In such cases, your strategy should focus on trying to increase income, as previously suggested. But consider too whether or not you're dealing with another form of grief: financial grief.

You'll recall that the death of a loved one sparks secondary losses, or so-called ancillary losses. Well, by the same token, when we lose someone close to us with whom we shared an economic connection, we not only experience personal grief but financial grief.

Financial Grief Explained

With financial grief, it's not just about the money. The impact of financial loss can be felt in many aspects of your life, from your daily routines to your long-term plans. Here are some ways that financial grief can manifest:

Your way of life: The lifestyle you once enjoyed with your loved ones may be drastically changed due to financial losses. Activities such as dining out, holidays, and hobbies may no longer be affordable, leaving you feeling like you've lost a piece of your identity.

Your family home: The possibility of having to sell your home to repay debts or cover mortgage payments can be incredibly distressing, adding another layer of grief to an already painful situation.

Your hopes, dreams, and aspirations: The financial plans you once envisioned for yourself and your family may be shattered, forcing you to reassess your future and rebuild your life from scratch.

Your self-image: Financial loss can affect how you view yourself as a provider, businessperson, or employee, leading to feelings of failure and self-doubt.

Emotional Responses to Financial Grief

As you cope with financial grief, you may experience various emotional responses, such as:

Confusion: Losing your financial footing can leave you feeling lost and uncertain about your identity and your future.
Anger: It's normal to feel angry and resentful about your financial situation and the circumstances that led to it.
Blame: You may find yourself blaming yourself or others for your financial losses as you try to make sense of the situation.
Guilt: You might experience feelings of guilt and self-blame, thinking that you should have been more vigilant or made different decisions.
Embarrassment: Financial loss can be a difficult subject to discuss, and you may feel ashamed to share your situation with others.
Sadness: The uncertainty and fear about the future can lead to deep sadness and despair.
Hopelessness: In extreme cases, feelings of hopelessness may lead to suicidal thoughts. If you experience these thoughts, it's important to seek professional help immediately.
Preoccupation: Your financial situation may become all-consuming, leading to mental and physical exhaustion.
Denial: You might try to ignore the reality of your financial losses or downplay the impact on your emotional well-being.
Shock: Disbelief and shock are common initial reactions to financial loss.
Withdrawal: You may find it difficult to face others or engage in social activities, preferring to be alone to process your feelings.
Helplessness: The prospect of starting over can be overwhelming, leaving you feeling helpless and lacking motivation.

Does any of this sound familiar? If so, you're definitely not alone. To better cope with financial grief, try to allow yourself to feel grief without shame or judgment, knowing that your feelings are normal and part of the healing process. As much as you may not want to, it's helpful also to reach out to supportive friends, understanding family members, or professional counselors for support. Be mindful also of your thoughts. Replace negative self-talk with positive affirmations.

If you find yourself considering suicide because your grief is just so overwhelming, know that there is help and places you can turn where people will listen and understand you. In July 2022, the US launched the 988 Suicide and Crisis Lifeline. It's a service Congress established to connect trained counselors with individuals experiencing mental health or substance use crises. Unfortunately, in 2023 a Pew study found that only 13% of Americans have heard of the 988 line. Therefore, it's likely being vastly underutilized, despite an increase in people needing this service.

Finally, recognize that crises can bring about personal growth and resilience. So draw upon your problem-solving skills and keep telling yourself that, even amid pain, you will learn something and become stronger from your experiences.

Again, *The Bounce Back Workbook* can help you more concretely put these strategies and ideas into action. For now, though, as you work on processing your financial grief, just remember that many people have faced similar challenges and emerged stronger and more resourceful. By acknowledging your feelings, seeking support, and focusing on your strengths, you can overcome what may seem like a nightmare situation and draw upon resilience and inner fortitude you probably never knew you had.

Death of a Loved One Resources

1. **GriefShare** – Nationwide grief support groups at churches.
2. **Modern Loss** – Publication and resource hub dealing with grief.
3. **National Alliance for Grieving Children** – Support for kids dealing with death.
4. **National Funeral Directors Association** – Network providing funeral services.
5. **National Widowers Organization** – Peer support for widowers.
6. **Soaring Spirits International** – Community for those who've lost a partner.
7. **The Compassionate Friends** – Organization providing hope to bereaved parents.
8. **The Dinner Party** – Community of young adults experiencing loss.
9. **The Heartfelt Institute** – Nonprofit focused on grief education and healing.
10. **Tragedy Assistance Program for Survivors** – Assistance for families of fallen military.

Chapter 6
Disability

"The best way to bounce back from adversity is to meet it head-on."

—Henry Ford

Christopher Powell is a remarkable individual—a groundbreaking mathematician, businessman, and motivational speaker. What makes his achievements all the more extraordinary is that he has accomplished them despite living his entire life with the most severe form of cerebral palsy, which caused him to spend most of his childhood and teenage years in a wheelchair.

"Cerebral palsy is often called a disability, but I call it a condition. It's something that you have to deal with on a daily basis," he says resolutely. In Christopher's case, he's done far more than just deal with his condition. Through steadfast determination and intense perseverance, he has defied the odds and far surpassed the expectations of others—but not himself.

For the first 22 years of Christopher's life, other people had to bathe, clothe, and feed him.

His condition is called quadriplegic, or quadriparesis, cerebral palsy, which means all of his limbs are affected; both arms and both legs. So his muscles are very stiff, and he has to make a concerted effort just to try to relax his arms. "An analogy I use is, 'Imagine if you have a speaker playing really good music, but in my case, the music is playing too loud. The volume is too high, and it's irritating.' So I try to find ways to turn the volume down by exercising or relaxing," Christopher shares, reflecting on the challenges he faces daily.

For instance, simply going to his kitchen or a brief walk presents countless obstacles. But Christopher's can-do spirit and practical nature shine through—traits he developed in his youth.

The early years of Christopher's life were marked by his mother, late aunt, and late grandmother tirelessly caring for him, and assisting with all his daily functions and activities.

As he got older, he became increasingly frustrated because he was always striving to do more, despite his physical limitations. But one thing always seemed to help: "I tried to maintain the mindset of having more than one solution to solve a problem," Christopher recalls, emphasizing his determination to overcome the obstacles that stood in his way.

In public school as a child, Christopher developed a deep love for mathematics while in high school. Even though he couldn't raise his hand or sketch out a math problem himself, his thirst for knowledge and self-improvement was unquenchable. "I couldn't write or hold a pencil. But I always had the mindset of striving to learn more about myself and the idea to say, how can I get better? My constant goal every day was: 'How can I get better and how can I improve my situation?'" he shares.

Setting goals became Christopher's driving force. He didn't waste time dwelling on what he couldn't do. "I was a big goal-setter, and that's what helped me stay motivated. If I set a goal, I wasn't concerned about what I *couldn't* do because I was focused on what I *needed* to do," he says.

His journey toward independence and education was not without its challenges, educational, physical, and more. As a youth, Christopher attended a homeroom with other children with disabilities. However, a teacher recognized his potential and paved the way for him to attend classes with non-disabled students, setting him on a path to take those math classes in high school. He excelled academically and that led to pursuing college.

Christopher's college years at Montgomery College and the University of Maryland College Park—where he earned a bachelor's degree in mathematics and was honored with the Dean's Award—presented him with an opportunity to pursue not only higher education but also independence. Transitioning from relying on his family and caretakers to accomplishing tasks independently became his paramount goal.

Setting the Bar Higher

"I lived in the dorms, and that's why I had the desire to have more independence," Christopher says. "I had a dual job in my college years: one was to get my degree, and the other was to become more independent."

"I was so used to having my parents do things for me" he adds. "I had to eventually do more on my own. When I decided to walk full-time, independently, that was another goal."

Just learning to walk, however, wasn't enough for Christopher. He then set the bar higher by attempting to run—a feat he wound up accomplishing in spectacular fashion. "I became an athlete, and I used to run track, and my legs got stronger," he says. "It led me to leave the wheelchair. I did many road races." Just as when he was a child striving to walk, he had many tumbles while running. Yet, those spills didn't deter him. "My college roommates would pick me up when I fell. But every year I got better, and my endurance got stronger," Christopher shares, highlighting the determination and progress he made in his physical abilities.

As he reminisced on the challenges he faced and the growth he experienced during his formative years, Christopher said he learned to rely on his inner voice and belief in himself. "The only voice I listened to was myself because it's hard for others to believe what you can do until you do it," he states, stressing the importance of self-belief and perseverance in overcoming obstacles.

Now, at the age of 53, Christopher Powell serves as the coordinator of the Mathematics Learning Center at Montgomery College. It's a position he's held for 24 years and counting. It's also a role where Christopher has inspired countless students to reach beyond their limits.

In addition to his career and personal achievements, Christopher purchased a house in Maryland in 2002. For well over 20 years, he has achieved his goal of living independently—a testament to his fighting spirit and unwavering determination.

Despite his awe-inspiring feats, Christopher doesn't sugarcoat his accomplishments—whether that's managing to live by himself or having run competitive races. "This was a process that took not days, weeks, months, or even years, but decades to learn," he says.

"It's very, very tough. It's not easy," he admits. "It takes an incredible amount of energy to do this (living alone). But I feel so fortunate and blessed to be able to do it despite the challenges. I know a lot of people who would love to spend a day in my shoes."

Reflecting on his life, Christopher said he is most happy about having put in the time and effort necessary to reach where he is today. He says people with disabilities and challenging conditions, like all individuals, "want to be recognized for their gifts and hard work." He said gratitude fills his heart for both "the highs and lows I've experienced." Both have shaped him into the remarkable individual he is today.

His advice to others: don't let a disability prevent you from identifying what you want to do—and going for it. "The thing that keeps me going is my goals. It keeps that drive alive," Christopher says. "If you don't have something to reach for, that's when you're going to have problems. It makes life exciting when you're striving for something."

He also emphasizes the importance of staying grounded and maintaining an even keel. He says that with his condition, he avoids letting himself get "too low or too high" emotionally—and that's the advice he gives to other people with disabilities too. "You have to be resilient in knowing that just because yesterday was a good day doesn't mean tomorrow will be."

Christopher Powell's story is one of resilience, perseverance, and grit. Despite the challenges he faced, he never allowed himself to be defined by his condition. Instead, he embraced his goals, pushed boundaries, and proved that with determination and a positive mindset, one can achieve greatness. Christopher just happened to be born with cerebral palsy. But disabilities can strike anyone, anywhere, and at any time. They might be the result of an illness, an accident, or a genetic condition, and they can significantly affect your life, including your finances.

Whether you personally have a disability, are caring for someone who does, or you know and want to support an individual navigating life with a disability, it's important to understand the scope of the challenges—as well as the resources available—for those with disabilities.

What Are Disabilities and How Prevalent Are They?

A disability is a physical or mental impairment that interferes with one or more major life activities. These activities could involve walking, talking, seeing, hearing, or learning. Disabilities can be temporary or permanent, ranging from mild to severe. Some common examples of disabilities include:

- Vision or hearing impairments;
- Mobility impairments;

- Chronic illnesses such as diabetes or heart disease;
- Mental health conditions such as depression or anxiety;
- Developmental disabilities such as Down syndrome or autism.

Disabilities are more widespread than you might think. The Centers for Disease Control and Prevention reports that about 61 million adults in the United States have a disability. That's roughly one in four adults.

Too often, when we think about people with disabilities, we envision only elderly senior citizens. While it's true that disabilities are more common among older adults—around 40% of those aged 65 and older have a disability—it's also true that many younger Americans will suffer a disability at some point. In fact, the Council for Disability Awareness reports that more than 25% of today's 20-year-olds will become disabled before retirement. This statistic highlights the importance of preparing for potential disabilities and safeguarding your financial and physical well-being. Long-term disability lasts 34.6 months, on average, according to the Council. During that time, you could run through any savings you may have, greatly increase your debt load, or simply not be able to make ends meet on a daily or monthly basis. And unlike many other setbacks, being disabled poses unique financial challenges—ranging from having limited work options or living on a fixed income to amassing large medical bills or having to budget for extra monthly expenses to pay for services you can no longer do for yourself.

Each of these situations poses significant financial challenges for individuals with disabilities and their families. For instance, a disability that hampers your work opportunities will result in income loss. Additionally, disabilities that require costly medical treatments can quickly drain your savings and cause debt to pile up. Furthermore, if you have a physical or mental disability, chances are you'll need to budget for extra monthly expenses to cover services you can no longer do for yourself, such as housekeeping, transportation, or personal care.

A Comprehensive View of Managing the Challenges Tied to Disabilities

Handling your finances when you have a disability can be tough, but there are other aspects you have to address too in order to protect your overall well-being. As people with disabilities can attest, managing and recovering from a disability is a multifaceted process, involving not only physical challenges but also emotional and economic aspects. One critical aspect that is often overlooked is disability coverage. Disability coverage is a type of insurance that provides income in the event you're unable to perform your work and earn money due to a disability. Despite its importance, there is a significant disability coverage gap, with many people lacking adequate insurance to cover them in case of disability.

Closing this gap is essential. You need to fully understand the risks of disability and the need for proper coverage. Unfortunately, most people tend to underestimate their chances of becoming disabled and overestimate the support they would receive from government programs. This can lead to financial hardship in the event of a disability.

The truth is if you face a disability, you won't have to go it alone—and you shouldn't. The systems around you—from your workplace if you're employed, to your local and federal government—also have a role to play. As far as employers, they can play a key role in closing the disability coverage gap because they can offer disability insurance as part of their benefits package and educate their employees about its importance. Moreover, policy changes at the governmental level can help ensure that more people have access to this critical protection. You can advocate for both of these things—with a private employer and with your elected officials.

Emotionally, support from family, friends, and professional therapists can also help you cope with the psychological effects of disability. Various therapeutic strategies, such as cognitive behavioral therapy, can assist in managing emotional responses and promoting resilience.

Physically, a comprehensive health care team, including doctors, physical therapists, occupational therapists, and others, can guide your recovery or adaptation process. They can help you regain as much function as possible, learn new skills, and adapt to your circumstances.

I hope you get my point: recovering from a disability is a holistic process that requires addressing physical, emotional, and financial aspects. Disability coverage is a significant part of this process, providing necessary financial support and peace of mind. And not just for the disabled person. Approximately 30 million Americans juggle work while also caring for a loved one. That's a big responsibility that greatly impacts their physical, mental, and financial health too. That's why I'll break down everything you need to know about disability coverage and more.

In this chapter, you will learn:

- The basics of disability insurance and how it can help you financially;
- All about Social Security Disability Income (SSDI);
- How to claim Social Security Disability Income or Worker's Comp benefits;
- What to do if you get sued for overpayment of disability benefits;

- The six primary sources of income if you become disabled and can't work;
- Federal and state resources that help the disabled and their caregivers;
- The mind-body connections that can help you overcome a physical disability,

The Basics of Disability Insurance and How It Can Help Financially

Disability insurance is an essential financial safety net for many individuals, as it can provide income replacement in the event of a disabling injury or illness. Here's an overview of disability insurance, its benefits, and how it can offer financial support when you're unable to work due to disability.

What Is Disability Insurance?

Disability insurance is a type of insurance policy that provides income replacement if you become disabled and are unable to work as a result. It can help cover your living expenses, medical bills, and other financial obligations during your period of disability. There are two main types of disability insurance:

Short-term disability insurance: This type of insurance provides income replacement for a short period, typically ranging from a few weeks to a few months. If your workplace offers disability insurance coverage, you can file a claim if you get sick or injured. Some short-term disability plans give benefits for as long as three months to 12 months per disability. Short-term disability usually covers a higher percentage of your income (e.g. 60% to 80%) but has a shorter waiting period before benefits begin, such as 7 to 14 days.

Long-term disability insurance: If you're unable to work for a longer time, long-term disability plans kick in with monthly benefits after a waiting period or after other benefits have run out. Long-term disability insurance offers income replacement for an extended period, which can range from a few years to the rest of your life, depending on the policy. It generally covers a lower percentage of your income (e.g. 50% to 70%) but has a longer waiting period before benefits begin, usually around 90 days.

But not every employer offers long-term disability, or LTD. In fact, the US Bureau of Labor Statistics reports that only 35% of civilian employees have access to LTD plans. And access to these plans can really differ based on what you're earning. For the lowest earners, only 9% had access, compared to 59% of the highest earners.

Even if your employer does offer group LTD, it might not be enough to keep you afloat financially if you're dealing with a serious injury or illness. If you do use the LTD insurance offered by your employer, the income benefit probably won't cover all your expenses when you have to stop working. The lower-end group plans usually only replace about 40% of your income, which leaves a pretty big income gap. And remember, the average LTD claim lasts 34.6 months, which could really eat into your emergency savings and cause major financial stress, or even bankruptcy. Also, be aware that some of you might not be eligible for LTD even if your employer provides it. This includes part-time, seasonal, and temporary workers. Check with your employer to be sure.

Benefits of Disability Insurance

Disability insurance offers several benefits that can help you maintain your financial stability in the event of a disability:

Income replacement: One of the primary benefits of disability insurance is that it provides a portion of your income when you're unable to work. This can help you maintain your standard of living and cover essential expenses such as housing, utilities, and groceries.

Protection of your financial future: Disability insurance can help you avoid draining your savings or accumulating debt due to the loss of income during your disability. This can protect your long-term financial health and ensure you have resources available for future needs, such as retirement or your children's education. Since the income provided by disability insurance can help you continue contributing to your retirement savings or other long-term financial goals this helps keep your financial future on track, despite your temporary or permanent inability to work.

Peace of mind: Knowing that you have financial protection in place can alleviate some of the stress and anxiety that often accompany disability. This peace of mind can allow you to focus on your recovery and rehabilitation, rather than worrying about how you will pay your bills.

Medical expenses: The income provided by disability insurance can also help cover medical expenses associated with your disability. This can include doctor visits, medications, physical therapy, or adaptive equipment.

Debt management: Disability insurance can help you manage your debt obligations during your disability. By providing a source of income, disability insurance can prevent you from falling behind on loan payments, credit card bills, or other financial obligations.

In conclusion, disability insurance is an essential financial safety net that can provide income replacement and financial support in the event of a disabling injury or illness. By understanding the basics of disability insurance and how it can help you financially, you can make informed decisions about whether this type of insurance is right for you and your family.

All About Social Security Disability Insurance

There's another benefit you've been earning while working that you might not even know about. It's called Social Security Disability Insurance (SSDI), and a lot of us just aren't aware it exists, even though it's such a big help for folks dealing with disabilities or serious illnesses. Social Security Disability Insurance and employer-provided disability insurance are different types of disability insurance.

SSDI is a federal insurance program administered by the Social Security Administration (SSA) in the United States. It provides income support to individuals who have a disability that prevents them from engaging in "substantial gainful activity." The disability must be expected to last for at least 12 months or expected to result in death. To qualify for SSDI, you generally need to have worked and paid Social Security taxes for a certain period of time and meet the SSA's definition of disability.

On the other hand, employer-provided disability insurance, also known as group disability insurance or employer-sponsored disability insurance, is typically offered by employers as part of their employee benefits package. This type of insurance (as described in the previous section) provides income replacement if you become disabled and are unable to work due to an illness, injury, or accident. The specific coverage and eligibility requirements can vary depending on the employer and the policy. While SSDI and employer-provided disability insurance both aim to provide financial assistance to people who are unable to work due to a disability, they have different eligibility criteria, coverage limits, and application processes.

Eligibility for SSDI

Let's be honest, none of us think we'll end up in a situation where we need disability aid. But remember that a whopping 61 million people live with some kind of disability. This could be anything from back pain and arthritis to mental health issues. Again, that's one in every four of us whose daily life is affected by what we broadly call a "disability."

When you're dealing with a disability, it can really hit you hard financially. That's why it's crucial to know about the financial support programs out there, such as Social Security Disability Insurance, which could come in handy when you and your loved ones need it most.

Even if you're working part-time, you could still get Social Security Disability Insurance benefits. It mostly depends on how much you're earning. In 2023, if you earned below $1,470 per month, or $2,460 a month for blind individuals, you could qualify for SSDI benefits. But most folks applying for SSDI have stopped working because of a severe disability.

So, why does SSDI have an earnings limit? It's because one of the main conditions to be eligible is that your injury or illness has to be serious enough to stop you from working. SSDI benefits are very hard to get, but they are there for those who have a good work history but can't work anymore because of a qualifying injury, disability, or illness. And believe it or not, more than 159 million US workers are insured for this federal disability program, according to the Center on Budget and Policy Priorities. However, the Center says just one out of three SSDI applicants gets approved.

A Profile of Who Collects SSDI

About 8.2 million people currently receive disabled-worker benefits from Social Security. Some of their relatives get payments too, including 104,000 spouses and 1.4 million children. So if a medical condition is stopping you from earning enough, SSDI benefits may be just what you need to give you and your family the support you deserve.

In decades past, men greatly outnumbered women in terms of SSDI recipients. For example, back in 1990, there was a 2-to-1 ratio of male SSDI recipients to female recipients. But these days, a roughly equal number of men and women receive SSDI payments. Research also shows that the risk of disability increases with age. So it's perhaps no surprise that people are twice as likely to receive SSDI at age 50 as at 40 and twice as likely to collect at age 60 as at

50, according to the Center on Budget and Policy Priorities. Generally, most people who receive SSDI benefits are older and experience significant physical or mental limitations. The average person receiving SSDI is in their late 50s, with 75% of beneficiaries being over 50 years old. Additionally, nearly 35% of recipients are 60 years old or older. These individuals suffer from severe impairments that affect their mental health, muscles, bones, or other aspects of their daily functioning. When looking at beneficiaries who are 50 years old or older, physical disorders are the most common. However, for those under the age of 50, about half of the beneficiaries have mental disorders. These mental disorders include conditions such as intellectual disability, mood disorders such as bipolar disease and severe depression, brain-related mental disorders caused by disease or damage, psychotic disorders including schizophrenia, and other mental impairments.

As mentioned, a lot of American workers aren't aware of SSDI as a huge source of help they've been earning while working. But both employees and employers pay into this federal program through Federal Insurance Contributions Act (FICA) payroll taxes. Here's the lowdown on what makes you eligible for SSDI:

- You've got a medical condition, illness, or injury that's severe enough to keep you from working for 12 months or could be terminal.
- You've worked and paid FICA taxes for at least five out of the last 10 years.
- You're between 21 years old and full retirement age.
- You're getting treatment from a health care professional who can vouch for the severity of your medical condition(s).

A Host of Benefits with SSDI

The SSDI approval process might take a few months, or maybe even longer. But trust me, if you qualify, it's worth it. The benefits can keep you out of poverty, particularly when dealing with chronic illnesses or disabilities. Here's what you get:

Monthly income: In 2023, the average benefit was $1,483 and could rise to as much as $3,627. The maximum SSDI benefit for 2024 is $3,822.

Medicare coverage: Medical and prescription drug coverage start 24 months after your SSDI cash benefits kick in.

Protected Social Security retirement benefits: When you're approved for SSDI, your Social Security earnings record gets frozen. This could mean a higher retirement income for you.

Dependent benefits: If you've got kids under 18, SSDI approval could mean more benefits for them, adding up to 50% more to your monthly payment.
Annual cost-of-living adjustments: Your benefits don't stay the same. They rise with inflation.
Return to work incentives: This is through Social Security's Ticket to Work. (More on this later.)

When you combine LTD insurance with the extra safety net of SSDI, it can make a huge difference in your life and the lives of the people you care about. It's super important to understand what kind of disability income programs are out there. These programs are key to helping us when we hit a gap in our working careers, especially when it comes out of the blue.

Claiming Social Security Disability Income or Workers' Comp Benefits

If you're unable to work due to a disability, Social Security Disability Income (SSDI) and Workers' Compensation benefits can provide crucial financial support. Figuring out how to go about this can sometimes feel overwhelming. But don't get flustered or despondent about the process. Once you understand the main requirements, it's far more manageable. So let me guide you through the four-step process of applying for and claiming these essential benefits.

To claim Social Security Disability Income benefits, follow these steps.

Step 1: Determine Your Eligibility

Before applying for SSDI, make sure you meet the eligibility requirements. These include two main criteria: First, you need to have a qualifying disability that is expected to last at least 12 months or result in death. Additionally, you must have accumulated enough work credits through your employment history to qualify. Typically, you need 40 credits, 20 of which were earned in the last 10 years before becoming disabled.

Step 2: Gather Necessary Documentation

You'll need to provide several documents when applying for SSDI benefits, such as:

- Your Social Security number;
- Your birth certificate or proof of US citizenship;
- Medical records and contact info for health care providers who treated your disability;

- A detailed work history, including job titles and duties;
- Information about any Workers' Compensation claims you've filed.

Step 3: Apply for SSDI Benefits

You can apply for SSDI benefits online, by phone, or in person at your local Social Security office. To apply online, visit the Social Security Administration's (SSA) website and follow the instructions provided. If you prefer to apply by phone, call the SSA at 1-800-772-1213. When applying in person, make an appointment with your local Social Security office.

Step 4: Wait for a Decision

The SSA will review your application and make a decision, usually within three to five months. If your application is approved, you'll receive a letter with information about your benefits. If it's denied, you can appeal the decision within 60 days.

Getting Workers' Compensation Benefits

If your disability is the result of a work-related injury or illness, follow these steps to claim Workers' Compensation benefits.

Step 1: Report the Injury or Illness to Your Employer

Notify your employer as soon as possible after the injury or illness occurs. Each state has different deadlines for reporting, so it's essential to act promptly. Your employer should provide you with a claim form to complete.

Step 2: Seek Medical Treatment

Get medical treatment for your injury or illness as soon as possible. Make sure to inform the health care provider that your condition is work-related, and ask them to document this in your medical records.

Step 3: File a Workers' Compensation Claim

Complete the claim form provided by your employer, and submit it to your state's Workers' Compensation agency. Be sure to include all necessary documentation, such as medical records and proof of employment. Keep a copy of the claim form for your records.

Step 4: Wait for a Decision

Your state's Workers' Compensation agency will review your claim and make a decision. If your claim is approved, you'll receive benefits according to your state's guidelines. These benefits can include wage replacement, medical treatment coverage, and vocational rehabilitation. If your claim is denied, you can appeal the decision within your state's specified time frame.

Applying for and claiming SSDI or Workers' Compensation benefits can provide vital financial support when you're unable to work due to a disability. By following the steps outlined in this section, you can navigate the application process and secure the benefits you need to maintain your financial well-being during a challenging time.

What to Do If You Get Sued for Overpayment of Disability Benefits

In some cases, you might receive an "overpayment" of disability benefits, due to you working and earning too much, an error by the Social Security Administration, or as a result of a miscommunication or misunderstanding. This is probably the last thing you want to deal with when facing a hardship such as a long-term disability. But it's important to be prepared for such scenarios because they do happen more often than you might suspect. According to the Social Security Office of Retirement and Disability Policy, only about 2% of disability insurance beneficiaries received a work-related overpayment. However, among people with earnings sufficient to put them at risk of a work-related overpayment, 71% were overpaid. Work-related overpayments lasted for a median of nine months and accrued a median amount of $9,282. And guess what. If you are flagged as being overpaid, it's on you to pay that money back to the federal government—which is typically done by the SSA reducing your monthly disability benefits. In such cases, it could take years to repay those funds, and that's a big financial burden likely to result in a diminished standard of living. So here's what to do to navigate this complex situation if you receive word of this issue or get sued for overpayment of disability benefits.

Don't Ignore the Situation

If you receive a notice that you have been overpaid disability benefits or are being sued, it's crucial not to ignore the situation. Ignoring notices or legal actions can lead to further complications, such as garnished wages, liens on your property, or even more significant legal consequences.

Gather Documentation

Start by gathering all relevant documentation related to your disability benefits. This can include payment records, medical records, correspondence with the insurance company or SSA, and any other documents that can help establish your case. Having this information organized and readily available will be helpful when working with an attorney or discussing your situation with the insurance company or SSA.

Contact an Attorney

Navigating a lawsuit for overpayment of disability benefits can be complex, and it's wise to have professional legal help on your side. Contact an attorney who specializes in disability law, or even a pro bono legal service, to discuss your situation and determine the best course of action. They can help you understand your rights and responsibilities, as well as represent you in court or negotiations with the insurance company or SSA.

Communicate with the Insurance Company or SSA

Once you have legal representation, your attorney will likely communicate with the insurance company or SSA on your behalf. They can work to negotiate a settlement, request a waiver or reduction of the overpayment, or establish a repayment plan that is manageable for your financial situation. Keep in mind that you should not communicate with the insurance company or SSA without first consulting your attorney, as they may use anything you say against you in the legal proceedings.

Consider Possible Defenses

There are several possible defenses against a lawsuit for overpayment of disability benefits. Some of these include:

Statute of limitations: If the lawsuit is filed after the statute of limitations has expired, you may be able to have the case dismissed. The statute of limitations varies depending on the type of benefits and the jurisdiction in which the lawsuit is filed.

Financial hardship: If repaying the overpayment would cause you significant financial hardship, you may be able to negotiate a waiver or reduction of the overpayment amount.

Lack of knowledge: If you can prove that you were unaware of the overpayment and had no reason to suspect that you were receiving more benefits than you were entitled to, you may have a valid defense.

Your attorney can help you determine which defenses may apply to your situation and how best to present them in court or negotiations.

Prepare for Court (If Necessary)

If your case goes to court, it's essential to be prepared. Work with your attorney to develop a strong defense and gather all necessary documentation and evidence. Your attorney will guide you through the court process and represent your best interests throughout the proceedings.

Here's the bottom line: If you find yourself advised of or sued for overpayment of disability benefits, it's crucial to take the situation seriously and act promptly. By gathering documentation, seeking legal representation, and considering possible defenses, you can increase your chances of resolving the issue favorably and minimizing the financial impact on your life.

Six Alternative Income Sources When You Have a Disability and Can't Work

When you're dealing with a disability that prevents you from working, finding alternative sources of income becomes crucial. There are six primary income sources worth exploring that can tide you over financially when you have a disability. These sources include government benefits, disability insurance, personal savings and investments, passive income, support from family and friends, and reverse mortgages. Here's a look at each option.

Government Benefits

There are several government programs designed to provide financial assistance to people with disabilities who can't work. Some of the most common programs include:

Social Security Disability Insurance (SSDI): As previously explained, SSDI is a federal program that offers monthly benefits to individuals who have worked long enough and paid Social Security taxes but can no longer work due to a qualifying disability. The amount of SSDI benefits you receive depends on your work history and earnings.

Supplemental Security Income (SSI): SSI is a needs-based program that provides financial assistance to individuals with limited income and resources who are disabled, blind, or elderly. SSI benefits can help cover basic needs such as food, clothing, and shelter.

Workers' Compensation: As mentioned, if your disability is a result of a work-related injury or illness, you may be eligible for workers' compensation benefits. These benefits can include wage replacement, medical treatment coverage, and vocational rehabilitation.

Disability Insurance

As explained earlier, disability insurance is a type of insurance policy that provides income replacement if you become disabled and unable to work. There are two main types of disability insurance:

Short-term disability insurance: This type of insurance typically covers a portion of your income for a short period, often between several weeks up to six months. It's designed to help you maintain your financial stability while you recover from a temporary disability.

Long-term disability insurance: Long-term disability insurance provides income replacement for an extended period, often up to retirement age. The benefit amount and duration depend on the policy's terms and your specific situation.

Disability insurance policies can be obtained through your employer or purchased individually. It's important to review the coverage, waiting periods, and benefit amounts when choosing a disability insurance policy.

Personal Savings and Investments

Having a solid emergency fund and investment portfolio can provide a source of income if you become disabled and unable to work. Your emergency fund should cover at least three to six months' worth of living expenses, which can help you cover immediate expenses while you explore other income sources.

Investments, such as stocks, bonds, and mutual funds, can generate returns that can help you maintain your financial stability during your disability. But if you're investing in the financial markets, do have a diversified portfolio to minimize risk and ensure a more stable income.

Passive Income

Passive income is money earned with little to no ongoing effort on your part. Some common sources of passive income include:

Rental properties: If you own rental properties, the rent you collect from tenants can provide a steady source of income.
Dividend stocks: Investing in dividend-paying stocks can generate a regular stream of income through dividend payments.
Peer-to-peer lending: By lending money to individuals or businesses through peer-to-peer lending platforms, you can earn interest on your loans.
Royalties: If you have created intellectual property, such as a book, music, or invention, you may receive royalties from the ongoing use or sale of your work.

Support from Family and Friends

In some cases, your family and friends may be willing to provide financial assistance if you become disabled and are unable to work. This support can come in the form of direct financial aid, help with daily expenses, or even offering a place to live. While relying on family and friends may not be a long-term solution, their support can be invaluable during a rough patch and can help you maintain your financial stability.

Reverse Mortgages

Finally, for older adults aged 62 and above who are disabled and own their homes, a reverse mortgage can be a valuable source of income. A reverse mortgage is a type of loan that allows you to access the equity in your home without having to sell it or make monthly mortgage payments. Instead, the loan is repaid when the homeowner passes away, sells the home, or moves out permanently.

The funds from a reverse mortgage can be disbursed in several ways, such as a lump sum, monthly payments, or a line of credit. These funds can be used to cover disability-related expenses, supplement other income sources, or pay for home modifications to accommodate your disability.

There are specific eligibility requirements for obtaining a reverse mortgage, such as:

- The homeowner must be at least 62 years old.
- The home must be the borrower's primary residence.

- The homeowner must have sufficient equity in the home.
- The homeowner must meet the financial eligibility criteria set by the lender.

Carefully consider the implications of a reverse mortgage before deciding to pursue this option. While it can provide financial relief and help you maintain your independence, a reverse mortgage will reduce the equity in your home, which may impact your estate or the inheritance you leave to your heirs.

Safeguarding Your Earnings During a Disability

To recap: If you or a family member faces a disability and can no longer earn money, it's essential to have a safety net. Here's a quick summary of just the insurance-related income replacement options in the event of disability:

State-sponsored Temporary Disability Insurance: States including California, Hawaii, New York, New Jersey, and Rhode Island offer limited-duration paid leave for those with disabilities.

Short-term Disability Plans from Private Insurers: These offer coverage for a short duration in case of disability.

Long-term Disability Through the Social Security Administration: However, these benefits might not fully compensate for lost income, and qualifying can be challenging.

Long-term Disability Policies from Private Insurers: Another option for extensive coverage.

Workers' Compensation: Benefits for employees who become disabled due to work-related incidents.

Veterans Benefits: For those who served in the military.

The duration and amount of these benefits can differ widely, depending on the source. Notably, state funds and workers' compensation cater exclusively to employed individuals. Therefore, if you're self-employed, or are an independent contractor, look into private insurance options for comprehensive coverage.

Beyond insurance, other income sources are available for individuals who become disabled and can't work. By exploring disability insurance, government benefits, personal savings and investments, passive income, support from family and friends, and reverse mortgages for older adults, you can find the financial resources you need to manage your disability and maintain your quality of life.

Federal and State Resources That Help the Disabled and Their Caregivers

Navigating the challenges of living with a disability or caring for a loved one with a disability can be overwhelming. Fortunately, there are special federal and state resources and programs that can assist disabled individuals and their caregivers. In this section, we'll explore these resources, covering topics such as financial assistance, health care, housing, employment, and educational support.

Financial Assistance

There are several financial assistance programs available to disabled individuals and their caregivers. These programs can help cover the costs of daily living, medical care, and other expenses associated with disabilities.

Supplemental Security Income (SSI): As mentioned earlier, SSI is a federal program that provides financial assistance to individuals with limited income and resources who are disabled, blind, or elderly.

Temporary Assistance for Needy Families (TANF): TANF is a state-administered program that provides cash assistance and support services to low-income families with children. Eligibility and benefit amounts vary by state.

Medicaid: Medicaid is a state and federal program that provides health coverage to low-income individuals, including those with disabilities. In addition to health care services, Medicaid may also cover long-term care services, such as personal care assistance and nursing home care.

Health Care Resources

Access to health care is crucial for individuals with disabilities and their caregivers. Here are some resources to help you navigate health care services and support:

Medicare: Medicare is a federal health insurance program for individuals aged 65 and older, as well as certain younger individuals with disabilities. Medicare can help cover hospital stays, doctor visits, prescription medications, and more.

State Health Insurance Assistance Programs (SHIPs): SHIPs offer free, unbiased information and assistance to Medicare beneficiaries and their caregivers. They can help you understand your Medicare benefits, compare health care plans, and resolve issues with your coverage.

Children's Health Insurance Program (CHIP): CHIP provides low-cost health coverage to children in families that earn too much to qualify for Medicaid but cannot afford private insurance. In some states, CHIP also covers pregnant women.

Housing Assistance

Accessible and affordable housing is essential for individuals with disabilities. Several resources can help you find suitable housing options and financial assistance:

Department of Housing and Urban Development (HUD): HUD offers resources and programs to help individuals with disabilities find affordable, accessible housing. These programs include public housing, housing choice vouchers, and the Section 811 Supportive Housing for Persons with Disabilities program.

State Housing Agencies: State housing agencies can provide information on affordable housing options, rental assistance programs, and home modification grants or loans for individuals with disabilities.

Employment Support

Employment opportunities can improve the financial well-being of individuals with disabilities and their caregivers. There are various resources available to help you or a disabled person you know find and maintain employment:

Vocational Rehabilitation (VR) Agencies: VR agencies provide a range of services to help individuals with disabilities prepare for, find, and maintain employment. Services can include job training, job placement assistance, and workplace accommodations.

Ticket to Work Program: The Ticket to Work program is a free, voluntary program offered by the Social Security Administration that helps Social Security disability beneficiaries explore employment options and become financially independent.

Educational Support

Education and training can empower individuals with disabilities and their caregivers. Here are some resources that can help with educational support:

Individuals with Disabilities Education Act (IDEA): IDEA is a federal law that ensures children with disabilities have access to a free, appropriate public education tailored to their individual needs. IDEA covers children from birth through age 21.

State Education Agencies (SEAs): SEAs can provide information on special education services, resources, and support for students with disabilities and their families.

Parent Training and Information Centers (PTIs): PTIs offer training and information to help parents of children with disabilities understand their rights and responsibilities under IDEA. They also provide support for parents in advocating for their child's educational needs.

Transportation and Mobility Resources

Accessible transportation options are vital when you have a disability and want to live independently and participate in your community. Thankfully, there are resources available to help with transportation and to improve your mobility:

Paratransit services: Many public transportation systems offer paratransit services for individuals with disabilities who are unable to use traditional public transit. These services typically provide door-to-door or curb-to-curb transportation and may require advance reservations.

State and local transportation agencies: Contact your state or local transportation agency for information on accessible transportation options and services in your area.

Support for Caregivers

Caregivers play a critical role in supporting individuals with disabilities, and it's important for them to have access to resources and support as well. Here are some resources for caregivers:

National Family Caregiver Support Program (NFCSP): NFCSP provides grants to states and territories to fund a range of support services for family caregivers. These services can include information and assistance, counseling, respite care, and training.

Family Caregiver Alliance (FCA): FCA offers information, resources, and support for family caregivers of adults with disabilities, chronic health conditions, or cognitive impairments. Their services include educational materials, webinars, and an online caregiver support group.
ARCH National Respite Network and Resource Center: ARCH provides information on respite care services and resources for family caregivers, including a searchable respite provider database and a guide to respite funding and services by state.

As you can see, there are numerous federal, state, and local resources and programs to assist disabled individuals and their caregivers in navigating the challenges they face. By exploring these resources, you can find support in areas such as financial assistance, health care, housing, employment, education, transportation, and caregiving. These resources can help improve your quality of life and enable you and your loved ones to live more independently and engage as much as possible within your local community.

The Mind-Body Connections That Can Help You Overcome a Physical Disability

The mind and body are interconnected, and understanding this relationship can be crucial in overcoming the challenges presented by a physical disability. In this section, we'll explore the power of the mind-body connection and discuss various strategies that can help you manage and even thrive in the face of physical limitations.

Embrace a Positive Mindset

Maintaining a positive mindset can have a significant impact on your overall well-being and ability to cope with a physical disability. Focus on your strengths, accomplishments, and potential for growth, rather than dwelling on limitations. A positive attitude can help you build resilience and adapt more effectively to your situation.

Practice Mindfulness and Meditation

Mindfulness and meditation are powerful tools that can help you manage stress, reduce anxiety, and improve your mental and emotional well-being. By practicing mindfulness and meditation, you can cultivate greater self-awareness, acceptance, and compassion for yourself and your situation. These practices can also help you cope with pain and discomfort associated with your disability.

Engage in Regular Physical Activity

While your physical disability may undoubtedly limit certain activities, it's still a good idea to stay as active as possible. Regular physical activity—whatever you're able to do—can help improve your physical and mental health, reduce stress, and increase your sense of self-efficacy. Work with your health care team to develop an appropriate exercise plan tailored to your abilities and needs.

Seek Social Support

Connecting with others who understand and support your journey can be incredibly valuable in overcoming the challenges of a physical disability. Join support groups, attend community events, or engage with online forums to build a network of people who share your experiences and can offer encouragement, advice, and friendship.

Utilize Therapy and Counseling

Professional therapy and counseling can help you address the emotional and psychological challenges that often accompany a physical disability. A therapist or counselor can help you develop coping strategies, improve your self-esteem, and provide guidance on managing stress, anxiety, and depression.

Consider Complementary and Alternative Therapies

Complementary and alternative therapies, such as acupuncture, massage, or yoga, can provide additional support in managing the physical and emotional aspects of your disability. These therapies can help reduce pain, improve mobility, and promote relaxation. Consult with your health care team before starting any new therapy to ensure it is safe and appropriate for your situation.

Develop Adaptive Strategies

Learning to adapt and find new ways to perform daily tasks can help you maintain your independence and improve your quality of life. Work with occupational therapists, physical therapists, or other professionals to develop adaptive strategies and tools that can help you navigate your daily life more effectively. (See *The Bounce Back Workbook* for 10 ways to utilize adaptive strategies and better manage a disability or physically challenging condition.)

Foster a Sense of Purpose

Having a sense of purpose and meaning in life can help you maintain motivation and resilience in the face of a physical disability. Pursue hobbies, interests, or volunteer opportunities that align with your values and passions. Engaging in activities that give you a sense of purpose can contribute to your overall well-being and help you overcome the challenges associated with your disability.

Leveraging the power of the mind-body connection can play a significant role in overcoming the obstacles presented by a physical disability. By embracing a positive mindset, practicing mindfulness, seeking social support, and engaging in adaptive strategies, you can improve your overall well-being and thrive despite your physical limitations.

Bouncing Back from Disability

Living with a disability undoubtedly makes life more challenging—particularly because there are numerous aspects of bouncing back from disability, including physical, financial, emotional, and social hurdles to tackle. The best way to address these challenges is to employ all the tools and techniques discussed in this chapter, from getting financial support and tapping a range of resources to maintaining a healthy mindset and using adaptive strategies. By taking this multifaceted approach, individuals with disabilities and their caregivers can better overcome challenges, improve overall resilience amid adversity, and gain greater independence too.

Disability Resources

1. **American Association of People with Disabilities** – Advocacy and support organization.
2. **Autistic Self Advocacy Network** – Advocacy and support for the autistic community.

3. **Job Accommodation Network** – Workplace inclusion and compliance insights.
4. **National Association of Councils on Developmental Disabilities** – Policy advocacy group.
5. **National Association of Disability Representatives** – Help with Social Security benefits.
6. **National Disability Institute** – Promoting economic empowerment.
7. **National Federation of the Blind** – Support and resources for blind Americans.
8. **Respect Ability** – Nonprofit that fights stigmas and advances opportunities for those with disabilities.
9. **The Arc** – Advocates for the rights of people with intellectual disabilities.
10. **United Spinal Association** – Services for individuals with spinal cord injuries.

Chapter 7
Disease

"I can be changed by what happens to me. But I refuse to be reduced by it."
—Maya Angelou

Chronic diseases such as heart disease, cancer, and diabetes are the leading causes of death and disability in the United States, affecting roughly 6 in 10 adults, according to the CDC. A disease, medical illness, or health scare can bring all your best-laid plans to a screeching halt—and throw your finances out of whack for years. That could have happened to my family after my husband, Earl, was diagnosed with atrial fibrillation, or AFib, in 2021. AFib is a heart condition or disorder characterized by irregular and often rapid heartbeats, and it can lead to heart attack or stroke. We always knew that health care costs in the US are astronomical. But can you imagine us getting a hospital bill for more than $400,000 after Earl was in the hospital for only *one day*? I fretted that just seeing that huge bill was almost enough to give my husband the heart attack he was trying to avoid! Read on to learn what led to that enormous medical bill and how we handled it. Spoiler alert: we had insurance, but far too many people aren't fortunate enough to have really good health care coverage. And even those with insurance can still wind up with costly bills.

Earl's heart saga began after our first post-COVID vacation. After we got our vaccinations, we traveled to Mexico for five weeks in 2021. During our getaway, we totally lived it up, eating and drinking whatever we wanted. But one night, toward the end of our trip, Earl noticed his leg swelling. At first, he thought it was due to dehydration. But I suspected that it was really tied to excessive alcohol, so I urged him to lay off the adult drinks and to load up on water instead. That seemed to do the trick and the swelling soon subsided. Still, the whole episode worried Earl enough that he made a point to visit his doctor as soon as we got back to the US. At his doctor's appointment, his primary care physician checked his heart and said: "I think you're in AFib, and I want you to see a cardiologist today." That pronouncement immediately set off alarm bells. Unfortunately, stroke runs in Earl's family. His mom had a stroke, and she passed in 2018. His father had a stroke and subsequently died in 2021. And Earl's grandfather had previously also had a stroke and died. So we took this medical news very, very seriously. At the cardiologist's office, AFib was immediately confirmed, and Earl was put on a blood thinner, Eliquis, for a few months.

After a battery of tests, EKGs, bloodwork, and other doctor visits, Earl was scheduled for a procedure called a cardioversion, in order to fix his AFib. With cardioversion, doctors shock the heart to try to bring it back into a normal sinus rhythm. On the day of surgery, Earl was put under general anesthesia in the operating room; meanwhile, I prayed outside in the waiting room and hoped for the best. After just 15 minutes or so, however, the interventional cardiologist came out and told me he had to abort the procedure. He didn't do the cardioversion, he said, because he noticed a blood clot on Earl's heart. If he had shocked Earl, that blood clot could have traveled to his brain, and he could've had a stroke right there on the operating table and died. I was so grateful that his doctor had taken the time and care to first perform something called a TEE—a transesophageal electrocardiogram—which is where they put a scope down the patient's throat and use a camera to look at the heart from all different angles. It was because of the TEE procedure that the cardiologist spotted the blood clot. At that point, the doctor also realized Earl's blood thinner, Eliquis, hadn't worked. It's supposed to break up any blood clots, but obviously, it didn't. So the cardiologist switched Earl's medicine to a different blood thinner called Xarelto.

A few months later, the cardiologist was able to successfully perform the cardioversion, and it went off without a hitch.

Unfortunately, it didn't last.

A couple of months later, Earl's AFib returned—something we've since learned is not uncommon after cardioversion. It was such an emotional blow to Earl, who just wanted to put this whole episode behind him. We were advised that Earl could undergo yet another cardioversion. But we discussed our options and decided for Earl to get a different procedure called cardiac ablation. This is where the $400,000+ bill comes in.

With a cardiac ablation, a surgeon uses a special catheter (a long, thin tube) with a tiny tip that can emit heat energy. They carefully guide this catheter to the problem areas of the heart and deliver heat energy to destroy the tiny bits of tissue that are causing the electrical signals to misbehave. It's like fixing the faulty switches in the heart's electrical system.

When the new cardiologist, an electrophysiologist, performed the cardiac ablation, he not only saw the AFib going on in Earl's heart, but he also detected a separate condition called atrial flutter. Thankfully, he fixed that too during the same surgery. Then came the bills. From the hospital. From the doctor. From the anesthesiologist, and more. One day the bill from his cardiac ablation arrived in the mail: everything topped $420,000 in total! Because of our health insurance, we only had to pay around $2,500. But I often think of individuals and families who have diseases and conditions that require life-saving care, but they simply can't afford it. That's a travesty.

The episode with Earl's AFib happened over a period of one year. My husband and I make a point to go with one another to all of our medical appointments, no matter how minor or routine. So for both of us, the fall of 2021 through the summer of 2022 was spent waiting for appointments, getting results from tests, doing various forms of heart monitoring, and scheduling surgeries. It was also a time for us both to dramatically change our lifestyles. We read everything we could about AFib. We found out that obesity is highly linked to this condition, as well as a number of lifestyle factors within our control. Earl was obese (and I was too), so he resolved to drop the weight immediately. We started walking together five miles a day every day, and the results were dramatic. In that year, he lost 65 pounds, and I lost 85 pounds. Both of us had high cholesterol and were prediabetic. The weight loss and lifestyle changes helped with those too. It wasn't easy. And it required consistency and dedication. But we now marvel at the "new and improved us," and the energy we have. We often say we feel like we're 30 years old, instead of in our 50s!

Earl's doctors call him a "model patient" since he has continued to stick to their advice regarding his weight loss and he's abstained from anything that can remotely trigger AFib. For example, he has dramatically reduced his salt intake and stopped drinking coffee entirely—even though he used to drink about five cups of java each day. He also completely quit drinking alcohol, even socially, because alcohol consumption is also linked to AFib. (I stopped drinking too, just to support him.) Earl jokingly tells people: "There's nothing like the fear of death to make you act right!" But recently he told me that, in all seriousness, his main fear wasn't death, but *dependency* on others. "The thought of being physically unable to do certain things because of a stroke was one of the worst things I could imagine," he said. "I dread dependency," he added, noting that avoiding that scenario was his primary motivation in getting healthy, changing his lifestyle, and beating AFib. "I also wanted to be around for you and the kids," he told me.

Addressing his AFib has had other benefits too. Earl's prior sleep apnea and (very loud) snoring—two other issues linked to AFib—have now been eliminated. Earl had also been considered borderline for having hypertension for most of his life. Then, in 2001, he was put on hypertension medication to control his blood pressure. He still takes that medicine, but his hypertension is much better managed now.

"This whole process has been transformative," Earl says. "It wasn't enough to just survive the COVID pandemic, but to go right into dealing with AFib was surreal. The weight loss has made me feel like I conquered something that has been plaguing me all my life."

He knows that his health improvements are the exception rather than the rule. Many people backslide and regain weight or fall back into bad habits that lead to or aggravate diseases and other health conditions. "I've become more physically resilient after changing my diet and lifestyle," Earl notes. "I don't get sick as often, and my mental clarity is better too."

"In my previous condition, my odds of living with AFib were pretty slim," he says. "I had no choice but to change."

Disease Can Spark a Cascade of Medical Bills

Dealing with disease and chronic health conditions can be scary on a personal level and financially. Once you or any of your loved ones are diagnosed with a disease, a seemingly never-ending stream of health care bills can roll in from hospitals, clinics, specialty medical providers, and others. If you're lucky enough to physically recover after an illness, it's possible that your financial struggles will continue long after your medical treatments end. That's because even if you have health insurance, you can nonetheless wind up in bankruptcy due to overwhelming medical bills from co-pays, deductibles, and out-of-pocket costs. If you're sick and tired of dealing with the financial aspects of being sick, rest assured that you can return to good physical health and proper fiscal health too.

When you're initially dealing with a disease, however, I recognize that it can hit you hard, both financially and emotionally. It's like a storm that rolls in and disrupts everything in its path, leaving you feeling shaken and uncertain about what lies ahead. But here's the thing—storms pass, and the sun eventually breaks through the clouds.

In this chapter, we're going to tackle the challenge of bouncing back from disease, not just in terms of your physical health, but also when it comes to your financial and emotional well-being. Think of it as a road map that will guide you through the twists and turns of this journey, helping you regain control and find your way back to a place of stability and strength.

First things first—let's talk money. When illness strikes, it often brings a hefty price tag along with it. Medical expenses can pile up like an avalanche, and navigating the complex world of health care and insurance can feel like wandering through a dense forest with no map. But fear not. I'm going to shed light on understanding those financial consequences and show you practical ways to manage them. From tackling medical bills to exploring financial assistance programs, I'll highlight the tools and strategies you can use to regain control of your finances.

And remember, you don't have to face this storm alone. Building a support system is crucial, just like having a trusty life raft in rough waters. Your family, friends, and loved ones can provide the strength and encouragement you need. Also, don't forget the power of shared experiences—seeking out support groups and connecting with others who have gone through similar journeys can be a source of immense comfort and inspiration.

Now, let's get down to the nitty-gritty of your recovery plan. It's time to assess where you stand financially and set realistic goals. Think of it as drawing up a battle plan, but instead of combatting the disease, you're tackling financial hurdles. I'll help you manage expenses and explore financial assistance programs and grants that can provide the relief you deserve.

Oh, and don't worry, we'll also navigate the maze of medical billing and insurance, showing you how to communicate effectively with health care providers and insurance companies, advocating for yourself, and seeking alternative treatment options when needed. It's like learning a new language—one that empowers you to navigate the health care system with confidence and get the best care possible without drowning in a sea of paperwork.

But recovery isn't just about finances. It's about nurturing your emotional well-being too. Dealing with a disease can take a toll on your mental health, leaving you feeling overwhelmed, anxious, or even isolated. So we'll explore strategies to cope with these emotional challenges, from seeking therapy or counseling to engaging in self-care practices and stress management techniques. Because healing isn't solely about your body—it's about nurturing your soul too.

Ultimately, this journey isn't just about bouncing back; it's about embracing life after illness. It's about redefining your priorities, celebrating small victories, and planning for a brighter future. It may not always be smooth sailing, but remember, storms don't last forever. You have an incredible capacity for resilience, and as you navigate your current challenges, you'll discover newfound strength within yourself that you never knew existed.

In this chapter, you will learn:

- How to handle lost income and employment challenges;
- The importance of building the right support system;
- How to communicate with health care providers;
- How to deal with insurance companies;
- Appealing a denial from your health insurer;
- What medical providers and health care systems can do to help patients;
- How to handle medical debt;
- The vicious cycle of chronic illness, disease, and medical debt;
- Strategies for dealing with medical debt;
- All about charity care programs;
- Drawbacks to charity care programs;
- Using "no surprising billing" legislation to your advantage;
- Steps for taking care of your emotional health;
- How to develop a financial recovery plan.

How to Handle Lost Income and Employment Challenges

Dealing with a disease often goes hand in hand with challenges related to employment and lost income. Illness can force you to take time off work for treatment, recovery, or necessary accommodations. In some cases, it may even result in a reduction in your working hours or the inability to continue working in your previous capacity.

Facing these employment challenges requires careful consideration and proactive planning. Start by familiarizing yourself with your employee benefits and understanding your rights. Research and determine if you have short-term disability insurance or other forms of income replacement programs available to you. These resources can provide financial support during periods when you are unable to work due to your illness.

If returning to your previous job is not feasible or no longer aligned with your health needs, consider exploring alternative work arrangements. Remote work, part-time positions, or freelance opportunities may offer greater flexibility and the ability to manage your health while still generating income. Additionally, vocational rehabilitation services and retraining programs can provide valuable guidance and support in navigating career transitions and exploring new employment opportunities that accommodate your condition.

Assessing Your Work Abilities and Limitations

One of the first steps in bouncing back from employment challenges is to assess your work abilities and limitations. Understand the impact of your illness on your ability to perform certain tasks or maintain a regular work schedule. This self-assessment will help you identify the adjustments or accommodations you may need to continue working or explore alternative employment options.

Consider consulting with your health care provider or a vocational rehabilitation specialist who can provide guidance and support in assessing your abilities and limitations. They can help determine any necessary workplace adjustments, explore suitable job roles or industries, and identify potential career paths that align with your health needs.

Exploring Workplace Accommodations and Flexibility

Employers are legally required to provide reasonable accommodations for individuals with disabilities or health conditions. These accommodations can help you perform your job effectively while managing your health needs. Openly communicate with your employer or human resources department about your condition and discuss potential workplace adjustments that could enhance your productivity and well-being.

Examples of workplace accommodations may include flexible work hours, modified duties, ergonomic equipment, or telecommuting options. By working together with your employer to identify and implement suitable accommodations, you can create a supportive work environment that allows you to thrive despite the challenges posed by your illness.

Seeking Vocational Rehabilitation and Career Transition Services

If your illness significantly affects your ability to continue in your current job or industry, vocational rehabilitation services can be instrumental in helping you transition to a new career path. These services are designed to assist individuals with disabilities or health conditions in acquiring new skills, exploring alternative career options, and finding suitable employment opportunities.

Contact vocational rehabilitation agencies in your area to inquire about available services and programs. These agencies can provide career counseling, skill development, job training, and job placement assistance. They can also guide you through the process of applying for vocational rehabilitation benefits, which may include financial support for education or job training programs.

Exploring Freelance, Part-time, or Remote Work Opportunities

In some cases, traditional full-time employment may not be feasible due to the limitations imposed by your illness. However, there are alternative work arrangements that offer flexibility and may better accommodate your health needs. Exploring freelance, part-time, or remote work opportunities can provide you with greater control over your schedule and workload.

Freelancing or working on a contract basis allows you to take on projects or assignments on your terms. This flexibility can be especially beneficial when managing a fluctuating health condition. Additionally, part-time employment or remote work options can provide a better work-life balance and reduce the physical demands of commuting or adhering to rigid schedules.

Research online job platforms, freelancing websites, or remote work job boards to explore opportunities that align with your skills and interests. Networking and reaching out to professional contacts or industry groups can also help you uncover hidden job opportunities that may not be publicly advertised.

Bouncing back from employment challenges requires patience, resilience, and adaptability. Embrace the opportunities that arise and be open to new career paths that may lead to fulfilling and rewarding experiences. By assessing your abilities, exploring workplace accommodations, seeking vocational rehabilitation services, and considering alternative work arrangements, you can regain financial stability and find a path forward in your career despite the challenges posed by your illness.

The Importance of Building the Right Support System

Dealing with a disease can be an isolating experience, but you don't have to face it alone. Building a strong support system is essential in navigating the financial and emotional complexities that arise during this challenging time. Just like a sturdy life raft, your support system provides stability and reassurance as you navigate the unpredictable waters of illness.

The Role of Family, Friends, and Loved Ones

Your family, friends, and loved ones are your anchors in times of turbulence. They offer a listening ear, a shoulder to lean on, and unwavering support when you need it most. Don't be afraid or reluctant to lean on them and share your worries and concerns. Allow them to be there for you, and let their love and understanding provide comfort during the toughest moments.

Communicate openly with your loved ones about your financial situation and the challenges you are facing. Sometimes, they may have ideas or resources that can help alleviate some of the financial burdens. Remember, they are invested in your well-being and want to support you in any way they can. Together, you can brainstorm creative solutions and find ways to ease the financial strain. In fact, if you're facing a disease that's hereditary and that runs in your family, certain relatives may have already coped with the issues you're contending with and might be great resources and points of emotional support too.

Seeking Emotional Support and Counseling

Coping with a disease not only takes a toll on your physical health but also impacts your emotional well-being. It's crucial to prioritize your mental health and seek emotional support during this journey. Just as a lighthouse guides ships to safety, seeking professional counseling or therapy can provide guidance and illuminate a path toward emotional healing.

Consider reaching out to a licensed therapist or counselor who specializes in helping individuals navigate the emotional challenges associated with illness. They can provide a safe and nonjudgmental space for you to express your feelings, fears, and frustrations. Through therapy, you can develop coping strategies, gain a new perspective, and build resilience as you navigate the emotional roller coaster of your journey.

Engaging with Support Groups and Online Communities

Finding a community of individuals who are going through similar experiences can be immensely comforting and empowering. Support groups and online communities can provide a lifeline, connecting you with others who understand the unique challenges you face. These communities act as buoys, keeping you afloat and offering valuable insights and encouragement.

Join local support groups in your area or explore online communities dedicated to your specific disease or condition. Engage in discussions, share your experiences, and learn from others who have walked a similar path. You'll discover a wealth of knowledge, resources, and emotional support that can guide you through the ups and downs of your journey.

Identifying and Utilizing Local Resources and Organizations

Communities often have local resources and organizations specifically designed to support individuals dealing with illness. These resources act as beacons, guiding you toward the assistance and services you need. Take the time to research and identify organizations that can provide financial guidance, emotional support, and practical assistance.

Reach out to local nonprofits, charities, or religious organizations that may offer financial assistance programs, support services, or resources tailored to individuals facing health challenges. These organizations can provide information on navigating the health care system, financial planning, and accessing essential services.

Additionally, social workers or patient navigators at hospitals or treatment centers can be valuable allies in connecting you with local resources. They can provide guidance and support in accessing available programs or funding that may help alleviate financial burdens.

Remember, building a support system takes time and effort. Don't hesitate to reach out and ask for help when needed. Your support system is there to guide you, uplift you, and provide strength during the toughest moments. Together, you'll navigate the financial and emotional complexities of your disease, finding solace in the knowledge that you are not alone on this journey.

How to Communicate with Health Care Providers

Navigating the health care system can be overwhelming, but effective communication with health care providers is crucial in ensuring you receive the care and services you need. Let's explore some strategies to help you advocate for yourself and navigate this complex landscape with confidence.

Understanding Medical Billing and Basic Insurance Terminology

Whether you're dealing with the office manager of a clinic, a representative in the billing department, a health care practitioner, or someone else, it's helpful to familiarize yourself with common medical billing and insurance terminology. Understanding terms such as deductible, co-payment, out-of-pocket maximum, and prior authorization can empower you to have meaningful conversations and understand your coverage.

Take the time to educate yourself about the specific terms and concepts related to your insurance policy. Review the explanation of benefits (EOB) statements you receive from your insurance company to gain insights into how your coverage works. If you come across unfamiliar terms or have questions, don't be shy about seeking clarification from your insurance provider or the billing department of your health care provider.

Negotiating Medical Bills and Seeking Financial Assistance

Medical bills can quickly accumulate, leaving you feeling overwhelmed. However, it's important to remember that you have the right to negotiate and seek financial assistance when necessary. Treat medical bills like any other financial obligation and approach them with a proactive mindset.

Review your medical bills thoroughly to ensure their accuracy. Mistakes can happen, so if you notice any discrepancies or questionable charges, reach out to the billing department of your health care provider for clarification and resolution. Keep records of all communication, including names, dates, and details discussed.

If you're struggling to pay your medical bills, inquire as soon as possible about options for financial assistance. Many health care providers offer financial aid programs based on income and need. These programs can provide discounts, payment plans, or even full or partial forgiveness of medical debt. Reach out to the billing department or financial counselors at your health care facility to inquire about available assistance programs and application processes.

Additionally, research local nonprofit organizations, foundations, or charitable programs that provide financial support to individuals facing medical challenges. These organizations may offer grants or assistance with specific medical expenses. Exploring these resources can significantly alleviate the financial burden associated with your health care costs.

Advocating for Yourself and Your Health Care Needs

As a patient, it's vital to advocate for yourself and ensure your health care needs are met. Effective communication with your health care providers is key to achieving this. Here are some tips to help you advocate for yourself:

Be prepared: Before appointments or discussions, make a list of questions, concerns, and symptoms you want to discuss. This will help you stay focused and ensure you address all important matters during your interactions.

Be clear and concise: Clearly communicate your symptoms, medical history, and concerns. Provide specific details and avoid assumptions or generalizations. It's crucial for your health care provider to have a comprehensive understanding of your situation.

Ask for explanations: If something is unclear or you don't understand a medical term or procedure, don't just gloss over the issue; ask for clarification. Your health care provider should be willing to explain things in a way that you can comprehend.

Take notes: During appointments, take notes or ask a trusted companion to do so. This will help you remember important information and instructions provided by your health care provider.

Seek a second opinion if needed: If you have concerns about your diagnosis or treatment plan, don't hesitate to seek a second opinion from another health care professional. It's your right to have confidence in your health care decisions.

Seeking Alternative Treatment Options and Exploring Cost-saving Strategies

Part of advocating for yourself involves exploring alternative treatment options and cost-saving strategies. Openly discuss your financial concerns with your health care provider, as they may be able to suggest more affordable alternatives without compromising your care.

Consider asking your health care provider if there are generic medication options available or if there are cost-saving measures for diagnostic tests or treatments. In some cases, they may be able to recommend alternative therapies or approaches that are equally effective but more cost-effective.

Additionally, research prescription assistance programs or patient savings programs offered by pharmaceutical companies. These programs can provide significant discounts or even free medications to eligible individuals. Take advantage of any resources or cost-saving strategies available to reduce the financial burden of your health care needs.

Effective communication and advocacy are key when dealing with health care providers and insurance companies. By understanding the terminology, negotiating medical bills, advocating for your needs, and exploring cost-saving strategies, you can navigate the health care system more confidently and ensure that you receive the care and coverage you require.

How to Deal with Insurance Companies

Insurance can often be a complicated web of policies, coverage limits, deductibles, and co-payments. Navigating the health care insurance system requires keeping a cool head—even when things seem illogical. You'll also need perseverance and a solid understanding of your policy.

Again, start by taking time to thoroughly review your insurance policy and familiarize yourself with the coverage it provides. Understand the scope of benefits, limitations, and any exclusions that may apply to your specific condition. This knowledge will empower you to make informed decisions about your health care and effectively advocate for what's in your best interests.

When dealing with medical procedures or treatments, open and clear communication with both your health care provider and your insurance company is essential. Be proactive in discussing treatment plans, cost estimates, and any potential coverage issues with your health care provider. They can provide guidance and support in navigating the insurance process and may be able to suggest alternative treatment options that are more cost-effective without compromising your care.

Make sure you know what procedures or treatments are considered routine, what's in and out of network, and what requires a prior authorization. Don't assume anything when it comes to health insurance. It can be a big mistake to take something at face value because it seems like "common sense" or simply because that's what's always been done. Rules change. Policies change. Benefit levels change. So you have to ensure that each and every contact you have with a health care provider is either fully covered by your insurance or partially covered to an extent that you can foot the other part of the bill. Keep up with renewals too. You don't want a lapsed premium to cause you to lose coverage right when you need it most.

You must also make yourself aware of the explanation of benefits (EOB), which is a document that outlines what treatments and services your insurer has paid for on your behalf. This document can sometimes be complex, filled with jargon, codes, and figures. It is important to carefully go through this document and understand each and every detail because it helps in spotting any errors, discrepancies, or charges for services you didn't receive. A minor misunderstanding or error can cost you a lot, so don't hesitate to call your insurer if there are any areas that you do not understand. They are obligated to explain it to you in a language you can comprehend.

Managing medical paperwork is another important aspect of dealing with insurance companies. It can often seem overwhelming, but it's crucial to keep track of all documents, from medical records and bills to EOBs and prior authorizations. Establishing a system for organizing these documents can save you considerable time, stress, and potentially, money. This may mean keeping a binder or digital folder of all records, categorizing by date or type of document, and making notes of any relevant discussions with your health care provider or insurer.

Additionally, don't shy away from negotiating with your insurer. It may sound intimidating, but insurance companies, like any other business, are often open to negotiation, especially when it comes to expensive procedures. This involves having a conversation with your insurance company about the cost of treatment and whether there is any flexibility. If you are faced with a hefty bill for a procedure, it might be worth it to discuss the situation with your insurance company and see if they might be willing to cover more of the cost.

Finally, it's essential to know that there are numerous resources available if you need additional support. Patient advocacy groups, nonprofit organizations, and even social workers in hospitals can provide invaluable assistance in navigating the health care insurance maze. They can help you understand your rights, assist in the appeal process, and sometimes, negotiate on your behalf with insurance companies. There are also online communities and forums where people share their experiences and offer guidance to others dealing with similar insurance challenges.

Remember, the ultimate goal is to ensure that you receive the care you need without causing a significant financial burden. This often involves navigating a complex and sometimes frustrating system, but with knowledge, organization, perseverance, and assertiveness, it is entirely possible to effectively manage your dealings with insurance companies. So stay informed, stay organized, and most importantly, stay proactive in advocating for your health and your rights.

Appealing a Denial from Your Health Insurer

If you encounter challenges or denials from your insurance company, don't be discouraged. Remember that you have the right to appeal their decisions. Take advantage of the appeals process, and provide any additional documentation or information that supports the medical necessity of the treatments or services you require. Persistence and advocacy can often lead to successful resolutions and the coverage you deserve.

When confronting such obstacles, it's key to remember that an initial denial does not represent the end of the road. Not by a long shot. Oftentimes, insurance companies deny claims due to simple mistakes or a need for more information. Be diligent in following up with both your health care provider and insurer to correct errors and provide any missing details. It's wise to keep a log of all conversations and correspondence, documenting dates, times, names, and discussed information.

In the appeals process, involve your health care provider as they have expertise in establishing medical necessity and might help articulate your case in a language that insurance companies understand. Additionally, familiarize yourself with your state's insurance regulatory agency, as they may provide guidance and assistance in the appeals process. You could also consider seeking assistance from a patient advocate or a legal advisor if your case is complex.

You should also know that most health care insurance policies do include a section that outlines the process for appealing decisions, as it's a fundamental right for policyholders. This section is usually found in the policy documentation or the member handbook provided by your insurer. Here are a few pieces of advice about that:

Thoroughly review your policy: Before you initiate an appeal, ensure you read and understand the appeals process as outlined in your policy. This will give you a clear understanding of what steps to follow, the timelines involved, and what you'll need to provide in terms of paperwork or documentation.

Understand the types of appeals: Typically, insurance companies have two types of appeals—internal and external. An internal appeal is reviewed by the insurance company, while an external one is reviewed by an independent third party. If your internal appeal is denied, you have the right to an external review.

Documentation is crucial: As part of your appeal, you'll need to provide supporting documentation, including medical records and a letter from your doctor indicating why the treatment is necessary. Keep copies of all correspondence with the insurance company and track all calls or meetings.

Strict deadlines: Each insurer sets deadlines for filing an appeal, which can range from 30 to 180 days from the date you received the denial. Ensure you meet these deadlines, as failing to do so can result in an automatic denial of your appeal.

Seek assistance: If the process becomes overwhelming, consider seeking help from a patient advocate or a health care lawyer. They can guide you through the process, making sure you're effectively presenting your case.

The insurance appeal process might be time-consuming and require patience. However, being persistent, proactive, and armed with thorough documentation could tip the scales in your favor, securing the crucial coverage you need for your health and well-being. By standing up for your rights, you not only advocate for yourself but also pave the way for others who might face similar challenges.

What Medical Providers and Health Care Systems Can Do

As I stated earlier in *Bounce Back*, you're more financially resilient when the systems in which you operate support you in various ways. That includes the health care system you deal with. But "the system" won't just work in your favor on its own—or somehow magically benefit you. We have to advocate and fight for policies and practices that would boost our physical and financial health. Remember, your physical health and financial health are intertwined. Financial stress has negative effects on your physical and emotional health. Here are some ways that health care providers and systems can help us all to prevent, reduce or better manage medical debt, thereby enhancing our physical and emotional well-being too:

- Improve financial assistance and repayment programs;
- Support informed patient decision-making;
- Proactively identify the risk of medical debt;
- Supply price transparency tools for providers (if physicians and health care providers don't even know the cost of the procedures, services, or medicines they're recommending—and most don't—they won't realize why people forgo certain suggested medical treatments).

Pat Merryweather-Arges, executive director of Project Patient Care, an advocacy organization for patients, their families, and caregivers, contends that we need far more enforcement of price transparency regulations in the health care system. Providers are supposed to be posting their prices, but they're not, she says.

Again, all of these ideas improve patient outcomes too, by decreasing people's stress, avoiding needless hospitalizations, and preventing premature deaths. It's a disservice to you as a patient if you can only speak to the billing department about the cost of your care. Health care providers should talk to patients as well. That's why Merryweather-Arges also suggests that hospitals and clinicians put on patient experience surveys questions about whether they were asked about the financial considerations of their care. If patients don't believe they can afford it, they won't follow through on their care plan, she says.

With regard to outpatient services, common sense tells us that various preventative services or preventive diagnostic services will be underutilized if folks feel that they're too costly. And it's definitely the case that more health care costs have shifted to the outpatient side. Stuff like bigger out-of-pocket costs or higher co-pays. Remember when co-pays were very manageable, like around $10 or so?

Today, depending on your insurance plan, you might have a co-pay as high as $1,000 or even $2,500 for certain procedures and services. All of this explains, in part, why there's so much medical debt outstanding in the US.

How to Handle Medical Debt

A recent report from the Consumer Financial Protection Bureau (CFPB) indicates that unpaid medical bills in America account for more than half of all debt in collections, with medical debt outstanding exceeding $88 billion. We often hear about people in the US with gigantic health care bills—and that certainly happens. But the typical medical debt owed in America isn't measured in the hundreds of thousands or even thousands of dollars. The average overdue medical debt in America ranges from $400 to $800. That might not sound like a lot. But consider that one-third of all Americans don't have enough money to deal with a $400 emergency and you can see why unexpected medical bills can throw many people's budgets out of whack. Like so many other financial issues, medical debt also most severely impacts vulnerable people and marginalized populations.

Medical debt disproportionately affects:

- **People of color:** 28% of Black households and 22% of Latino households have medical debt, versus 17% of white households.
- **Persons with disabilities:** 27% of households where at least one person has a disability owe medical debt, compared to 14% of households where no one has a disability.
- **Poor people:** 11% of households living below the poverty line have medical debt, far more than the 3% of households above the poverty line that owes medical debt.
- **Uninsured individuals:** Nearly 50% of uninsured people owe medical debt or report that they are paying off medical debt over time.

As mentioned, simply having insurance doesn't always protect against the cost of medical care. High-deductible medical plans and a litany of out-of-pocket expenses can still dramatically affect your budget.

According to the National Community Law Center, medical debt can harm your financial health in numerous ways, such as debt going into collections, legal action being taken against you if you can't afford to pay past-due medical bills, potential damage to your credit rating, or even bankruptcy if you need to get medical creditors off your back.

One bit of good news is that medical debt below the $500 threshold doesn't hurt your credit rating anymore. Since the first half of 2023, the three major credit reporting agencies, Equifax, Experian, and TransUnion, no longer include medical debt in collections under $500 on credit reports. This change is part of a broader shift in how these agencies are handling medical debt reporting. They also no longer include paid medical debts on credit reports since July 1, 2022, and they've increased the period before medical debt in collections appears on your credit reports from six months to one year. The aim of these changes is to give consumers more time to negotiate or pay their medical debts and avoid the negative impact on their credit reports

The Vicious Cycle of Chronic Illness, Disease, and Medical Debt

As someone living with a chronic illness or disease, you may be well aware of the added burden of medical debt, creating a vicious cycle of financial and health problems. It's estimated that about two-thirds of all bankruptcies in the United States are tied to medical issues and expenses, with many people unable to afford the high cost of health care and insurance premiums.

You likely require ongoing medical care for your chronic condition, which can lead to long-term debt as you struggle to cover the costs of treatments, medications, and other health care services. According to the CFPB, about 56 million American adults, or 20% of the population, have medical debt reported on their credit reports, negatively impacting their financial well-being. Additionally, medical debt can lead to a decline in your ability to work, worsening your financial situation.

To mitigate the impact of medical debt on people like you with chronic illnesses, several solutions have been proposed. Some experts suggest that policy changes at the federal level could help alleviate the burden, such as expanding Medicaid and implementing more comprehensive health care coverage. Others argue for the need to address the root causes of high medical costs, including negotiating lower drug prices and limiting out-of-pocket expenses for consumers.

All this underscores the detrimental effects of the relationship between chronic illness and medical debt, emphasizing the need for systemic change in the health care industry. By addressing the root causes of high medical costs and implementing policy changes, the financial drain on those living with chronic diseases can be significantly reduced.

Strategies for Dealing with Medical Debt

If medical debt is weighing you down, you don't have to live with this burden. Here are some approaches to take to chip away at—or outright eliminate—those burdensome medical bills.

Negotiate with the Medical Provider

Doctors and health care providers are often willing to negotiate on the amount of debt owed. They would rather receive partial payment than no payment at all, and therefore, are open to discussing lower lump-sum payments or interest-free payment plans. It's not uncommon for providers to accept as little as 25 to 50 cents on the dollar of what you owe.

Work with Independent Advocates and Government Agencies

There are several organizations such as RIP Medical Debt, HealthWell Foundation, and the Patient Advocate Foundation that work with individuals to help pay off medical debts. (See *The Bounce Back Workbook* to learn more about RIP Medical Debt, which buys up medical debt in bulk and then cancels the debt to relieve people of that financial burden.) Also, if you qualify for Medicaid, you may be eligible to have retroactive medical bills covered. It's worth exploring these options if you have a disease that's left you struggling with medical debt.

Consider Debt Consolidation

If you have multiple medical debts, consolidating them into a single debt can make repayment more manageable. This can be done through a personal loan from any number of institutions, including traditional banks, credit unions, online lenders, or peer-to-peer loan companies. This strategy not only gets the medical provider or collections agency off your back but also eliminates any potential negative remarks on your credit score. Plus, you can repay the debt at a pace that suits your financial situation.

Apply for a 0% APR Credit Card

If your credit score hasn't been severely damaged, you could apply for a credit card that offers a 0% intro APR. This allows you to pay off the medical provider or collections agency and then repay the credit card issuer in a time frame you're comfortable with. You may also earn some credit card rewards in the process. Be careful about some of those medical credit cards offered by many doctors' offices. They often have hefty interest rates, compounding the debt you owe.

All About Charity Care Programs

I'm guessing that you don't have a medical degree. So you might not be able to talk about various diseases at a high level with your doctor or other health care experts. But you are an expert in your own finances. You *can* talk about your money—what you have or don't have. Which is why if you're on a tight budget and you need medical care, you should inquire about charity care programs.

Charity care programs, also known as financial assistance programs or indigent care programs, are initiatives offered by hospitals and health care systems designed to help patients who are unable to pay for their medical services due to financial hardship. These programs can be a lifeline when you're dealing with costly medical conditions, chronic illnesses, or unexpected health emergencies. But they're not without their hurdles and issues, as I'll explain shortly.

Eligibility for these programs typically depends on several factors, including your income level, assets, family size, and the federal poverty level guidelines. The criteria can vary widely between institutions, so you'll need to check the specific requirements of the charity care program at the hospital or health care facility where you received or plan to receive care.

Once you're approved, these programs can cover a broad range of services, from hospital stays and surgical procedures to medications, laboratory tests, and outpatient services. The level of assistance can vary, from discounted care to complete coverage of all medical costs. In some cases, charity care programs can even *retroactively* cover bills for services that were provided to you *before* you applied for assistance.

Charity care programs are not only vital for easing the financial burden of medical costs, but they can also have profound emotional and psychological benefits. Medical debt or the fear of incurring it can lead to significant stress, which can exacerbate health problems, particularly for those with chronic illnesses. By providing a safety net, these programs can alleviate this source of stress, allowing you to focus more on recovery and less on your financial situation. Moreover, these programs can offer a sense of hope and reassurance for you and your family during challenging times. Knowing that there are options available to help manage the financial aspects of medical care can provide peace of mind and contribute to your overall well-being.

In addition to charity care programs, many hospitals and health care systems also provide other resources such as case managers or financial counselors. These professionals can guide patients through the process of applying for assistance, help them understand their bills, and inform them about other available resources and programs such as Medicaid or state-funded health insurance programs.

It's important to note that charity care programs are typically a last resort for those who are uninsured or underinsured and have exhausted all other options. Patients are usually expected to apply for Medicaid or other state or federal programs for which they may be eligible before they can be considered for charity care.

Drawbacks to Charity Care Programs

While charity care programs offer crucial support to many, they are not a substitute for comprehensive health insurance. They're typically designed to help with costs associated with care provided at a specific hospital or health system and may not cover services elsewhere. So I would still encourage you to explore all options for health insurance coverage to ensure that you have access to a broad range of health care services.

Furthermore, according to a CFPB report, "Some hospitals create barriers to accessing charity care, such as requiring patients to request applications multiple times, using extremely lengthy applications, asking patients to submit detailed financial documentation multiple times a year, or requiring that patients first pursue other funding sources. Documentation requirements for charity care may be burdensome for the unbanked, those in informal or gig employment, or those without access to the internet." As a result of these and other factors, the CFPB says, charity care utilization is low.

Finally, you should also be aware that using a nonprofit hospital alone won't save you from getting hefty medical bills. In fact, the Financial Health Network and Kaiser Health News both report that 45% of nonprofit hospitals still send bills to patients who qualify for charity care. If that happens to you, push back and try to get those bills eliminated or reduced. Here's the approach I would take:

Contact the billing department first: If you receive a bill despite qualifying for charity care, the first step would likely be to get in touch with the billing department of the hospital or health care provider. They should be able to clarify the situation and adjust your bill accordingly if you indeed qualify for charity care. Keep copies of all correspondence, including emails and letters, and take note of any phone calls, including the date, time, and the name of the person you spoke with.

Provide proof of eligibility: You may need to provide documentation to prove your eligibility for charity care. This could include income statements, tax returns, or other proof of financial hardship.

Seek help from a patient advocate: Many hospitals and health care systems have ombudspersons, also known as patient advocates or patient representatives. These individuals work to resolve complaints, concerns, or issues patients have related to their care or treatment. They serve as intermediaries between patients and health care providers or administrators, helping to navigate complex health care systems and advocating for your rights and needs. Patient advocates can also help in navigating complex health care billing issues. They may be able to aid you in ensuring that your charity care benefits are correctly applied.

Formally dispute or appeal the bill: If your attempts to resolve the issue with the health care provider are not successful, you may need to formally dispute or appeal the bill. This would involve writing a letter to the health care provider explaining the situation and providing evidence of your charity care eligibility.

Seek external help: If your appeal is unsuccessful, or if the hospital or provider is unresponsive or unhelpful, consider reaching out to your state's health department or attorney general's office for assistance. They may be able to provide advice, intervene on your behalf, or direct you to further resources.

Stay informed and keep copies: Be sure to stay informed about your rights as a patient. Laws and regulations regarding medical billing and charity care vary by state, so it's important to know the rules that apply in your area. Always keep copies of all your medical bills, as well as any correspondence or documents related to your charity care application or approval.

Using "No Surprising Billing" Legislation to Your Advantage

You can also use federal law to your advantage to keep medical costs down. As you probably already know, navigating the often-convoluted landscape of medical billing can be daunting. Unexpected bills and out-of-network charges can quickly turn a health concern into a financial nightmare. Thankfully, recent legislation gives you protections against these surprise medical bills. This legislative measure is known as the No Surprises Act.

The No Surprises Act took effect on January 1, 2022, and it offers comprehensive safeguards for people enrolled in both group and private health plans. It eliminates the shock of surprise medical bills when you use emergency services, certain nonemergency services from out-of-network providers while at in-network facilities, and services from out-of-network air ambulance service providers. In simpler terms, if you're receiving treatment, the bill you receive should align with your in-network cost-sharing amount, even if the services were technically out-of-network.

Prior to the enforcement of the No Surprises Act, health insurance didn't always cover the entire cost of out-of-network services. Consequently, patients often found themselves facing exorbitant bills that far exceeded their expected in-network costs. This discrepancy between what the health plan paid and what the provider billed is known as "balance billing," a notorious source of those "surprise" medical bills.

However, with the enforcement of the No Surprises Act, several key changes have revolutionized patient billing:

- Emergency services, regardless of whether they're in-network or out-of-network, cannot result in surprise bills.
- Out-of-network cost-sharing for most emergency and some nonemergency services is now banned. So you can't be charged more than in-network cost-sharing for these services.
- Certain additional services provided by out-of-network providers during your visit to an in-network facility are also protected from balance billing.
- Health care providers and facilities are now required to provide you with a clear notice explaining these billing protections, and they must obtain your consent to waive any of them.

These protections are not exclusive to insured patients. If you're uninsured or self-paying, the No Surprises Act ensures you can receive a good faith estimate of your care costs *before* your visit. This transparency helps you avoid any unexpected charges. Furthermore, if your final charges exceed your good faith estimate by at least $400, you have the right to dispute the bill within 120 days of the date on your bill.

People covered under programs such as Medicare, Medicaid, TRICARE, the Indian Health Services, or the Veterans Health Administration were already protected against surprise medical bills. However, the No Surprises Act also serves as a baseline for consumer protections against surprise bills, supplementing state laws and ensuring that patients don't get saddled with excessive out-of-network charges or higher cost-sharing.

By minimizing the risk of unexpected out-of-network costs, the No Surprises Act helps ensure that the focus remains where it should be: on your physical health and emotional well-being.

Steps for Taking Care of Your Emotional Health

Dealing with a disease can take a toll on your emotional well-being, but it's important to prioritize your mental health as you navigate the ups and downs of your journey toward recovery. Managing the emotional impact requires self-care, support from others, and strategies to cope with the challenges you face. Let's examine some effective approaches to help you maintain emotional health and find the support you need.

Embracing Self-care Practices

Self-care is a vital component of managing the emotional impact of a disease. It involves taking intentional steps to nurture your physical, mental, and emotional well-being. Just as you care for your body by following medical treatments, self-care focuses on nurturing your inner self.

Prioritize activities that bring you joy, relaxation, and a sense of calm. This could include engaging in hobbies you love, practicing mindfulness or meditation, spending time in nature, journaling, or engaging in creative outlets. Make time for activities that recharge and rejuvenate you, even if it's just for a few minutes each day.

Physical self-care is equally important. Ensure you're getting adequate rest, nourishing your body with nutritious food, and engaging in regular physical activity to the extent that your health allows. Remember, self-care is not selfish; it's a necessary investment in your well-being.

Self-care is also crucial for caregivers of people with disease or illness. When you're dedicated to supporting someone else, you often overlook your own needs. Amid the constant demands for your attention, it becomes second nature to prioritize others. This tendency can lead you to sideline your own well-being, often neglecting essential self-care. However, taking time for yourself is not only beneficial for you but also ensures you're in the best position to care for your loved ones.

Seeking Emotional Support

Navigating the emotional challenges of a disease is not something you have to face alone. Seeking emotional support from trusted individuals can provide comfort, understanding, and guidance during difficult times. Reach out to family members, close friends, or loved ones and share your feelings openly. Allow them to be a source of comfort and support as you navigate the emotional journey.

If you prefer a more structured support system, consider joining a support group specifically tailored to individuals facing similar health challenges. These groups provide a safe space to share experiences, exchange advice, and receive validation from individuals who truly understand what you're going through. Support groups can be in-person or online, depending on your preference and accessibility.

In addition to personal connections, professional support is also beneficial. Consider working with a therapist or counselor who specializes in supporting individuals with chronic illness or health challenges. They can provide a confidential space to discuss your emotions, fears, and concerns. Therapy offers tools and coping strategies to help you navigate the emotional impact of your disease and develop resilience in the face of adversity.

Exploring Mind-body Techniques

Mind-body techniques, such as relaxation exercises, deep breathing, guided imagery, and meditation, can be powerful tools in managing stress, anxiety, and emotional turmoil. These practices promote a connection between your mind and body, allowing you to cultivate a sense of inner calm and emotional balance.

Engage in regular relaxation exercises to alleviate stress and tension. Practice deep breathing exercises, where you inhale deeply through your nose, hold the breath for a few seconds, and exhale slowly through your mouth. This simple technique can activate the body's relaxation response and reduce anxiety or feeling overwhelmed.

Guided imagery involves using your imagination to create a calming and peaceful mental scene. Close your eyes, visualize a serene environment, and focus on the details, such as sights, sounds, and sensations. This practice can help shift your focus away from stressors and induce a sense of relaxation.

Meditation, whether through formal meditation practices or mindfulness techniques, can help cultivate a present-moment awareness and reduce emotional distress. Set aside dedicated time each day for meditation or integrate mindfulness into your daily activities. As you develop a regular practice, you'll find it easier to cope with the challenges you encounter.

Engaging in Peer-to-peer Support

Connecting with individuals who are going through similar experiences can provide a unique form of support and understanding. Peer-to-peer support networks allow you to share your journey with others who can relate to your challenges, triumphs, and concerns. These networks act as a valuable lifeline, offering empathy, practical advice, and a sense of belonging.

Explore peer-to-peer support organizations, online communities, or local meet-up groups focused on your specific health condition or disease. These communities offer a platform to share experiences, exchange resources, and find solace in knowing that you are not alone on your journey. Engaging with peers who understand your unique experiences can be profoundly healing and empowering.

Managing the emotional impact of your disease is an ongoing process that requires patience, self-compassion, and resilience. Prioritize self-care, seek emotional support from loved ones or professionals, explore mind-body techniques, and connect with peer support networks. Together, these strategies will help you navigate the emotional challenges, maintain your well-being, and find strength in the face of adversity.

How to Develop a Financial Recovery Plan

In the face of disease, developing a financial recovery plan is essential to regain control over your economic and emotional well-being. Think of it as a compass, guiding you toward a path of stability and resilience. By setting realistic goals and taking proactive steps, you can navigate through the challenges and lay a solid foundation for your recovery.

Assessing the Current Financial Situation

To begin, it's important to take stock of your current financial situation. This involves gathering all relevant financial documents, such as bank statements, bills, and credit reports, and evaluating your income, expenses, assets, and liabilities. Understanding where you stand financially provides the necessary groundwork for developing an effective recovery plan.

As you assess your finances, identify areas of strength and areas that require attention. Take note of any outstanding debts, medical expenses, or financial obligations that need to be addressed. This assessment serves as a starting point to create a road map that will lead you in the direction of financial stability.

Setting Realistic Goals and Timelines

Once you have a clearer understanding of your financial situation, it's time to set realistic goals that align with your circumstances. These goals will serve as the milestones on your journey to recovery. Make sure they are specific, measurable, achievable, relevant, and time-bound (SMART goals).

Consider short-term and long-term goals. Short-term goals may include managing immediate expenses, creating a budget, or seeking financial assistance. Long-term goals could involve paying off debt, building an emergency fund, or saving for future health care needs. By breaking down your recovery plan into manageable steps, you'll maintain focus and motivation along the way. It's important to be realistic with your goals and timelines too. Recovery takes time, and progress may not always happen as quickly as you hope. Be patient with yourself and celebrate each milestone, no matter how small. Remember, every step forward counts.

Creating a Budget and Managing Expenses

A budget is your fiscal compass. It helps you track your income and expenses, ensuring that your financial resources are allocated wisely. Creating a budget involves examining your income sources, categorizing expenses, and identifying areas where you can adjust your spending.

Start by listing all sources of income, including wages, benefits, or disability payments. Next, categorize your expenses into essential categories such as housing, utilities, food, and health care, and nonessential categories such as entertainment or dining out. Review each expense carefully, identifying areas where you can reduce or eliminate unnecessary spending.

Don't forget to account for medical expenses in your budget. Keep a record of all medical bills, insurance premiums, and out-of-pocket costs. Consider setting aside funds each month specifically for health care–related expenses to ensure you are prepared for future medical needs.

Managing expenses also involves exploring cost-saving strategies. Look for discounts or generic alternatives for medications, compare prices for medical services, and inquire about financial assistance programs offered by hospitals or pharmaceutical companies. Every dollar saved contributes to your financial recovery.

Exploring Financial Assistance Programs and Grants

During times of illness, financial assistance programs and grants can provide invaluable support. They act as a life preserver, offering relief from the weight of medical expenses and helping you stay afloat financially.

Research and explore government-funded programs, nonprofit organizations, and charitable foundations that provide financial assistance to individuals facing health challenges. These programs may offer grants, scholarships, or funds to cover specific medical expenses or basic living needs. Additionally, consider reaching out to disease-specific organizations or advocacy groups, as they often have resources and financial aid available to support individuals in similar circumstances.

Be diligent in gathering the necessary documentation and completing the application processes for these programs. Keep in mind that eligibility criteria and funding availability may vary, so it's important to explore multiple avenues and stay persistent in your search for financial assistance.

Developing a financial recovery plan is an ongoing process. Regularly revisit your goals, adjust your budget as needed, and stay open to opportunities for financial support. By taking proactive steps and staying committed to your recovery plan, you'll create a solid foundation for your economic well-being as you navigate through the challenges of your disease.

Disease Resources

1. **Alzheimer's Association** – Help for Alzheimer's patients and caregivers.
2. **American Cancer Society** – Support for cancer patients and research.
3. **American Diabetes Association** – Resources for diabetics to manage health.
4. **American Heart Association** – Helps improve the lives of those with heart disease.
5. **American Lung Association** – Supports lung health and those with illnesses.
6. **Epilepsy Foundation** – Offers services to improve the lives of epileptics.
7. **Family Caregiver Alliance** – Provides education, services, and advocacy for caregivers tending to people with disease or illness.
8. **Lupus Foundation of America** – Support for those diagnosed with lupus.
9. **National Alliance on Mental Illness** – Education and advocacy for mental health.
10. **National Kidney Foundation** – Provides resources for kidney disease patients.

Chapter 8
Disasters

"It's not whether you get knocked down; it's whether you get up."

—Vince Lombardi

Krissy Henderson (not her real name) and her family have endured more than their fair share of natural disasters. Krissy—as she prefers to be called—is 43 years old, but she still recalls the first time she survived a major hurricane at age three. "I just remember being very scared," Krissy says of Hurricane Alicia, which pummeled the Houston area where Krissy and her parents lived. The year was 1983. That catastrophe uprooted them and began what would become a series of dislocations from unrelenting storms, bone-chilling tornadoes, and other acts of Mother Nature's wrath. Hurricane Katrina in 2005. Hurricane Harvey in 2017. And plenty of storms in between and since then. One time, Krissy says, when she was a kid playing with her neighbors, nature's fury erupted. They all went into the bathroom for shelter. When they came out, numerous homes around them were ripped apart.

In many ways, these natural disasters have wreaked havoc on Krissy and her relatives' lives and taken an immeasurable toll, both financially and emotionally. Her mother lost a home in the wake of Harvey, and Krissy's sister has what the family calls "tornado dreams." At the same time, Krissy notes, these tempests have given her an enormous amount of resilience and the ability to handle just about anything.

That capacity to bounce back has been much needed over her lifetime, as Krissy has battled a number of other Dreaded Ds and survived them too. Krissy is a business attorney currently living in Tampa, Florida. She married and divorced at a young age and then had around $15,000 worth of debt that she had to work arduously to pay off while in law school. She says tackling the debt was the biggest financial challenge she's faced. But it was Hurricane Harvey, perhaps, that left the biggest emotional impact.

As Krissy explains, by the time this mega-disaster hit, her parents were already divorced for many years. Her mother owned a home in Spring, Texas, and she didn't want to leave because the area was not yet hard hit, and even though the power was out, she had a gas stove. Nonetheless, city officials ordered the evacuation of all residents in her neighborhood. "They took her and her neighbors to a nearby recreation center—and then they flooded the people's homes by opening up the dams to allow the water to flow from Houston. It was to save the downtown area of the city," Krissy says.

In other words, it wasn't the massive downpour of rain from Harvey itself but the actions of local authorities that flooded this neighborhood; officials sacrificed those homes to save other parts of the city, namely downtown Houston.

As the floodwaters from the dam and Hurricane Harvey receded, a new horror emerged in the form of opportunistic contractors. They descended upon the ravaged homes, promising restoration but leaving trails of broken promises in their wake. Krissy's mother fell victim to one such scammer, who promised to put in new kitchen cabinets, but simply took around $6,000 and never returned to do the work. It was just another example of how the vulnerability of those in the aftermath of catastrophe was exploited, compounding their anguish and pushing them further into a hole.

At one point, Krissy couldn't help but wonder why her parents didn't have insurance to protect their home and its belongings after enduring multiple storms. She later learned it was because of discriminatory lending practices. For residents in her mother's predominantly African American community, including Krissy's mom, securing proper insurance was an impossible task because their mortgage agreements forbade it. According to Krissy, there was a clause in the mortgages stipulating that no insurance could be obtained because the homes were in a zone that had not flooded in 100 years. This left these homeowners immensely vulnerable to the ravages of natural disasters.

When it got to the point that her mother's home became unaffordable—due to both financial mismanagement and a predatory loan, Krissy says—the family attempted to get a loan modification. But the relentless demands of mortgage modifications spanned five grueling years, an epic journey riddled with bureaucratic red tape and frustration. Paperwork vanished, the system seemed designed to break their spirits, and her mother grew exhausted with the entire process.

"In the end, she lost her home after Harvey through foreclosure," Krissy says. "Then a developer bought her house, fixed it up, and sold it for twice as much as it was originally worth."

All these years later, the whole saga still stings. "I feel like I could've done more," Krissy says ruefully. "I had my own trauma to deal with. But I still have a lot of guilt," about her mother's home being lost to foreclosure.

Krissy says she witnessed the mental and financial toll that other neighbors in similar circumstances endured. "They were mostly Black, single women there and they all had a similar story of how it was 'a miracle' that they were able to get their homes in the first place." But after Harvey, "they all ended up short-selling their homes," Krissy says.

No Aspect of Life Untouched

The recurring cycle of natural destruction has left no aspect of her family's existence untouched, impacting them emotionally, straining personal relationships, and shaping their outlook on life in profound and lasting ways. These aren't just haunting memories either. "Tornados, hurricanes, flooding, and other disasters have just permeated our lives so much," Krissy says, noting that they're an indelible part of her family's narrative, something that persists to this day. "My sister has tornado dreams. She always has since we were little," Krissy adds. These dreams, symbolic of the storms they faced both literally and metaphorically, no doubt leave a serious imprint on their psyches.

As for her, Krissy acknowledges that nature's fury has also impacted her in somewhat troubling and unexpected ways. Describing the emotional fallout of enduring so many relentless storms, Krissy confessed: "There's something about me that struggles to settle down. I have the need to move around. Kind of like a transient thing," she says. "As a child, every few years we would have to move for some reason, whether it was a storm or a job change, or something else. Now, I always have a feeling like something is going to happen, so don't get too used to it, or don't be too happy." The wounds left by the tempests run deep and seem to have left her in a constant state of vigilance, always waiting for the next disaster to strike. That's affected her work as well as her personal relationships, Krissy says. "There's a form of stoicism [that I have]. Thank God I have my daughter now. Besides her, I could never be attached to a place or people, or a thing because those things have always been temporary and transient."

Krissy's experiences show that storms and natural disasters can leave lasting scars, not just on the outside but on the inside too. As if that weren't enough to handle, she's had to face other recent personal challenges, including the breakup of a cherished relationship and the loss of a second baby through miscarriage. "I'm currently dealing with a lot of grief," she says.

But even in her darkest moments, Krissy says she also feels strength and comfort. "I'm grateful for God's grace and mercy that carried me through. This (breakup) is not a disaster. I'm seeing this as an opportunity to be free and do what I really want to do instead of sacrificing."

"Getting through storms and other types of traumas has actually given me a lot of resilience to deal with my current challenges," she says. "I feel like I'm OK, and I'm going to be OK," she adds, with steely determination.

Another upside: her experiences with the chaos of Mother Nature have taught her the value of preparedness, the necessity of meticulous planning—and the importance of being very well insured. "Homes can be replaced," Krissy says. "I have plenty of insurance. I'm probably *too* insured now," she says with a laugh.

When I ask Krissy what she wants for her beloved and precocious 15-month-old daughter, Krissy pauses for a very long time and gives it some serious thought. Finally, she says this: "I definitely want her to have a place that she can call *home*. But I think in this day and age, she has to learn to find that place *inside* herself too."

As a mom, that's something I can identify with and want for my kids as well. Krissy's story serves as a poignant reminder to us all: Even amid life's most unnerving and difficult times, if you can cultivate and tap into your inner strength, you're building the strongest foundation of all—one that can withstand any storm.

The Long-lasting Impact of Natural Disasters

While Krissy's story is unique, her family isn't alone in their circumstances. When Hurricane Katrina struck New Orleans and the Mississippi Gulf Coast in 2005, millions were affected, and hundreds of thousands fled Mother Nature's wrath. Years later, scores of displaced residents battled insurance companies while others never returned to their former homes. A similar scenario played out in the aftermath of Hurricane Sandy's pummeling of the East Coast in 2012. More than a decade later, many New York and New Jersey residents still lacked permanent housing. I was living in Northern New Jersey when Sandy hit; we lost power for days but were spared the full brunt of the storm. Our next-door neighbors, however, weren't as lucky. The Hurricane sent a tree crashing through their roof. Fortunately, no one was hurt. More recently, in 2022, Hurricane Ian ravaged Florida. And 2023 saw the deadly impact of even more hurricanes, not to mention ferocious wildfires, such as those in Hawaii in August 2023. In the wake of the devastating inferno that erupted in the town of Lahaina in Maui, more than 100 people died, making the Hawaii wildfire the deadliest blaze in modern US history.

Natural disasters—including tornadoes, earthquakes, or fires—can total cars, level homes and businesses, and even wipe out entire towns. There is always the risk of man-made problems too amid natural disasters. Whether an unscrupulous home contractor swindles you or an insurance company gives you the runaround and refuses to pay a claim, disasters are a Dreaded D you need to bounce back from in order to get your life back to normal.

Understanding Billion-dollar Weather and Climate Disasters

Weather and climate disasters are not just dramatic news stories; they come with a heavy price tag. As of this writing (September 2023), since 1980, the United States has faced 371 weather and climate disasters where the costs reached or exceeded $1 billion each. This includes damages to properties and assets, as well as cleanup and recovery efforts. When we adjust these costs for inflation to 2023 levels, the total cost of these 371 events surpasses an astonishing $2.62 trillion.

Let's break down these numbers a bit. From the year 2000 to 2009, the US experienced 67 such events, averaging about 6.7 per year. The cost of these events during this decade was $594.6 billion, which averages to $59.5 billion per year. These disasters also took a heavy toll in human terms, leading to the loss of 3,102 lives, or about 310 deaths per year.

Fast-forward to 2023, and the frequency of these high-cost disasters was on the rise. As of September 11, 2023, the US had already faced 23 weather or climate disasters, each costing over $1 billion. These include two flooding events 18 severe storms, one tropical cyclone, one wildfire, and one winter storm. Unfortunately, these disasters also resulted in the deaths of 253 people. (Notably, this data doesn't even include Tropical Storm Hilary. In August 2023, Hilary brought record-breaking flooding and caused a first-ever tropical storm watch to be issued for Southern California. As of this writing, damage estimates for Hilary were still unfolding.). If we compare these numbers to the past, we can see that the average number of billion-dollar weather and climate disasters was 8.1 per year from 1980 to 2022. However, in the most recent five years (2018–2022), the annual average more than doubled to 18.0 events.

More recently, the first half of 2023 was marked by severe hail storms in Florida and Texas and a series of tornadoes and hail storms across several central states, causing severe damage to homes, businesses, vehicles, farms, and other infrastructure. The prior record for billion-dollar disasters occurred in 2017, when 22 natural calamities each caused over a billion dollars in damages, totaling an estimated $383.7 billion, marking a high since 1980. With 23 such incidents reported by early September 2023, the US already set a new disaster record for the full year of 2023.

These figures are compiled and analyzed by the National Centers for Environmental Information (NCEI), an organization that monitors and assesses the climate, and tracks and evaluates climate events that have significant economic and societal impacts. The NCEI uses the most comprehensive public and private sector sources to estimate the total costs of these events. These costs include physical damage to residential, commercial, and municipal buildings, vehicles, public assets such as roads and bridges, and agricultural assets. However, the estimates do not include certain types of losses, such as natural capital or environmental degradation, mental or physical health care–related costs, or supply chain interruption costs. Therefore, the actual losses may be even higher than reported.

Huge insurance losses are also upending the overall insurance industry. The price of flood insurance is exorbitant in places such as Florida. Meanwhile, in states such as California, insurance firms Allstate and State Farm have stopped insuring homes altogether, citing increased wildfire risk and skyrocketing construction costs.

Even reinsurers are sounding the alarm bells. Reinsurance companies insure insurance firms. A reinsurance firm helps insurance companies cover their losses by taking on some of the risk, so that no single company faces too much financial strain from large claims. In August 2023, one giant reinsurer, Swiss Re, put out a statement affirming its projections of a 5–7% annual growth trend in insured losses. Swiss Re officials said the major contributor to US insurance claims were "severe convective storms—storms associated with thunder, lightning, heavy rain, hail, strong winds, and sudden temperature changes."

Jérôme Jean Haegeli, Swiss Re's Group chief economist, also said: "The effects of climate change can already be seen in certain perils like heatwaves, droughts, floods, and extreme precipitation. Besides the impact of climate change, land use planning in more exposed coastal and riverine areas, and urban sprawl into the wilderness, generate a hard-to-revert combination of high value exposure in higher risk environments. Protective measures need to be taken for insurance products to remain economical for such properties at high risk. It is high time to invest in more climate adaption."

Most insurance experts agree: hurricanes and other meteorological occurrences are becoming more intense and taking place with greater frequency.

While we can't completely stop powerful natural disasters from happening, understanding the economic impact of these violent events can help us prepare and potentially mitigate some of the damages. It underscores the importance not only of individual preparedness—but of also investing in infrastructure that can withstand extreme weather events and creating policies that help communities recover quickly when disasters do occur. It's evident that these major catastrophes are not one-off occurrences but quite predictable scenarios that merit all of our collective efforts to combat. These numbers are also a stark reminder of the real costs of weather and climate disasters—costs that are measured not only in dollars and cents but in the lives impacted and lost.

In this chapter, you will learn:

- An insider's view of how disaster recovery works;
- All about free money from the Red Cross;
- What to do the first 24 to 72 hours after a disaster;
- What to do the first week to 10 days after disaster strikes;
- How to secure FEMA aid after a disaster;
- How to handle living with disaster six months later;
- How to cope with long-term disasters six months to six years and beyond;
- All about the new federal effort designed to help disaster survivors;
- How to deal with the two most common insurance claim problems;
- How to address trauma and manage your emotions;
- How to plan for future natural disasters.

An Insider's View of How Disaster Recovery Works

Chris Burt has spent 35 years as an emergency management and public health expert, offering a multidisciplinary perspective and an insider's look at disaster recovery from various angles. His extensive career spans work in every sector of government—federal, military, state, and local—as well as in the nonprofit and nongovernmental organizations (NGOs) world. He's done stints with FEMA (Federal Emergency Management Agency), working in disaster recovery, and is now a disaster program manager with the Red Cross.

Burt's impressive credentials—an MS-MBA in applied management and health care administration and an MPH with a concentration in emergency management and epidemiology—further augment his expertise. Because of his multifaceted background, Burt is always mindful of three related areas: the physical, financial, and policy aspects of natural disasters.

"I look at things from a scientific perspective, a business perspective, and a policy perspective," he says, adding that his ultimate goal is to "ensure that people are healthy and cared for, especially at-risk populations."

According to Burt, "Disasters don't know color, race, religion, or sexual orientation. They come when they come." However, during his years of service in emergency management and disaster recovery, he's recognized that some communities, particularly communities of color, often face additional challenges in the wake of disasters. That's why, he said he's committed to public health, equality, and inclusion in his approach to disaster management. "Everybody has the ability to recover, but not everybody has the capacity to recover," he points out, emphasizing the need for equitable recovery strategies. For example, Burt notes that not everyone has insurance, money, or a place to stay if their house gets leveled.

In terms of disaster response, Burt stresses the importance of understanding the intricacies of federal aid. A crucial component of this is the Stafford Act, which triggers federal assistance when the president makes a declaration of disaster. Every federal agency has a mandate under the Stafford Act and plays a role in recovery, from clearing roads to ensuring the continuity of education.

"When the president makes a federal declaration, that's when the floodgates open for federal assistance to come in," Burt explains. The Act mobilizes every federal government agency, each with a specific mandate for recovery. This structure brings not only technical expertise but also critical resources to disaster-stricken areas.

Despite wide-ranging federal help for survivors navigating the aftermath of a disaster, Burt says there are definite limits to federal assistance. "People always think the feds are going to bail them out, or that the Red Cross is going to put them up in a hotel. But the need or delivery of services is based on what the agencies and government have decided is going to be the best recourse for recipients," he warns. He cited an instance where a tornado struck Alabama in 2023. The storm survivors didn't get put up in hotels. Rather, "they gave out tents and sleeping bags," as temporary shelter, Burt says. A wide array of factors shapes disaster assistance, from the extent of damage to the number of people impacted and the anticipated recovery duration, he adds.

People or families aren't the only ones impacted by disaster. So are businesses. "Their infrastructure is impacted," Burt notes. "Their workforce and operations are impacted." Therefore, the Small Business Administration (SBA) provides them with assistance. That's what happened with the Paycheck Protection Program (PPP) during the COVID disaster. Business owners got forgivable PPP loans and low-interest recovery loans called EIDL, or Economic Injury Disaster

Loans. Because of his public health background, during the COVID pandemic, FEMA detailed Burt to the SBA to handle financial requests made by doctors' offices and medical practices. The goal was to make sure the loan requests were legitimate. "There's even tax relief in disasters," Burt says. "Anything that you put forth or pay for in your recovery can be tax deductible, like cleanup supplies, tarps, and so on."

But the real success in recovery, according to Burt, is based on partnerships and everyone coming together for the common good. The Red Cross is one such organization that plays a pivotal role in disaster assistance, providing initial financial assistance, setting up shelters, and offering health services. "Our goal at the Red Cross is to alleviate human suffering," Burt says. "We tend to be the initial boots-on-the-ground organization after a disaster. We're a local organization, but 95% of our workforce is volunteers."

"Disaster recovery begins at the local level, and it ends at the local level," Burt notes. "You have greater success when it's a local-led effort and with stakeholders involved in the process."

All About Free Money from the Red Cross

For many people, blood donations are the first thing that comes to mind about the Red Cross in the wake of a disaster. But the organization also offers critical cash assistance when it's urgently needed—along with other support. "One time I went out at 1:00 a.m., and I saw a house was burned down," Burt recalls. He immediately gave the people funds for shelter. "I can give you a debit card and a Zelle [payment] within a matter of minutes. The generosity of our donors helps with our relief."

"We also stand up the shelters, we're there to give you a warm blanket and someone to talk to. We help if you need eyeglasses or you lost your medication in a disaster," Burt says.

Regarding cash assistance, Burt says it's provided free from the Red Cross and ranges from $350 to $1,200. The money can be used to buy food or clothing, secure shelter, and address other pressing needs. "It's just temporary, and we suggest people take advantage of other resources," Burt says.

"To qualify for the free money," he adds, "we do damage assessments based on FEMA criteria." FEMA guidelines attribute various levels of damage to a structure after a disaster: affected, minor, major, and destroyed, each of which determines the type of assistance given.

What to Do the First 24 to 72 Hours After a Disaster

In the wake of a natural disaster, you may be reeling from the shock of everything—or simply grateful to be alive. Whatever the case, you need to manage your physical, emotional, financial, and overall well-being when disaster strikes. Here's what to do in the first 24 hours to 72 hours after a disaster to best support your recovery efforts.

Ensure Safety

Above all, ensure your and your family's safety. This could mean evacuating to a designated area or moving to a safer location within your home. The benefit of taking this step is straightforward but profound: it will protect your life and the lives of your loved ones. Moving to a safe location will also lessen the chance of injuries and further trauma, allowing you to remain physically capable of addressing the situation.

Seek Help and Inform Authorities

Once you are safe, reach out to emergency services and notify them of your situation. This is crucial for ensuring that help and resources are directed your way as soon as possible. By informing the authorities, you enable a more swift and effective response, which can lead to a quicker resolution and potentially limit the extent of damage and loss.

Document Damage

As soon as it's safe to return, document the damage to your property for insurance purposes. Take photos, videos, and make a written account of what you observe. This step is key for building a strong insurance claim. Proper documentation can lead to a more favorable settlement, helping you recover financially and start the rebuilding process sooner.

Secure Temporary Accommodation

If your home is uninhabitable, secure temporary accommodation for you and your family. Emergency shelters or hotels or even staying with friends or family can be options. Securing a safe, comfortable place to stay can provide the stability you need in the aftermath of a disaster. It will offer a base for recovery operations and provide essential physical and emotional respite.

Begin Cleaning Up

Start the cleanup process by disposing of hazardous materials and removing water or debris, if safe to do so. Doing so will mitigate the risk of further damage to your property and belongings. This step also accelerates the path to normalcy and helps create a safer environment for when repair work begins.

Start Replacing Vital Documents

Initiate the process to replace vital documents that were lost in the disaster. This includes passports, driver's licenses, Social Security cards, and birth certificates. Contact your bank, credit card companies, and other financial institutions about the loss of financial documents. Replacing these documents quickly will ensure you have the necessary identification for various recovery processes. It also helps protect you from potential identity theft, provides proof of residence, which is often required for aid applications, and allows you to access financial services needed for your recovery.

Contact Your Insurance Company

Contact your insurance company to report the loss and start the claim process. The sooner you begin this process, the sooner you could potentially receive the necessary funds for recovery. Starting this early also helps you understand what your policy covers, helping you better plan your next steps.

Take Care of Yourself and Your Family

Look after your emotional health. Reach out to friends, family, or mental health professionals. Dealing with a disaster is stressful, and it's essential not to ignore the emotional and psychological impact. Taking care of your emotional well-being will give you the strength and resilience needed to navigate the challenging road to recovery.

Returning Home Safely

When you are able to return home, the American Lung Association recommends several key steps to ensure your safety:

Do wear protective gear: This includes N-95 masks, gloves, and sturdy shoes. This gear will protect you from potential hazards such as dust, mold, and debris.

Do ventilate your home: Open doors and windows to let fresh air in and circulate. This will help clear out any lingering contaminants.
Do inspect for structural damage: Look for signs of damage that might make your home unsafe. This includes checking the stability of the floors and walls.
Don't rush to enter: Don't enter your home until local officials have declared it safe.
Don't ignore mold: Mold can cause severe health issues. If you find mold, have it professionally removed.
Don't immediately use gas or electrical appliances: Wait until these appliances have been checked by a professional. These could pose fire risks if they've been damaged.

These steps are designed to ensure your safety and health when you return home, helping to avoid additional damage and potential health risks.

The immediate aftermath of a disaster is primarily about ensuring survival and safety. Despite the desire to begin recovery, it's essential to meet immediate needs first. Reach out to professionals for assistance, rely on your community for support, and focus on staying safe and healthy. This phase lays the foundation for your recovery journey.

What to Do the First Week to 10 Days After Disaster Strikes

As the initial shock of the disaster begins to fade, you may find yourself in a new phase of recovery—one marked by a blend of relief, frustration, and uncertainty. It's been a week or perhaps 10 days since the disaster struck, and your life is still far from what it used to be. You've secured immediate needs and begun the process of seeking financial aid, but the path to complete recovery seems long and daunting. There may be a gnawing worry about temporary housing, concerns about your damaged property, or anxiety about lost income. The emotional toll can be heavy as you navigate unfamiliar bureaucracies, deal with insurance claims, and continue to cope with the stark reality of the disaster. It's an uneasy and challenging time, but know that these feelings are entirely normal and shared by many in similar situations. With patience, perseverance, and the right guidance, you can overcome these hurdles and start rebuilding your life.

Access Local Resources

In the aftermath of a disaster, the world may seem overwhelming. The road to recovery, however, often begins right in your community. Numerous local resources can be invaluable during this time, and it's essential to understand their availability and how to leverage them.

Nonprofit organizations, churches, and community centers often offer immediate assistance to those affected by disasters. These organizations typically provide necessities such as food, clothing, and sometimes temporary shelter. By reaching out to these local resources, you can secure the essentials for you and your family. This allows you to focus on the next steps toward recovery.

The benefits of accessing these local resources are multifaceted. Not only do they provide immediate physical relief, but they also offer emotional support. Connecting with others in your community who are also affected by the disaster can bring about a sense of unity and shared resilience. You're not alone in your recovery journey.

"When disasters hit, people should always go to a DRC, a disaster recovery center," says Burt, the emergency management and disaster expert. "That's where the SBA, Red Cross, Team Rubicon, every nonprofit, and the Salvation Army are—everyone is there to offer assistance to the members of that community."

Team Rubicon is a veteran-led, global nonprofit that provides humanitarian assistance before, during, and after disasters and crises. Founded after the Haiti earthquake in 2010, the organization now has more than 150,000 volunteers across the United States and has launched more than 1,100 operations domestically and internationally.

Additionally, there's the National VOAD, or Voluntary Organizations Active in Disasters, an organization that collaborates with multiple nonprofit entities to provide aid to those impacted by natural disasters. When a disaster strikes, they mobilize a network of experienced disaster relief organizations that provide critical services such as damage assessment, home repair, and cleanup efforts. Additionally, they support the affected communities throughout the recovery process and help in the coordination of resources among various disaster response organizations. It's an essential resource for anyone who needs assistance in the wake of a natural disaster, providing much-needed relief and support during challenging times.

Apply for Aid

As the dust settles, it's crucial to start thinking about the long-term impact of the disaster on your financial well-being. The federal government offers several programs to help victims of disasters get back on their feet.

One of these programs is managed by FEMA, which provides temporary housing assistance, home repair and replacement grants, and low-interest disaster loans for homeowners, renters, and businesses affected by a disaster. It's vital to apply for this aid as soon as possible to help manage the immediate financial impact of the disaster.

To apply for FEMA assistance, visit their official website and follow the application process. You'll need to provide information about your situation, including details of your losses, a description of your dwelling, and insurance details if applicable. (See the next section also for a step-by-step guide to applying for FEMA aid.)

The benefits of applying for aid extend beyond immediate financial relief. Government assistance can offer the means to start rebuilding your life after a disaster, providing some sense of normalcy in a challenging time. Securing emergency housing can provide a safe space for you and your family to stay while you begin the recovery process. Disaster assistance loans, on the other hand, can provide you with the means to repair or rebuild your home, replace essential personal property, and even help you restart a business disrupted by the disaster.

It's worth noting that the process of applying for aid can sometimes be complex and time-consuming, with various forms to fill out and documents to provide. However, the potential financial relief and stability it can bring make it a worthwhile endeavor.

Remember, these steps are just the beginning of the recovery process. It's OK to feel overwhelmed at times; what's important is to keep moving forward. Take each day at a time, lean on the resources and support available to you, and know that with every passing day, you're one step closer to regaining your footing and rebuilding your life.

How to Secure FEMA Aid After a Disaster

In the aftermath of a catastrophic event, FEMA is there to provide crucial support. If you're a survivor of a disaster and need help, here's a step-by-step guide on applying for FEMA assistance and the important documents you'll need throughout the process.

Step 1: Understand Eligibility

First, it's important to understand whether you are eligible for assistance. Typically, FEMA provides aid to individuals and businesses who have suffered losses due to disasters such as floods, hurricanes, earthquakes, and wildfires. To be eligible, the disaster must have been officially declared by the president of the United States and you must reside in a declared disaster area.

Step 2: Prepare Essential Documents

Before beginning your application, gather the necessary documents to support your claim. This typically includes:

Proof of identity: This could be a driver's license, passport, or any government-issued ID that verifies your identity.
Proof of occupancy or ownership: This could be a lease, mortgage statement, utility bill, or property tax bill.
Insurance information: Details of your coverage, such as policy number and the insurance company's contact information.
Documentation of damage: Take photographs or videos that clearly demonstrate the extent of the damage caused by the disaster. Also include any records of repairs or quotes for repair work.

Step 3: Apply for Assistance

You can apply for FEMA assistance online at `DisasterAssistance.gov`, via the FEMA mobile app, or by calling the FEMA helpline at 1-800-621-FEMA (3362). You will need to provide details about your situation, the damage incurred, and your financial needs. You should try to apply as soon as possible after the disaster to ensure timely support.

Step 4: Inspection and Follow-up

Once you have submitted your application, FEMA will schedule an inspection of your property to verify the damage. This can be a virtual or in-person visit, depending on the circumstances. The inspector will need to see your ID and proof of occupancy or ownership.

After the inspection, FEMA will review your case and send a letter outlining their decision. If approved, the letter will also detail how much assistance you will receive and how it should be used.

Step 5: Appeal, If Necessary

If you're not satisfied with FEMA's decision, you have the right to appeal. To do this, you must send a letter explaining why you believe the decision was incorrect within 60 days of receiving FEMA's decision. Include any supporting documents that were not initially provided.

We all wish it could be simple and very straightforward. But the reality is that securing assistance after a disaster can be a complex process. The key is to stay organized, document everything, and start the process as soon as possible. FEMA is there to help, and these steps can increase your chances of receiving the aid you need to recover.

How to Handle Living with Disaster Six Months Later

In the half-year that has passed since the disaster, you might have begun to notice a deceptive sense of normalcy set in. Streets are clear, repairs are underway, and life seems to be returning to a rhythm. But look closer, and you'll see the undercurrent of lingering stress and upheaval. The truth is: six months is often not enough time to completely erase the impacts of a catastrophic event. The disruption, loss, and aftermath of a disaster leave profound marks, both tangible and intangible, that demand your attention, patience, and resilience.

Monitoring Your Mental Health

Coping with the emotional aftermath of a disaster is as critical as tackling its physical destruction. Six months in, the adrenaline rush that propelled you through the immediate aftermath has likely subsided, replaced by the reality of everyday struggles and uncertainties. Stress, anxiety, and trauma might surface, appearing as sleepless nights, mood swings, or feeling overwhelmed.

Taking steps to monitor and care for your mental health is paramount. Do not hesitate to seek help. The Substance Abuse and Mental Health Services Administration (SAMHSA) has a Disaster Distress Helpline, which provides 24/7/365 crisis counseling and support. Calling this helpline can connect you with trained professionals who understand the unique stressors you're facing and can provide practical advice and emotional support.

Remember, taking care of your emotional well-being isn't a sign of weakness; rather, it is a step toward resilience. It allows you to heal and regain the strength to continue rebuilding. Plus, a healthy mental state can improve your problem-solving skills and decision-making ability, both of which are crucial during this recovery period.

Continuing Insurance Claims

While your immediate survival needs might be covered, a major part of your recovery will hinge on how your insurance claim progresses. This process is often complicated and requires constant attention and follow-up. Just fix your mind to know that it won't last *forever*, but it'll probably take longer than you'd like.

Maintain regular contact with your insurance company and be persistent. Inquire about the status of your claim, what is being covered, and what isn't. If there are delays or disputes over the claim, do not hesitate to stand up for your rights. Be aware of your policy's terms and conditions, and keep all documentation and communication with the insurance company.

Understanding the intricacies of your coverage can save you from unexpected financial burdens. Keeping the claims process moving will ensure you receive the funds needed to repair or rebuild, replace lost belongings, and regain your footing financially.

Addressing Financial and Housing Issues

As you navigate the tangle of emotions and insurance claims, you may still be grappling with the pressing issue of housing. Displacement is a challenging reality for many disaster survivors. Even six months later, you might be living in temporary housing or staying with friends or relatives. If your home was severely damaged, the repair or rebuilding process can be a lengthy one.

Here's what you can do to address ongoing financial and housing issues:

Secure long-term temporary housing: Begin by exploring long-term temporary housing options. These could include rentals within your community or in nearby areas. Prioritize a location that allows you to maintain a semblance of normalcy—proximity to work, school, and supportive social networks can play a significant role in your mental well-being and recovery process.

Seek out assistance programs: Look into ongoing assistance programs, such as those offered by FEMA or other nonprofit organizations. While assistance from these organizations often targets the immediate aftermath of a disaster, some programs can provide extended support. FEMA's Individual Assistance program, for instance, can help with rent for temporary accommodation, home repairs, and even longer-term transitional housing in some cases.

Conduct financial planning: Managing financial stress is crucial during this period. You might be dealing with lost income, increased expenses, and looming repair costs. If you haven't already, consider sitting down with a financial advisor or a disaster recovery financial counselor to discuss your situation. They can provide valuable advice on managing your money during this challenging time, navigating insurance claims, and planning for the expenses involved in getting back to normal.

It's perfectly normal to feel exhausted or frustrated by financial and housing issues at this stage. You might be in smaller, more cramped quarters. Or you may be residing with relatives during this rough patch and perhaps everyone is getting on your nerves! Recovery takes time, and everyone moves at their own pace. Keep taking small steps toward progress, and before you know it, you'll have traversed the seemingly insurmountable mountain of post-disaster recovery.

This six-month mark is not just a reminder of the disaster, but a testament to your resilience. By taking care of your mental health and diligently handling your insurance claims, housing, and financial issues, you can turn this milestone into a stepping stone toward recovery and rebuilding.

How to Cope with Long-term Disasters Six Months to Six Years and Beyond

As the dust settles and the immediate crisis fades, the long-term impact of a disaster becomes apparent. This period, extending from six months to several years after the disaster, may be challenging as you come to grips with the full extent of the damage. You might find yourself grappling with a plethora of issues ranging from property loss and persistent financial instability, to prolonged displacement. It's a time filled with uncertainty but also a time for resilience and recovery.

Rebuilding and Repairing

After a disaster, your home, your sanctuary, may be in ruins, or require extensive repairs. This stage is not merely about restoring a physical structure; it's about re-creating a safe, secure environment for you and your loved ones. Work closely with contractors, architects, or city planners to ensure all repairs and reconstructions comply with local codes and regulations. This will not only ensure your home is structurally sound, but can also make the rebuilding process smoother and possibly prevent future disaster-related damage. Remember, rebuilding is not a race, it's a marathon, and every small progress brings you one step closer to normalcy.

Seeking Long-term Aid

In the face of such immense challenges, remember you don't have to face them alone. There are several organizations offering long-term assistance to disaster survivors. FEMA, for example, provides continued assistance programs, including disaster loans and grants for repairs and replacements not covered by insurance. It also offers crisis counseling for people dealing with emotional distress from the disaster.

Local nonprofit organizations can also be instrumental in providing support during the long-term recovery phase. These organizations can help with home repairs, provide financial assistance, and even offer job placement services if you've lost your work due to the disaster.

Lastly, keep engaging with your community. Community resilience can play a critical role in long-term disaster recovery. Participate in local recovery efforts, attend town meetings, and stay informed about resources available to you. Remember, the road to recovery is long and often filled with hurdles, but with perseverance, resilience, and the right support, you can navigate through it and come out stronger on the other side.

All About the New Federal Effort Designed to Help Disaster Survivors

Navigating the aftermath of a disaster can be an overwhelming experience, made even more stressful by the complexity of securing aid from various sources. Recognizing this challenge, the federal government has launched a new initiative aimed at streamlining the disaster assistance process, making it more efficient, intuitive, and accessible for individuals affected by disasters. This initiative, part of the broader strategy to enhance the federal government's customer experience, seeks to minimize the burden on disaster survivors and empower them to bounce back from financial shocks.

The initiative's goal is to centralize and simplify the process of accessing and managing federal disaster assistance. Traditionally, survivors had to navigate different agencies and processes, a task that was often daunting and confusing. Under this new approach, the government aims to create a more seamless, integrated process, reducing bureaucratic red tape, speeding up the recovery process, and improving survivors' experience.

The federal project is part of a series of initiatives focused on improving service delivery by understanding experiences from the customer's point of view. This is conducted under the organizing framework of "Life Experiences." These experiences are significant events or transitions that often require interactions with multiple federal agencies and different levels of government.

The goal is to make these interactions less complex and more responsive to the needs of the people, moving away from bureaucratic silos and preconceived solutions.

The specific life experience initiative focusing on disaster recovery and financial shocks was one of the priority life experiences selected by the federal government and the President's Management Council (PMC) for the 2022 designation cycle and is ongoing in the year 2024 and beyond. Other experiences included approaching retirement, birth, and early childhood for low-income mothers and children, and transitioning to civilian life. The process involved speaking directly to a diverse representation of members of the public to understand how people interact with the government during these moments in their lives.

In terms of the initiative's approach to helping people recover from a disaster, federal employees began by listening to people's stories nationwide. They collected feedback on people's experiences and identified areas where the government process could have been simpler and more helpful. In the end, one solution they came up with involves creating a unified portal where survivors can access information and apply for assistance from various federal programs. This not only saves survivors time but also reduces the stress associated with navigating disparate aid programs. The portal will offer personalized guidance, enabling survivors to understand which programs they qualify for, how to apply, and how to track their applications.

The initiative also prioritizes clear, understandable communication. The government recognizes that complex jargon and legalese can be a significant barrier for survivors seeking aid. Therefore, all communications, from the portal's interface to individual assistance letters, are designed to be as clear and concise as possible.

Streamlining the process also means faster delivery of aid. The government aims to expedite the approval process and disburse funds more quickly, reducing the financial strain on survivors and helping them to recover faster.

This initiative reflects the government's commitment to a new people-centered approach, placing the needs and experiences of disaster survivors at the heart of its services. By simplifying the disaster assistance process, the government hopes to not only aid recovery but also bolster resilience, enabling individuals and communities to emerge stronger from the trials of natural disasters.

Overall, this federal initiative represents a significant step forward in disaster recovery. It acknowledges the realities and challenges faced by disaster survivors and seeks to offer practical, tangible solutions. By centralizing and simplifying the process of securing aid, the government is easing the burdens you may experience, letting you focus on recovery and rebuilding your life.

Since the initiative's primary goal is to leverage technology to make the disaster recovery process as efficient and user-friendly as possible, here are some specific strategies the initiative aims to implement:

Unified digital portal: One of the key proposals is the creation of a unified digital portal where individuals can access all the information they need about federal disaster assistance. This online platform will offer personalized guidance, enabling users to understand which programs they are eligible for and how to apply for and track their applications.

Electronic applications and approvals: To expedite the process, the initiative aims to make it possible for individuals to apply for assistance and receive approval electronically. This means that survivors can access the help they need from the comfort of their homes, without the need to visit multiple agencies or wait for in-person appointments.

Rapid response: The government aims to significantly reduce the time between a disaster event and when survivors receive aid. The goal is to provide disaster survivors with an initial response within 24 hours (yes, 24 hours!), including an outline of the available federal support, how to access it, and guidance on the next steps. In fact, the government has set the following goals for Americans seeking crucial services:

- You should be able to apply in 20 minutes;
- You should be able to enroll in 24 hours;
- You should receive vital services within a week;
- You should get equitable, high-quality service experiences including wraparound supports.

This initiative will hopefully one day touch every aspect of our dealings with the federal government, from getting your passport to filing your taxes, and more.

Centralized communication: The Life Experiences initiative also aims to centralize communication so disaster survivors receive updates and information from a single source. This will make it easier for individuals to stay informed about the status of their applications and any changes to the available assistance.

Clear, user-friendly language: Recognizing that jargon can be a significant barrier for individuals seeking assistance, the initiative is committed to using clear, understandable language. This will make it simpler for survivors to understand the available assistance, their eligibility, and the application process.

Integration with local resources: The federal portal will also aim to integrate with local resources. This could mean providing information about local aid organizations, shelters, food banks, and other community services that could be of assistance to disaster survivors.

Regular updates and improvement: The government plans to use feedback from users to continually improve the platform, ensuring it remains user-friendly, efficient, and responsive to the needs of disaster survivors.

By implementing these strategies, the government aims to make the disaster recovery process less stressful and more efficient, giving you more of a fighting chance to bounce back after a disaster. I'd suggest you stay abreast of this federal effort by regularly visiting this website: `https://www.performance.gov/cx/projects/`.

How to Deal with the Two Most Common Insurance Claims Problems

Tackling insurance claims in the aftermath of a disaster can be a daunting task. You're likely already dealing with the emotional toll of the disaster and the upheaval of your life, and navigating complex insurance policies and paperwork can add an additional layer of stress. However, addressing common insurance claim problems proactively and effectively is crucial to your financial recovery. It's a process, often challenging, but with patience, organization, and determination, you can manage it successfully.

Problem #1: Inadequate Documentation

The cornerstone of a successful insurance claim is thorough and accurate documentation. Without this, you may face significant hurdles in getting the compensation you need to rebuild and recover.

Before disaster strikes, if possible, create a home inventory. List out items room by room, detailing their make, model, serial number, and estimated value. Periodically updating this list will make post-disaster claims smoother.

Immediately after the disaster, once it's safe, prioritize your personal safety. Only then should you begin documenting the aftermath.

Start by taking detailed photos and videos of all the damage. Ensure good lighting and capture images from multiple angles to provide a comprehensive view. This includes both structural damage to your property and damage to personal belongings. If you had taken photos of your property before the disaster, those can be particularly useful as "before" shots for comparison.

Compile receipts, appraisals, or any other proof of value and ownership for damaged items. If original receipts are lost, bank statements or credit card bills might help. For items that are irreplaceable or have sentimental value, consider obtaining a professional valuation.

For repairs or replacements, keep detailed records of costs. This should include quotations, invoices, and payment receipts. Engage with reputable contractors or repair services, and always get multiple quotes when possible.

Finally, maintain a log of all communication with your insurance company. Note down names, dates, and the essence of discussions. This might come in handy if there's any discrepancy or delay in processing your claim.

This meticulous approach ensures you present a strong case to your insurance company and helps prevent disputes over the extent of damage or cost of repairs.

Problem #2: Lack of Advocacy

Despite your best efforts, there may be instances where your claim is denied or you believe the payout offered is insufficient. In such situations, it probably behooves you to bring on an advocate who can help.

Before reaching out to a professional, try to understand the reasons for the claim denial or the low insurance payout. Insurers should provide a written explanation, and you can then address these specific points when you appeal.

Hiring a public adjuster or an attorney who specializes in insurance claims can be beneficial. Public adjusters work on your behalf to assess the damage and help negotiate with the insurance company. Before hiring one, research their background and reputation. Seek out testimonials or references to ensure they have a track record of success and are respected in the industry. If they are well versed in insurance policies and claims procedures, their expertise may help ensure you receive a fair settlement. However, be clear about their fee structures. Some might charge a percentage of your claim payout, while others might have a flat or hourly rate.

Similarly, if your claim is denied, an attorney can review your case, offer legal advice, and if necessary, represent you in any legal proceedings against the insurance company. Ensure that any attorney you consider has experience in insurance claim disputes. Some law firms even provide free initial consultations, allowing you to gauge your case's strength before committing financially.

While hiring a professional involves costs, the potential benefit of a fair payout can significantly outweigh the expense. But remember to factor their fees into your financial planning, especially if they take a percentage of the settlement.

Joining local support groups or community organizations can also be beneficial. These groups can share experiences, recommend reliable professionals, and sometimes even offer emotional support during challenging times.

It's important to fight for what you need and deserve. And no, it shouldn't have to be a battle—on top of the disaster you've already dealt with. But remember, your insurance claim is a key aspect of your financial recovery. Ensuring it's handled properly can help speed up your return to normalcy. Stay organized, be proactive and persistent, and don't hesitate to seek professional help when needed. It's not just about surviving the disaster; it's about effectively rebuilding your life afterward.

How to Address Trauma and Manage Your Emotions

The emotional recovery after a disaster is as critical as the physical and financial recovery. It's a journey that can seem overwhelming, filled with frustration, sadness, anxiety, and even guilt. According to FEMA, it's also common to want to strike back at people who have caused great pain. These feelings are normal and expected. Addressing this trauma and managing your emotions are integral to your overall well-being and your capacity to move forward. Here's how you can navigate this complex emotional landscape.

Reach Out

Don't face your emotional turmoil alone. Connection and communication are powerful tools in processing trauma. Reach out to friends and family; their support and understanding can provide immense relief during this difficult time. For example, you could arrange regular check-ins with loved ones, use video calls for face-to-face interaction when physical meetings aren't possible, or create a support group with others who have experienced similar disasters.

Additionally, consider seeking professional help. Mental health professionals are trained to help you navigate your feelings and can provide strategies to manage stress, anxiety, and other post-disaster emotions. Resources such as the SAMHSA Disaster Distress Helpline, at 800-662-HELP (4357) offer immediate counseling to anyone in need, providing a listening ear and useful techniques to cope.

Be mindful also that children and older adults may have specific worries in the aftermath of disasters. Kids may feel a profound sense of loss or anxiety over not having their normal routine or usual surroundings. Older people may struggle to adapt to unfamiliar surroundings or may simply feel depressed or mistakenly think that they are a burden to others. Even those who experience a disaster secondhand through exposure to extensive media coverage can be emotionally affected, FEMA says.

Prioritize Self-care

In the aftermath of a disaster, it's easy to neglect your own needs. However, self-care is a vital part of addressing trauma and managing emotions. Aim to maintain a balanced diet; nourishing your body can also nourish your mind. Try to ensure you get adequate rest; sleep is a restorative process and can impact your emotional resilience.

Engage in regular physical activity as well. This doesn't necessarily mean rigorous exercise; even simple activities such as walking, stretching, or gardening can have significant benefits. Physical activity releases endorphins, known as feel-good hormones, which can help reduce feelings of stress and anxiety.

After a disaster, you shouldn't spend all your time worrying about the bills, battling insurance companies, and fretting over damaged or lost property. Remember to also engage in activities that bring you joy and relaxation. Whether it's reading, listening to music, or practicing mindfulness exercises, such activities can offer a respite from your current circumstances and contribute to your emotional healing.

For instance, you could start your day with a simple stretching routine, followed by a healthy breakfast. During the day, find pockets of time for activities you enjoy, and at night, establish a sleep routine that promotes restful sleep.

Addressing trauma and managing emotions after a disaster is a unique journey for everyone. It's OK to have bad days. The key is not to isolate yourself and to prioritize self-care. Seek help when needed and know that it's OK to take this one day at a time. You're stronger than you know, and with time and support, you can navigate this emotional terrain.

How to Plan for Future Natural Disasters

Natural disasters can strike anytime, anywhere. They're a part of life on Earth, but that doesn't mean we're helpless. By making smart, proactive choices, we can prepare for natural disasters and mitigate their impact. Here's how.

Understand Your Environment and Risks

Know the disaster likelihood of where you are living or planning to buy a home or property. If it's in a flood plain or a flood-prone area, buyer beware. Consider the physical and financial risks involved in living in certain areas. "Think about the fact that not only do you run the risk of losing your home, but your automobiles, or if you're a farmer, you also have livestock at stake," says Burt, the disaster recovery expert. He adds: "If you want to live in paradise, be prepared to pay the premium for paradise. There's a cost for paradise, and it isn't always milk and honey."

Be Insured

Always be insured, whenever possible. This applies to renters, homeowners, and business owners alike. Admittedly, the cost of homeowners insurance isn't cheap. Residents in disaster-prone states such as California, Oklahoma, or Florida sometimes pay more than $5,000 annually for coverage. Nationwide, in 2023 it cost an average of $146 a month, or $1,754 per year, for a policy with $300,000 in dwelling coverage, according to PolicyGenius. But insurance can cover your personal property and protect you against major losses.

In terms of frequency, impact, and cost, floods are the most common and destructive natural disasters in the US. Hurricanes with flooding most frequently occur between June and November. But flooding affects every state and can happen at any time of the year, resulting from a variety of causes, including heavy rainfall, coastal storms, storm surges, and the melting of ice and snow. The extensive damage floods cause to infrastructure, homes, and businesses, coupled with their frequency, makes them the top natural disaster in the country.

Save on Insurance

Can't afford flood insurance? Then evaluate your housing options. Do you have to live in the location where you currently reside? Could you get to higher ground or possibly relocate? These are unique and personal considerations. And I realize that you might have a knee-jerk reaction to moving and automatically think, "I don't want to move!" Whatever the case, review *The Bounce Back Workbook* for some exercises that will help you reflect on your housing and overall disaster preparedness.

Remember, too, that insurance companies underwrite the National Flood Insurance Program, which can help manage the high premiums common with this coverage. Ensure you have adequate coverage for different types of disasters common in your area. This proactive financial planning provides peace of mind and secures the funds necessary for recovery and rebuilding in the aftermath of a disaster.

Here are some tips to maximize your savings on property insurance:

- **Bundle policies:** One of the best ways to save money on your homeowners' insurance policy is to bundle it with another policy from the same carrier, typically car insurance. Bundling can save you anywhere from 5% to 25% on your premiums. If you already have an auto insurance policy and money is tight, consider purchasing your home insurance policy with the same company.
- **Look for discounts:** Most providers offer several insurance discounts. Some are easier to qualify for, such as outfitting your home with security systems or enrolling in automatic payments, while others are more difficult to attain, such as having a new home or recently purchasing one.
- **Make renovations:** Although this can be costly up front, insurers will see an updated and repaired home as a lower risk to insure and offer lower premiums. Conversely, you may find yourself paying extra if your home has an older roof or outdated systems.
- **Maintain good credit:** Although you likely won't have time to improve your credit when shopping for home insurance, it's a great thing to keep in mind over time. By gradually improving or maintaining your credit, you may see a discount on your home insurance premiums at renewal.
- **Avoid small claims:** Filing a home insurance claim, even a small one, is likely to increase your home insurance premiums at your policy's renewal date. Consider whether reporting a claim is worth this uptick in cost. For example, if a covered loss will cost less than your deductible to replace or repair or you filed a claim in the past few years, you may not want to alert your home insurance company.
- **Compare providers:** Not all home insurers calculate risk the same way. If you're about to purchase home insurance or you already have home

insurance but want to save money on your premiums, get quotes from several insurers to compare prices. In addition to price, compare coverage options, customer reviews, and third-party ratings.

Understand Your Insurance Policy

Read the limitations of your insurance policy thoroughly. Insurance companies may try to limit their payout in certain circumstances. Be prepared for this and understand what is and isn't covered. Knowing what is covered and what is not can prevent unpleasant surprises after a disaster. In some instances, "The insurance company is going to do everything it can to not pay the claim," says Burt, the disaster recovery expert. "When there are Acts of God or acts of terrorism—that's where the nonprofits come in," he adds.

Typical homeowner insurance doesn't cover damages from earthquakes, floods, mudflows, landslides, or tsunamis. Additionally, in areas often affected by wildfires, hurricanes, or tornadoes, insurance might either limit or not offer coverage. However, you can potentially extend your coverage for wind or wildfires by adding a special provision called an endorsement, or you might consider buying specific earthquake, windstorm, or wildfire insurance through regional programs. If you live in California, for example, and you want to protect your home against tremors, you may be able to get insurance through the California Earthquake Authority.

Prepare a Go Bag

A "go bag" is a packed case that you grab on your way out of the door in an emergency. It should contain important documents, cash, necessary medication, and other essentials. This can be a lifesaver in last-minute evacuations. Keep a go bag ready with must-have items such as three days of clothing, water, 10 to 15 days of any medicines you take, important items for pets, and $500 or so in cash. You may need cash during a natural disaster because ATMs and card systems might be out of service. Also, consider keeping a pair of boots and blankets in your car.

Stockpile Emergency Supplies

The aftermath of a disaster often disrupts normal services, such as electricity and the water supply. Having a stockpile of essential supplies can make all the difference. To be ready in an emergency, store water, nonperishable food, first-aid supplies, flashlights, batteries, a battery-powered radio, a portable phone charger, personal hygiene items, and important medications. Update your supplies regularly to ensure they remain fresh and usable. The aim is to have enough supplies to sustain you and your family for at least three days in the event of a disaster. By doing this, you ensure immediate access to crucial items during a crisis, mitigating potential health risks, and offering a semblance of normalcy in an otherwise chaotic situation.

Pad Your Pantry Wisely

In addition to your emergency supplies, keep your pantry well-stocked with non-perishable food items. Think beans, rice, canned vegetables, pasta, and other staples. In the event of a prolonged disaster, these items can provide nourishment when fresh food is unavailable.

Develop an Evacuation Plan

It's always smart to have a solid evacuation plan. This plan should detail a safe route to exit your home and an established meeting place for family members. Practice this plan regularly to ensure everyone in the household is familiar with it. This proactive step can save valuable time during an emergency, ensuring the safety of your loved ones and reducing the potential for panic.

Secure and Digitize Important Documents

Always digitize your documents. Take pictures of important papers and store them in the cloud, where you can easily access them. Laminated physical copies can also be kept in your go bag. This applies to policies, birth certificates, and other important records. Also, take pictures and videos, keep receipts of purchases, and document the condition of your property before a disaster. This will help when filing insurance claims or applying for federal aid.

Build Your Savings

Work on amassing a healthy amount of savings, including money specifically for insurance deductibles. Not everybody has the up-front money to make a claim, and having a fund for this can significantly smooth the recovery process. An emergency fund is a financial safety net, meant to cover unexpected expenses.

Aim to save enough to cover three to six months' worth of living expenses. Start small if necessary, and remember, every bit helps.

Make Legal Preparations

It's also advisable to have a will prepared. This ensures that your final plans will be carried out according to your wishes, minimizing the potential for estate or legal issues and avoiding unnecessary stress for your relatives in case the worse happens. "The last thing you want is for there to be estate problems for your family in the event of a death," Burt cautions.

Make a Financial Recovery Kit

A financial recovery kit contains important documents you might need after a disaster. This includes identification documents, proof of address, insurance policies, financial account details, and medical information. Keep these documents in a waterproof, fireproof container, and consider storing copies in a secure cloud storage service.

Explore Earthquake Insurance

Most homeowner's insurance and renter's insurance policies do not cover earthquake damage. Earthquakes are among the most unpredictable of disasters and can strike at any time. If you live in an earthquake-prone area, you might want to consider purchasing additional earthquake insurance. This can cover repairs to your home and other structures and may also cover temporary living expenses if your home is uninhabitable.

Fight Off Forest Fires

If you reside in a fire-prone area, create a defensible space around your home by clearing flammable vegetation. Regularly clean your roof and gutters of leaves and other debris, which can catch embers. Have a planned evacuation route and make sure all family members know it. Fire season generally lasts from May through August, peaking in late summer.

Get Hurricane Ready

Hurricane season runs from June 1 through November 30 in the US. If you live in a hurricane-prone area, preparation is key. Secure your property by installing storm shutters or plywood over windows, trimming trees near your home, and securing outdoor items that could become flying debris. Also, create a family evacuation plan and know your local evacuation routes.

Defend Against Drought

Droughts are the second-most frequent natural disaster in America, behind flooding. Droughts are more than just a lack of rainfall—they're sneaky culprits that can wreak havoc on your home's foundation. When drought hits, the earth beneath your home dries, contracts, and can pull away from your foundation. This can result in:

- Foundation cracks and leaks;
- Damage to both interior and exterior walls;
- Misaligned doors and windows; and
- Other structural issues.

To defend against drought, do the following:

Water Wisely. Consistent, deep watering around the foundation can help maintain the moisture levels in the soil. Use soaker hoses or drip irrigation systems early in the morning or late evening to reduce evaporation.

Embrace Landscaping Techniques. Opt for drought-resistant plants and strategic landscaping to reduce water runoff and maintain soil moisture. Ground covers, mulches, and shade plants can retain moisture and prevent soil from drying out too quickly.

Monitor Soil Conditions. Keep an eye on the soil around your home's foundation. If it's pulling away, it's a sign that the soil is too dry. But also be cautious not to over-water, as this can cause its own set of issues.

Consider Home Improvements

Finally, consider making home improvements to enhance your property's resistance to future disasters. These improvements may include reinforcing your roof, installing storm-resistant windows and doors, or improving your home's foundation. If you live in a flood-prone area, think about flood-proofing measures. To fight drought, use foundation vents that allow the crawl space to breathe, reducing humidity. Additionally, evaluate your home's drainage system to ensure that when rain does come, water is directed away from your foundation. Although this may require an up-front investment, it significantly reduces potential damage, saving you money in the long run.

Preparation is the best protection against the damage that natural disasters can cause. By being proactive, you can protect yourself, your family, and your property and ensure that you're ready to face whatever Mother Nature throws your way. Planning for future natural disasters may seem overwhelming, but these events are happening with greater frequency, and it's a matter of *when*—not *if*—we'll all have to face some kind of disaster. Every step you take toward preparedness is a move toward safety and peace of mind. Remember, the goal of preparedness isn't to eliminate all risks; it's to make you resilient, ready to bounce back quicker and stronger, regardless of what happens.

Disaster Resources

1. **All Hands and Hearts** – Disaster recovery support focused on rebuilding.
2. **American Red Cross** – Provides disaster relief and recovery assistance.
3. **Habitat for Humanity** – Helps people recover from disasters.
4. **Lutheran Disaster Response** – Provides long-term disaster recovery.
5. **National Voluntary Organizations Active in Disaster** – Coalition helping communities prepare and recover.
6. **Operation Blessing** – Humanitarian organization providing disaster relief.
7. **SBP** – Rebuilds homes for low-to-moderate-income people who can't afford to rebuild after a disaster.
8. **Southern Baptist Disaster Relief** – Faith-based disaster recovery assistance organization.
9. **Team Rubicon** – Utilizes veterans' skills for disaster response.
10. **United Methodist Committee on Relief** – Global humanitarian aid and disaster relief.

Chapter 9
Debt

"Been down, been up, been broke, broke down, bounced back. Been off, been on, been back, what you know about that?"

—Beyoncé

Most Americans are up to their eyeballs in debt, and the situation only seems to be getting worse. Mortgage debt stood at $12 trillion at the end of June 2023, according to the latest figures from the Federal Reserve Bank of New York. Student loan debt tops $1.6 trillion. Auto loans in the US exceed $1 trillion, and credit card balances topped $1 trillion too for the first time ever in 2023, and continue to climb. The Fed's data also show that the first quarter of 2023 was the first time in 20 years that Americans didn't pay down their credit card balances after the holidays—suggesting more people are struggling with their obligations.

Those debts don't even consider the growing number of people—especially millennials—taking out payday loans, or the group of Americans who've fallen behind on their taxes and owe big debts to Uncle Sam. Is any of this ringing a bell? Regardless of your age, income, gender, or ethnic background, chances are you owe some form of debt. Pew Charitable Trusts reports that 80% of Americans have debt, with mortgages being the most common liability and 39% of adults in the US carrying credit card debt.

Even though debt has become a way of life for so many people in the US, living a debt-free life truly is possible. At the very least, you can drastically slash your debt to affordable levels so that debt isn't stressing you out, limiting your savings, or holding you back from reaching important goals.

The statistics paint a clear picture: debt is a national issue that affects people across all walks of life. But while these figures may seem daunting, it's important to remember that they don't define your future. You may feel like you're drowning in debt, that you're stuck in a cycle you can't break out of. But take a deep breath. There is a way out. It won't be instant, and it won't be without effort, but a debt-free life truly is possible.

In this part of *Bounce Back*, you're going to learn practical strategies to tackle different types of debts. You'll come to understand that others, just like you, have faced these challenges and come out the other side. But most importantly, you're going to discover that debt is not a life sentence. It's a situation that can be changed, managed, and ultimately overcome.

So let's start this journey together, a journey toward freedom, peace of mind, and a life unburdened by excessive debt.

In this chapter, you will learn:

- How to recognize emotional spending;
- How one well-known financial expert overcame debt and became good with money;
- How to enter the no shame zone;
- A unique look at needs vs. wants;
- An inspirational tale of going from debt to wealth;
- What to do if your home mortgage has become unaffordable;
- How to navigate your home loan options;
- How to deal with your emotional burden;
- Fool-proof, effective strategies to knock out credit card debt once and for all;
- How to cut auto loan debt even if you're leasing or are upside down on a car loan;
- Smart ways to eliminate college debt, for federal student loans and private loans;
- How to get others, such as the government or an employer, to repay your college debt;
- Solutions to get out of payday loan traps;
- Easy fixes for worrisome IRS issues and tax debt.

How to Recognize Emotional Spending

Aja Evans is a licensed mental health counselor who decided at age 12 to become a therapist.

She knows what it's like to spend excessively, particularly when you don't feel like you measure up, personally or financially. Evans, who is originally from Albany, New York, remembers living in New York City in her early 20s for college and trying to keep up with friends who were socializing and living a lifestyle that exceeded her finances. "I was hanging out with friends, living above my means, paying my rent, going to brunches, and really just doing things that were luxuries for a 20-year-old."

"But I felt really bad about myself because of money," she adds. "I kept wondering: 'Is everybody else making more money than I am?'"

That experience contributed to Evans always making space in her private practice as a therapist for her clients to discuss money issues.

Like Evans, most of her clients are Black women. Many carry debt—and they talk to Evans about it. For the majority of them, she says, talking about identity is a central component of who they are. It shapes their values, decisions, and actions—including around the topic of finances. For example, she often encounters women, including some self-professed "shopaholics," who say: "I don't feel good about myself, so I shop" or "I feel OK, but I feel better if I get a new outfit."

In such scenarios, Evans says her role is to guide the individual to peel back the layers of why the spending is important to them or why they're masking their feelings and what's going on. For some individuals, the spending—and the debt—are tied to feelings of anxiety, insecurity, or other emotions.

"People don't give themselves enough time to feel their feelings," she notes. "We want to get rid of our feelings so quickly, so we don't feel any discomfort." But part of healing is to be "in those feelings, process them, and name them." And that includes coming to terms with feeling anxious, angry, needing to cry, or anything else.

Ultimately, Evans says she wants overspenders and people in debt to feel like they're "still worthy, beautiful, and attractive even if they show up somewhere in an outfit they already had."

How to Enter the No Shame Zone

Shame is a huge issue, especially for people in debt but even for those who aren't in debt, Evans says. In her practice, she commonly encounters salary shame, debt shame, shame around having a lack of financial education, and shame around not being able to establish family boundaries. For some people in debt, it's incredibly hard to say no to relatives who ask to borrow money, or who request cash outright. "It can feel as if you're going against the family if you try to set up healthy boundaries," Evans says. As a result, "I have clients who are putting themselves in dire circumstances," because they find it nearly impossible to turn down family members who request money.

Whether it's family problems, relationship trouble, career challenges, or other issues, it's important to not let those problems also contribute to a consumer debt overload. That's what happens when people engage in "retail therapy"—shopping to make themselves feel better. A better solution: simply talking, Evans says. You might not want to talk to a therapist, a friend, or a relative about what you're going through, perhaps out of shame or embarrassment about your predicament. Evans says it's perfectly fine to wait to talk—at least initially. "If you're not ready to talk, or you just need to cry, you can have a moment to do that, and that's OK," Evans says. "But you do need to talk about things eventually. Shame is multiplied when you're isolated because you think nobody has gone through what you have."

Cherry, the CFP and head of Concurrent Financial Planning, agrees that shame is a big challenge for many people struggling financially.

Cherry says people in debt are already financially and emotionally burdened. But on top of those pressures, they typically face a lot of "spend shaming" from society at large—or even professionals from whom they seek guidance. Some of these people question or outright bash others for their spending decisions. "But you don't owe anybody an explanation" for your spending choices, Cherry contends.

He bristles when he hears financial advice being doled out to individuals suggesting that they just hunker down and stop all spending. Such an approach is unsustainable and robs people of some of the joy of living, Cherry argues.

Instead of telling people to deprive themselves and never spend or enjoy themselves, Cherry suggests that you "maximize life now and optimize life later."

"The key word is 'and,'" he says, explaining that you have to strike a balance, considering both your current self *and* your future self. In other words, be reasonable in your spending today, and spend in the current moment in ways that won't disadvantage future you.

To ensure that you walk the tightrope between present happiness and future security with grace, consider these three quick tips:

1. **Practice Mindful Spending:** Before you make a purchase, especially an impulsive one, take a moment to reflect. Ask yourself: "Is this purchase bringing true value to my life or is it a temporary emotional fix?" This doesn't mean you should never indulge, but understanding the reason behind your spending can lead to more fulfilling choices.

2. **Allocate "Fun Money" in Your Budget:** Rather than completely cutting out nonessential spending, assign a specific amount in your budget for treats and self-indulgences. This gives you the freedom to enjoy the present without derailing your future financial plans. Enjoying yourself within set boundaries can help ease the potential feelings of guilt or shame associated with spending.
3. **Celebrate Small Financial Wins:** Every time you reach a financial milestone, whether it's paying off a particular debt, saving a specific amount, or resisting an unnecessary purchase, celebrate it. This positive reinforcement can help you feel good about your financial choices, without the need to spend excessively. It's about appreciating the journey toward financial wellness, recognizing that each step, no matter how small, is a move in the right direction.

Remember, your worth is not defined by your spending habits or the state of your bank account. You deserve to enjoy the present while responsibly preparing for the future. And in this journey, be kind to yourself and recognize that everyone's financial path is unique. No shame, just progress.

A Unique Look at Needs Versus Wants

You've probably heard it said that you have to distinguish between your wants and your needs. Cherry takes an unconventional approach to this topic. "Your wants are needs too," he says.

When I press him to elaborate further, he explains that wants are needs as well because they're fulfilling an emotional need you have. Cherry argues that it's flawed, and impractical, for financial experts, therapists, and others to only consider a person's basic human needs.

"Needs aren't just basic things, like food, clothing, and shelter," he says. "There are also social, relational, community, and pleasure needs," among others, Cherry notes.

In his viewpoint, the person living in a gated community is doing so, in part, because they're fulfilling their status needs. Ditto for the person taking a skiing trip to Aspen or vacationing in Italy. "People love to say, 'I don't buy material things; I'd rather have experiences and memories.' But all those things cost money too! And it's satisfying the person's emotional needs," Cherry says.

Should you fall into debt due to misfortune, such as job loss, divorce, or medical bills, don't expect much sympathy from the general public either. "We're in a society that tells us, 'Shake that off, have grit, and get it together,'" Cherry notes. But if we don't first process our emotions about the Dreaded Ds or setbacks we face, “now it’s not the event itself that holds us back,” he says. Rather, it’s the failure to address the emotional fallout from the event.

If you’re in debt due to a Dreaded D such as downsizing from a job, divorce, or disability, be sure to read those specific chapters of *Bounce Back* along with the first two chapters of this book for greater insights into tackling the emotional aspects of setbacks and building your mental well-being and resilience. Also check out *The Bounce Back Workbook* for specific activities, exercises, and crucial reflections to further explore why you’re in debt and whether there are any patterns you need to address.

An Inspirational Tale of Going from Debt to Wealth

When Tiffany Aliche dug herself out of debt, she had to acknowledge a number of things she says she did “wrong” that led to her debt woes—from being overly trusting of others to failing to have a financial nest egg.

Speaking on the MomForce podcast by Chatbooks hosted by Vanessa Quigley, Tiffany shared the following: “I was financially ‘perfect’ until I was 26. I invested with somebody who I thought was a friend that convinced me to take money off of a credit card to invest with him, and it ended up leaving me $35,000 in credit card debt. And then I just finished my master’s, and I had a student loan debt of about $52,000. And I decided that I was an adult, so I bought a condo which was another $220,000 of a mortgage. Then I lost my job. That was my financial rock bottom being about $300,000 in debt. And no income.”

Hitting rock bottom meant she had no choice but to turn to family for support.

“I’m fortunate because I was able to move back home at 29 and sleep in my middle school bed again. Although at the time it didn’t seem fortunate,” Tiffany says. “But it was there that I started my business from a place of like, here are all the things I did wrong, and here’s how I’m rebuilding.”

I happen to know Tiffany personally, as a friend and a colleague working in the same area as I do—helping to financially educate and empower people. She’s a former preschool teacher turned financial educator. Millions of people follow Tiffany’s wisdom and affectionately call her “The Budgetnista.” She’s written a *New York Times* bestselling book, *Get Good With Money,* and was featured in a Netflix docuseries called *Get Smart With Money*. Along the way, she overhauled her finances to such an extent that she’s bought homes for cash, helped retire her parents, and engages in meaningful philanthropy, supporting causes she believes in domestically and internationally. And that’s not all: because she understood the struggles associated with debt, and how it sapped people’s ability to build a future, Tiffany launched the highly impactful “Live Richer Movement,” an online financial course and community for like-minded people trying to improve their financial health. Through that effort, she's helped more than two million women collectively save, manage money, and pay off hundreds of millions in debt.

Overall, Tiffany has done a phenomenal job of not just getting out of debt and rebuilding her life but thriving personally, professionally, and financially—even in the face of adversity. In June 2023, Tiffany would have marked her sixth wedding anniversary to her husband, Jerrell Smith, whom she lovingly called "Superman." Sadly, he died suddenly of a brain aneurysm in late 2021. Jerrell was a well-known and beloved figure in their Newark, New Jersey, community—a man who hosted "Sunday Suppers" for the neighborhood, regularly gave local kids money for getting good grades, and routinely mowed the lawns of elderly residents. "I used to call him the Black Mr. Rogers," Tiffany says. "He was just the nicest guy."

Jerrell's unexpected passing sent Tiffany reeling, and forced her to reevaluate how much time she'd spent working, building her business and brand. She still has a passion for teaching financial education, but she places a premium on harmony and the connections in her life. She now prioritizes spending time with family and friends, engaging in self-care, and has even learned to finally let others care for her too—something she previously struggled with since her parents raised Tiffany and her four sisters to be fiercely independent. In the wake of Jerrell's death, Tiffany's community and family have been an enormous source of support. "I'm grateful that I don't have to navigate it alone," she said. And even amid her grief and loss, she said she has gratitude for the "soft landing" she's experienced. She realizes how many things Jerrell put in place to help her adjust to life without him. Likewise, she recognizes the blessing of having slowed down her workload in the year before Jerrell's death to spend more time together and enjoy their union. "Our marriage went from good to amazing to great," she says, adding: "I was fortunate enough to be in partnership with such an amazing person."

Tiffany's journey is a lesson to us all in how we can take seemingly insurmountable obstacles, such as major debt or the loss of a loved one, and not succumb to those challenges. Let's turn our attention now to specific areas of debt, and how to overcome them financially.

What to Do If Your Home Mortgage Has Become Unaffordable

A home is more than just a place to live. It's where you create memories, where you feel safe and secure. But when your mortgage becomes unaffordable, that sense of safety can quickly turn into a source of stress and uncertainty. You might feel trapped, overwhelmed by the sheer size of your mortgage debt and the worry of potentially losing your home.

The first thing to remember is that you're not alone. Many people find themselves in this situation, especially during times of economic downturn or personal financial crises. The second thing to remember is that there are options available to you, strategies designed to help make your mortgage more manageable.

Understanding Your Mortgage

A mortgage is a loan secured by property. When you agreed to the mortgage, you promised to repay the lender the loan amount, plus interest, over a set period of time. This agreement was based on your financial situation at that time. But circumstances change. You might have lost your job, had a reduction in income, or faced an unexpected financial emergency. Suddenly, the mortgage payments that once seemed manageable are now a heavy burden.

Loan Modification

One possible option is a loan modification. This is an agreement between you and your lender to change the original terms of your mortgage. The aim is to lower your monthly payment to a more affordable level. This can be achieved by extending the term of the loan, lowering the interest rate, or even reducing the principal balance. It's important to note that each lender has their own criteria for loan modification, and not everyone will qualify.

Refinancing

Another option is refinancing, which involves replacing your current mortgage with a new one. The new mortgage could have a lower interest rate or a longer term, both of which could result in lower monthly payments. However, refinancing usually requires good credit, and there may be costs involved, such as closing costs and fees.

Government Programs

There are also several government programs designed to help homeowners struggling with their mortgage payments. For example, the Federal Housing Administration (FHA) offers a Home Affordable Modification Program (HAMP) and a Home Affordable Refinance Program (HARP).

Selling Your Home

In some cases, it might be best to consider selling your home. This can be a difficult decision to make, especially if you have a lot of emotional attachment to your home. However, selling could allow you to downsize to a more affordable home, or even switch to renting for a while, which could free up your finances and allow you to regain control.

How to Navigate Your Home Options

Each of these options has its own pros and cons, and the right choice depends on your individual situation. It's important to do your research, seek advice from professionals, and weigh all your options before deciding.

Now, let's imagine a scenario. Say you're a middle-aged professional who worked in an industry that has just experienced a significant downturn. Your job, which once seemed so stable, is now gone. The mortgage payments for your family home, which once felt manageable, are now a looming monthly dread. Your savings are dwindling, and every day you worry about how to keep a roof over your family's head.

You research your options and decide to approach your lender about a loan modification. The process is lengthy and requires a lot of paperwork, but you persist. After several weeks of back-and-forth, your lender agrees to modify your loan. They extend the term of your mortgage and reduce your interest rate, bringing your monthly payments down to a level you can manage.

It's not a quick fix. You still have a long road ahead, and there will be sacrifices. But for now, you have some breathing room.

Short Sale or Deed-in-lieu

If selling your home or refinancing isn't a viable option, and a loan modification doesn't provide enough relief, there are still options available. A short sale or deed-in-lieu of foreclosure could be a potential solution. A short sale involves selling your home for less than what you owe on the mortgage. While this means you won't make any money from the sale, it can help you avoid foreclosure.

Deed-in-lieu of Foreclosure

When dealing with a home you can't afford, this is another option. In this scenario, you voluntarily transfer the title of your home to your lender to avoid foreclosure. This won't save your home, but it can somewhat alleviate the damage to your credit that a full-blown foreclosure would cause. You'll still take a hit to your credit though, even if you voluntarily turn over the keys to your mortgage lender.

These options should be considered as a last resort, as they can have serious implications for your credit and potential tax consequences. However, they could provide a way out if other options aren't feasible or have failed.

Communication Is Key

Throughout this process, it's important to communicate openly and honestly with your lender. Lenders would rather work with you to find a solution than go through the costly and time-consuming process of foreclosure. If you're proactive and reach out early, you may find that your lender is more willing to work with you on a solution that benefits both parties.

How to Deal with Your Emotional Burden

Finally, it's important to address the emotional aspect of facing unaffordable mortgage debt. The stress and worry can be overwhelming. It's normal to feel a sense of loss, failure, or fear. But remember, you are more than your debt. You have the power to take control of your financial future, and every step you take toward addressing your debt is a step toward financial freedom.

Now, let's return to the most recent scenario. You've managed to secure a loan modification, reducing your monthly payments to a more manageable level. But the experience has taken a toll. There were nights when you couldn't sleep, days where the worry felt all-consuming. But with each conversation with your lender, with each form filled out, with each step taken, you started to feel a little bit better. It wasn't easy, but you did it. You took control of your situation, and you're now on a path to a better financial future.

You know there will be more challenges ahead. But you also know that you have the strength and the resources to meet them head-on. You understand that your worth is not defined by your debt. And most importantly, you've learned that even in the face of daunting debt, there is always hope. There are always options. And there is always a way forward.

In the end, the most important thing is to take that first step. Reach out to your lender, start the conversation, and explore your options. You have the power to change your financial future. Know that there are resources and people out there who can help. Take a deep breath, gather your courage, and take that first step toward relief—or even a debt-free life.

Fool-proof, Effective Strategies to Knock Out Credit Card Debt Once and for All

Credit card debt is a common issue many Americans face, and it can feel like a never-ending cycle. The interest rates are high, and if you're only making the minimum payments, your balance may not be going down as quickly as you'd like. It can feel like you're stuck on a hamster wheel, constantly running but not getting anywhere. But there is hope. You can break free from this cycle. I did.

Understanding Your Credit Card Debt

Credit card debt is considered revolving debt, which means you can borrow against your credit limit as long as you make the minimum payments. The problem is, the interest rates on credit cards are often high, and if you're only making the minimum payments, a significant portion of that payment is going toward the interest, not the principal balance. This can make it feel like you're not making any progress.

Pay More Than the Minimum

The first step in tackling your credit card debt is to try to pay more than the minimum payment each month. Even a little bit more can make a big difference over time. This can help reduce your balance faster, and you'll pay far less in interest over time. I always tell people: "Minimum payments in the short run really mean maximum payments in the long run." Don't fork over needless interest and finance charges to credit card issuers if you don't have to. When I dug myself out of debt—back in 2001 to 2004—I started paying two and three times the minimum required payments on my credit cards. I realize this won't be feasible for everyone. But the point is: whatever extra you can put toward those credit card bills will help you eliminate debt (and the stress that goes with it) sooner rather than later. Even if you can only put an extra $10 or $25 toward your credit card payments, do it.

Debt Snowball Versus Debt Avalanche

There are two popular methods for paying off credit card debt: the debt snowball method and the debt avalanche method. The debt snowball method involves paying off your debts from smallest to largest, regardless of the interest rate. This can provide a psychological boost as you see debts being paid off quickly.

The debt avalanche method involves paying off your debts from the highest interest rate to the lowest. This can save you the most money in interest over time, but it might take longer to see a debt fully paid off. That's a factor you should consider (emotionally and economically).

While most financial experts typically suggest paying off your high-interest-rate credit card debt first, I don't subscribe to that philosophy—mostly because it doesn't work for most people. If it did, we wouldn't have so many folks in debt year after year! Instead, I tell people to "attack your area of pain." Here's what I mean by that: If sky-high interest rates are bothering you, yes, focus on those debts first. But maybe you're in a situation like I was. When I was deep in debt, I actually had very low-interest rates—4.9% or less on all my cards—because I called each one of my creditors and asked for lower rates. What bothered me was the fact that I was nearly maxed out on all my cards, bumping right up against my credit limits. If a card had a $10,000 limit, I often had $9,900 owed on it! So in these scenarios, your best bet is to attack the credit cards with the *highest* dollar balances—regardless of interest rates.

But perhaps you're not maxed out on most of your cards. Maybe your wallet is full of credit cards, including several with small balances, and you simply find it difficult to keep up with everything. You might have 10, 12, or more credit cards, and you've missed payments—simply because you just forgot about the due date, or you were traveling and didn't pay on time, or you neglected to put your bills on autopay. Whatever the case, late payments can trigger those nasty late fees, which typically run about $35. So if it's overwhelming for you to manage so many credit cards, your best strategy is to focus on paying down the cards with the *lowest* dollar balances first. That way, you knock out a couple of cards—say, with a $200 to $500 balance or so—and then you start working your way up to cards with bigger balances.

With the "attack your area of pain" method, you'll see progress quickly in the area that bothers you most, and that will keep you motivated to stick to your debt payoff plan.

Balance Transfers and Debt Consolidation

Another option to consider is a balance transfer credit card or debt consolidation loan. A balance transfer card allows you to transfer your credit card balances to a card with a lower interest rate, often 0% for a promotional period. A debt consolidation loan allows you to consolidate your credit card debts into one loan with a lower interest rate. Both of these options can save you money in interest and potentially allow you to pay off your debt faster.

Use Windfalls Wisely

Another way to rebound from debt is to wisely use the resources that come your way—especially windfalls. A windfall refers to any unexpected influx of money you get, separate from your regular paycheck. It could be a year-end bonus at work, a tax refund, a government stimulus payment, or even funds received from a life insurance payout or a divorce settlement. These substantial sums can significantly contribute to eliminating debt that might otherwise take years to repay. For instance, the average tax refund check amounts to over $3,000, according to the IRS. When you receive such a windfall, it's crucial to prioritize debt repayment rather than squandering the money.

Seeking Professional Help

If you're feeling overwhelmed by your credit card debt, it might be beneficial to seek professional help. Credit counseling agencies can provide advice and resources and may be able to negotiate with your creditors to lower your interest rates or create a debt management plan.

Now, let's imagine another scenario. You're a young professional who, fresh out of college, found yourself relying heavily on credit cards to cover expenses. Over time, these balances have grown, and you find yourself juggling multiple high-interest credit card debts. Each month, you make the minimum payments, but your balances don't seem to be going down.

You decide to take action. After evaluating your options, you decide to use the debt avalanche method, focusing on the card with the highest interest rate first. You also look into a balance transfer card with a 0% promotional period. You successfully transfer a portion of your highest-interest credit card balance to this new card, giving you a break on interest for a while.

This doesn't make the debt disappear overnight. You still have a long road ahead. But you've taken the first steps. You've stopped the cycle. And each month, as you make your payments, you see your balances going down. You know it's going to take time, but you also know that you're making progress. You're not just running on the hamster wheel anymore. You're moving forward, toward a future free from credit card debt.

How to Cut Auto Loan Debt Even If You're Leasing or Are Upside Down on a Car Loan

Having a car can provide a great sense of freedom and convenience, but when the debt attached to that vehicle becomes unmanageable, it can start to feel more like a burden than a benefit. Whether you're struggling with monthly payments or are upside down on your car loan, there are strategies you can employ to help reduce your auto loan debt.

Understanding Your Auto Loan

Auto loans are installment loans, meaning you borrow a certain amount of money and agree to pay it back, with interest, in monthly installments over a certain period. Being "upside down," or "underwater," on your auto loan means you owe more on the loan than the car is currently worth. This can happen if the car depreciates in value faster than you're paying off the loan, or if you took out a loan with a long-term and small down payment.

Refinancing Your Auto Loan

One option to consider if your car payments are too high is to refinance your auto loan. This means taking out a new loan with a lower interest rate or longer term to replace your current auto loan. While this can lower your monthly payments, be aware that a longer loan term means you'll end up paying more in interest over the life of the loan.

Selling Your Car or Trading It In

If you're upside down on your car loan, one option is to sell your car and use the money to pay off as much of the loan as you can. With inflation affecting nearly everything, used car prices have been through the roof lately. So you might get more money than you think by selling your car. Case in point, in early 2022, Earl and I sold our 2020 Ford Explorer ST. We'd purchased this SUV brand-new, and for the two years we owned it, we only put 12,000 miles on it—primarily due to being on lockdown during the pandemic. Even though we liked the car, the reason we sold it was that it seemed cursed! The vehicle was in two accidents—one while just parked in front of our home and the other while Earl was stopped at a red light and got hit from behind by a distracted driver. There were also multiple recalls on the car and issues with its sensors, panels, electronics, and more. It was all stuff that was under warranty. But we finally said enough is enough. When we sold it, we not only got insurance money, but a nice buyback price from the dealer, netting *more* than we'd paid for the car. So investigate how much money you can get from your own set of wheels. And be aware that if your car is worth *less* than what you owe, you'll need to make up the difference. You could also consider trading in your car for a less expensive model.

Leasing a Car Instead

Leasing a car instead of buying can result in lower monthly payments, but it's not without its drawbacks. At the end of the lease term, you won't own the car and will need to return it or buy it out. Leasing also usually comes with mileage restrictions and potential fees for wear and tear.

Seeking Professional Help

If you're struggling to manage your auto loan debt, consider seeking the help of a credit counseling agency. These organizations can provide valuable advice and resources, and may even be able to negotiate with your lender on your behalf.

Now, imagine this scenario.

You're a parent who, a few years ago, purchased a new car to safely transport your growing family. However, after a few unexpected financial setbacks, the monthly car payments have become a struggle. On top of that, you've discovered that you owe more on the car than it's currently worth. After some research, you decide to look into refinancing your auto loan. You manage to secure a loan with a slightly lower interest rate, which reduces your monthly payments. It's a small change, but it gives you a little more breathing room each month.

You also make the tough decision to sell some personal items to pay down the difference between what you owe on the car and its current value. It's not easy, but it's a necessary step toward getting your auto loan debt under control.

These changes don't solve everything overnight. There are still months when money is tight and the stress feels overwhelming. But little by little, you're making progress. Each payment brings you one step closer to owning your car outright, and each day brings you one step closer to a future free from the burden of this debt.

Smart Ways to Eliminate College Debt for Federal Student Loans and Private Loans

Student loan debt is a significant issue for many Americans, with balances that can feel overwhelming. However, there are strategies and programs available that can help you manage and even eliminate this debt.

Understanding Your Student Loans

Student loans can be either federal or private. Federal student loans often come with lower interest rates and more flexible repayment options than private loans, but both types can cause financial strain if the balances are high.

Repayment Plans

For federal student loans, there are several repayment plans available. Standard repayment plans divide your loan balance over a set number of years, typically 10. Graduated and extended repayment plans start with lower payments that increase over time or stretch the repayment period over a longer time, up to 20, 25, or even 30 years.

There are also income-driven repayment plans, which cap your monthly payments at a percentage of your discretionary income. These can be particularly helpful if you're experiencing financial hardship.

Federal Loan Forgiveness Programs

Certain professions may qualify for loan forgiveness programs. For example, the Public Service Loan Forgiveness (PSLF) program forgives the remaining balance of your Direct Loans after you have made 120 qualifying payments while working full-time for a qualifying employer, typically a government or nonprofit organization.

In June 2023, the US Supreme Court ruled that President Joe Biden's plan to forgive up to $20,000 in federal student loan debt for Pell Grant recipients and $10,000 for non-Pell Grant borrowers was unconstitutional. Biden then immediately announced three alternative ways that he would offer student loan relief. Under the first effort, the Secretary of Education used its authority under the Higher Education Act to initiate a rulemaking process that would give debt forgiveness to as many borrowers as possible. Additionally, the Department of

Education began a new repayment plan option under which many people who owe college debt will not have to make any payments on those obligations. Finally, to ease the transition for those who'd previously had their student loans paused for three years during the pandemic, the Department of Education also launched a so-called "on-ramp" to repayment—lasting from October 1, 2023, to September 30, 2024. During this "on-ramp" period, if you miss monthly payments, you won't be considered delinquent, nor will you get reported to credit bureaus, placed in default, or referred to debt collection agencies.

If you have student loans, I strongly suggest you look into the latest loan forgiveness and deferment options available, along with new benefits for borrowers. There is a student loan repayment tool online at `StudentAid.gov` that guides you through all the options and helps you choose the best repayment schedule for your goals. This online tool does side-by-side comparisons of loans and even lets you see what part of your student loans can be forgiven.

Critical to many student loan borrowers is an entirely different Income-Based Repayment program, dubbed IBR. It replaces the former PAYE (Pay As You Earn) and REPAYE (Revised Pay As You Earn) income-sensitive programs. Four important features of the new income-based program are worth mentioning. First, the amount of your student loan payments will be cut at least in half. That's because new formulas are being used to determine how much discretionary income you have to put toward student debt. In the past, you had to allocate 10% or 15% of your discretionary income toward student loans. The new guidelines require you to fork over just 5% of your discretionary income. Second, people with student loan debt less than $12,000 can qualify for loan forgiveness after just 10 years, instead of the previous 20-year repayment requirement. Third, you can qualify for $0 monthly payments and still have those "no payment" months count toward loan forgiveness. Finally, in a big change from past student loan repayment rules, if you're enrolled in the new income-based repayment program, your student loan balances can never *grow*—even if you're not required to make payments because your income is too low. This comes as good news to a lot of people in the past who'd complained about diligently paying their college debt only to see the balance keep increasing.

Refinancing and Consolidation

Refinancing is the process of taking out a new loan with a lower interest rate to pay off your existing loans, potentially saving you money over the life of the loan. Be cautious, however, as refinancing federal student loans with a private lender means you'll lose access to federal protections and benefits, such as income-driven repayment and loan forgiveness programs.

Consolidation is the process of combining multiple federal student loans into one loan. This can simplify your payments and potentially give you access to alternative repayment plans, but it could increase the overall cost of paying off your loans.

Getting Professional Help

If you're feeling overwhelmed by your student loan debt, consider seeking the advice of a student loan counselor or financial advisor. They can help you understand your options and create a plan for tackling your debt.

Now, picture this scenario.

You're a recent college graduate, trying to navigate the world of adulting, when you receive your first student loan bill. The balance is staggering, and you're not sure how you'll ever pay it off.

After doing some research, you decide to apply for an income-driven repayment plan for your federal loans, reducing your monthly payments to a more manageable amount. You also explore loan forgiveness programs and discover that your job at a nonprofit organization could make you eligible for Public Service Loan Forgiveness. You start the paperwork, marking each payment on your calendar.

These changes don't make your student loan debt disappear overnight, and there are times when it feels like you'll be paying off these loans forever. But each payment, no matter how small, is progress. Each month, you're chipping away at your debt, inching closer to the day when you'll be free from the burden of these loans. You've taken control of your student loan debt, and you're moving toward a less cash-strapped future.

How to Get Others, Such as the Government or an Employer, to Repay Your College Debt

Often, the burden of student loan repayment doesn't have to rest solely on your shoulders. There are options where other entities, such as employers or the government, can help you repay your college debt. Why would they do this? It's a competitive job market. Employers of all kinds know that offering fringe benefits such as help with student debt will allow them to better hire and retain top talent.

Employer Student Loan Repayment Assistance Programs

More and more companies are offering student loan repayment assistance as a part of their benefits package. These programs can vary greatly from one company to another, but generally, the company will make regular payments toward your student loans. This could be a flat amount or a match of your own payments, up to a certain limit.

Here's just a sampling of 15 companies that help repay their employees' student loans, according to *U.S. News & World Report*:

1. Abbott (a health care company);
2. Aetna (another health care giant);
3. Ally Financial (a financial services firm);
4. Brillient (a technology consulting company);
5. Chegg (an educational services company);
6. CVP (a health care technology and consulting firm);
7. Estee Lauder Companies (a global beauty brand);
8. Fidelity Investments (a financial services company);
9. Google (online search company);
10. MassMutual (insurance company);
11. New York Life (another insurer);
12. Nvidia Corporation (a visual technology company);
13. Raytheon (aerospace and defense firm);
14. SoFi (financial services company);
15. The Hartford (insurance company).

As you can see, employers of all types provide this perk. Before you get too excited, remember to check the specifics of your company's program. There might be conditions, such as a requirement to stay with the company for a certain period, or limits on which loans qualify.

Additionally, the federal Office of Personnel Management oversees the federal student loan repayment program, which allows federal agencies to pay off the college debt of government workers. These agencies can repay up to $10,000 a year of an employee's student loans for six years, for a total of $60,000 in federal loan repayment support. To qualify, you must stay employed by the agency for three years. If you work for a federal agency or are considering job hopping, look into this benefit.

There are also forgiveness programs targeted at specific professions, such as teachers and nurses, or those who serve in the military. These programs usually require a certain period of service in a high-need area or role.

Volunteer Work and Other Programs

Several volunteer organizations, such as AmeriCorps, Peace Corps, or National Health Service Corps, offer educational grants or loan repayment assistance as part of their service benefits. This can be an excellent option if you're interested in volunteer work or public service.

Getting Professional Help

If you're unsure of your options or need help navigating these programs, consider seeking the help of a student loan counselor or financial advisor. They can provide valuable insight and assistance in applying for these benefits.

Now, imagine this.

You've long been out of school and working a job you enjoy, but your student loan payments are a significant drain on your budget. Then, during an HR presentation, you learn that your employer offers a student loan repayment assistance program. After confirming that your loans are eligible, you enroll in the program.

Each month, your employer makes a payment toward your loans. It's not a huge amount, but over time, it adds up. And because these payments are in addition to what you're already paying, you see your loan balance start to decrease faster than you expected.

At the same time, you begin investigating loan forgiveness programs. As a teacher, you discover that you may qualify for Teacher Loan Forgiveness after a few more years of service in a low-income school. The combined impact of these programs doesn't make your student loan debt magically disappear, but it significantly accelerates your repayment timeline. The end is in sight, and with each passing month, you're one step closer to being free from the burden of student loans. You feel less alone in your debt repayment journey, knowing that there are resources available to help you reach your financial goals.

Solutions to Get Out of Payday Loan Traps

Payday loans can seem like a quick fix when you're in need of fast cash, but they often lead to a vicious cycle of debt due to their high-interest rates and short repayment terms. However, there are strategies you can use to escape this payday loan trap.

Understanding Payday Loans

A payday loan is a short-term, high-cost loan that's typically due on your next payday. These loans are often used by people who need quick cash for emergency expenses. While they can be easy to get, they carry extremely high interest rates, often equivalent to a 400% annual percentage rate (APR) or higher.

In a recent report, the Consumer Financial Protection Bureau noted that many payday lenders engage in unfair, deceptive, and abusive practices. The CFPB said of the illegal activity it found: "Lenders would put language in loan agreements that prohibited consumers from revoking their consent for the lender to call, text, or e-mail the consumers about collection on the outstanding balance. Lenders also made false collection threats that would often purport their authority to garnish wages of borrowers, when no such authority exists." In some cases, the CFPB added, payday lenders actually did unlawfully garnish people's wages, by duping employers into turning over the employee's wages with false claims that the full amount of the payday loan was due.

Attorney Lyle D. Solomon, of Oak View Law Group in California, says payday loans are such a financial scourge that he decided to become what he calls the "payday loan crusader." On his website, he explains why: "I have seen my close friend's life getting destroyed because of his addiction to the easy money of payday loans. It seemed too good to be true to walk into a payday loan store and walk out with $500. It also seemed too easy to only pay back $50/week.

Lo and behold, now in his mid-forties, he doesn't have a home, still lives in a shared apartment with housemates, and has paid more to the payday loan companies than on a mortgage down payment. I have seen this story repeat for hundreds of my clients. I realized I needed to do something to bring payday loan equity, and hence I became the payday loan crusader."

Alternate Solutions

Instead of relying on payday loans, consider other ways to access emergency funds. This could include savings, credit cards, a personal loan from a bank or credit union, or assistance from family or friends. While these options may not be without their own issues, they're often less risky than payday loans. Your job may even be a good option for quick cash. Many employers will provide payroll advances, and this is a way you can tap into no-interest funds without turning to predatory payday lenders.

Debt Consolidation Loans

A debt consolidation loan could be another option to help manage payday loan debt. This involves taking out a new loan, typically with a lower interest rate, to pay off multiple debts, including payday loans. This can simplify your debt payments and potentially save you money on interest.

Seek Professional Help

If you're struggling with payday loan debt, consider seeking help from a reputable credit counseling agency. These organizations can provide advice, educational materials, and potentially negotiate with your lenders on your behalf.

Now, picture this scenario. You're living paycheck to paycheck, just scraping by. An unexpected car repair throws your budget into chaos, and you turn to a payday loan for quick cash. The relief is immediate, but when your next payday rolls around, you find yourself unable to repay the loan in full, leading to high fees and an ever-growing balance.

Recognizing the danger of this cycle, you reach out to a local credit counseling agency. They help you to create a budget and guide you in negotiating a repayment plan with the payday lender. It's not an instant solution, but it's a start.

In the meantime, you take on a part-time job and begin building an emergency savings fund, determined to avoid falling back into the payday loan trap. You also explore options for a small personal loan from your local credit union, which offers much lower interest rates.

It's a slow process, and there are moments of frustration and fear. But with each step, you're moving away from the trap of payday loans and toward a more stable financial future. You're not just escaping debt; you're building the skills and habits that will help you avoid falling back into this trap in the future.

Easy Fixes for Worrisome IRS Issues and Tax Debt

For many Americans, the fear of taxes looms large. Even for many newcomers to the United States, the prospect of having an unwanted run-in with tax authorities is a huge concern. According to Simon Karmarkar, the founder and creator of MasRefund, a dual-language tax service in Spanish and English, many immigrants dread dealing with taxes because of fears of deportation if they make a simple mistake. Karmarkar recalls his own journey to the US as a child when his father brought the family to America. They had no money and didn't speak English. "He was the bravest person I know," Karmarkar says of his dad. "But one thing struck fear into his heart: taxes."

To be sure, dealing with the Internal Revenue Service (IRS) can feel intimidating, especially when you owe a significant amount in back taxes. However, there are ways to manage and even resolve your tax debt.

Understanding Your Tax Debt

The first step is understanding exactly how much you owe and why. This could be due to unpaid taxes, penalties, or interest. Remember, ignoring your tax debt won't make it go away and can lead to more penalties and interest, increasing the amount you owe.

Payment Plans

If you can't pay your tax debt in full, the IRS offers payment plans, also known as installment agreements. These allow you to pay your debt over time, in monthly installments. There are several types of payment plans, each with its own requirements and fees, so you'll want to choose the one that best fits your situation. There's a short-term payment plan option (to pay off tax debt in 180 days or less) and a long-term payment plan that lets you repay past-due IRS debt over a period of up to 72 months. Depending on how much you owe, you can likely simply request an online payment agreement from the IRS. You don't even have to talk to them directly if that scares you.

According to the IRS website, you qualify to apply online under these circumstances:

For individuals: You want a long-term payment plan, and you owe $50,000 or less in combined tax, penalties, and interest, and have filed all required returns. Alternatively, if you want a short-term payment plan, you must owe less than $100,000 in combined tax, penalties and interest.

For businesses: You may qualify to apply online for a long-term payment plan if you've filed all required returns and owe $25,000 or less in combined tax, penalties, and interest.

Note that if you're a sole proprietor or an independent contractor, you should apply for a payment plan as an individual. If you don't apply online through the IRS's Online Payment Agreement tool, you can apply by phone or by mail by submitting Form 9465, Installment Agreement Request.

Offer in Compromise

An offer in compromise is an agreement between you and the IRS that settles your tax debt for less than the full amount you owe. This option is only available to those who meet certain criteria and can't pay their tax debt in full or through a payment plan.

Innocent Spouse Relief

If your spouse or former spouse incorrectly reported items or omitted items on your joint tax return, you may be eligible for innocent spouse relief. This could relieve you of the responsibility for paying tax, interest, and penalties if your spouse (or former spouse) improperly reported items or omitted items on your joint tax return.

Getting Professional Help

Tax debt can be complex, and it's often beneficial to seek professional help. A tax professional or attorney can guide you through the process, help you understand your options, and potentially negotiate with the IRS on your behalf. If you have tax fears or deep money fears of any kind, be sure to read *The Bounce Back Workbook*, which will help you explore the sources of your money anxieties and better handle those concerns.

Now, imagine this scenario. You're a small business owner, and after a tough year, you find yourself unable to pay your full tax bill. The total amount owed to the IRS feels insurmountable, and you're not sure what to do.

After some online reading, you decide to apply for an installment agreement with the IRS. The process is straightforward, and you're able to set up a monthly payment plan that fits within your budget. It's not an instant fix, but it's a manageable solution.

At the same time, you seek help from a tax professional. They review your situation and find deductions you'd missed, which can minimize your tax liability. They also give you advice on managing your business finances to avoid future tax debt.

The process of paying off your tax debt is slow, and there are moments of frustration and worry. But with each payment, you're reducing your debt and moving closer to resolving your IRS issues. You've taken control of your tax debt, and you're working toward a more stable financial future. It's not an easy journey, but you're not alone, and with every step, you're moving toward a future free of tax debt.

Psychological and Emotional Recovery from Debt

Debt is not just a financial burden; it also takes a toll on your mental and emotional well-being. It's important to understand and address these psychological impacts as part of your overall debt recovery process.

Recognize the Emotional Impact of Debt

Debt can cause stress, anxiety, depression, and even relationship issues. Recognizing the emotional impact of your debt is the first step toward addressing it. Don't ignore these feelings or dismiss them as unimportant. They're a valid part of your debt experience.

Seek Support

You don't have to face your debt alone. Reach out to supportive friends and family members. Consider seeking professional help, such as a therapist or counselor, especially if your debt is causing significant distress. Joining a support group, either in person or online, can also be beneficial. Hearing others' experiences and knowing that you're not alone can provide comfort and practical advice.

Practice Self-care

While working to repay your debt, don't neglect your physical and emotional health. Regular exercise, a healthy diet, and adequate sleep can all contribute to better mental health. Try stress management techniques, such as meditation, deep breathing, or yoga. Make time for activities you enjoy and that help you relax.

Focus on the Future

Remember that your current situation is temporary. With each payment you make, you're moving closer to a debt-free future. Stay focused on your goals and the positive changes you're making in your life.

Now, imagine this.

You're a parent juggling lots of responsibilities. Between student loans, credit card debt, and your auto loan, you feel overwhelmed. The stress of your debt is causing sleepless nights and tension with your children. You feel that you're failing, not just financially but as a parent.

You decide to reach out to a therapist, who specializes in financial stress. In your sessions, you learn to recognize the negative thought patterns that are exacerbating your stress. You start practicing self-care, such as going for a run each morning and setting aside time each week for a hobby you love.

You also join an online support group for single parents dealing with debt. The stories and advice you hear from other group members help you feel less alone and give you practical strategies for managing your debt.

These changes don't erase your debt overnight, but they help you cope with the stress it causes. You start sleeping better and have more patience with your children. You feel less like a failure and more like someone who's taking control of their situation.

Remember, debt recovery is not just about regaining financial stability but also about restoring your mental and emotional well-being. It's a difficult journey, but with every step, you're moving closer to a future free of debt and the stress it causes.

The Path to a Debt-free Life

The path to becoming debt-free is not a sprint; it's a marathon. It's a journey filled with ups and downs, challenges, and victories. Maybe you've gone in and out of debt. Perhaps you've struggled to keep the credit card balances down and nothing—until now—has worked. Although it may feel daunting at times, every step you take is a step toward a more secure and stress-free financial future.

Remembering Your Why

Your why is the reason behind your goal to become debt-free. It could be to live a stress-free life, save for retirement, travel the world, or provide a better life for your family. Remembering your why can motivate you when the journey gets tough.

Staying Consistent

Consistency is key when it comes to debt repayment. Make your payments on time and stay on top of your repayment plan. Even when progress seems slow, remember that every payment brings you closer to your goal.

Celebrating Small Wins

Every debt you pay off, no matter how small, is a victory. Celebrate these wins. They serve as proof of your progress and can provide a much-needed morale boost.

Building a New Relationship with Money

Becoming debt-free is about more than just paying off what you owe. It's about building a new relationship with money—one that involves smart spending, saving, and investing.

Now, picture this. You're standing in your kitchen, looking at the pile of bills on your counter. Just a few years ago, these bills would have filled you with dread. But today, you're smiling. Because today, you're making the last payment on your credit card debt!

You remember the stress and anxiety you felt when you first decided to tackle your debt. But you also remember the relief when you created a repayment plan, the satisfaction when you made your first payment, the excitement when you paid off your first credit card.

Today, those feelings of stress and anxiety are replaced by pride and a sense of accomplishment. You did it. *You're debt-free!*

It wasn't easy. There were sacrifices, tough decisions, and moments of doubt. But it was worth it. Because now, you're not just debt-free. You're empowered. You have control over your money, instead of it controlling you.

I won't sugarcoat it: the journey to becoming debt-free is a challenging one. But with determination and a proper mindset, a solid game plan, and the right support, you can overcome your debt and build a brighter financial future. As Saundra Davis, the financial coach, says, knowing what to do isn't enough. You can have all the financial literacy information in the world, and that might not make a difference. "Financial education is necessary but insufficient," Davis says. You'll have to also address your relationship with money and notice what's gotten you to this point—the good and the bad. In doing so, you'll discover that the journey to a debt-free life is not just about the destination but also about the growth and lessons learned along the way.

Debt Resources

1. **Association for Financial Counseling and Planning Education** – Financial counselor education and resources.
2. `Credit.org` – Nonprofit credit counseling and debt management education.

3. **Debt Reduction Services** – Offers free budgeting and credit counseling for those struggling with debt.
4. **Financial Therapy Association** – Helps with the emotional aspects of money issues.
5. **GreenPath Financial Wellness** – Nonprofit focused on financial health.
6. **JumpStart Coalition** – Provides a wealth of financial literacy resources.
7. **National Association of Consumer Bankruptcy Attorneys** – Aid for bankruptcy filers.
8. **National Foundation for Credit Counseling** – Financial counselors.
9. **Operation HOPE** – Offers financial dignity and inclusion programs.
10. **Take Charge America** – Nonprofit credit counseling and debt assistance.

Chapter 10
Damaged Credit

"Don't let failure define you; let your ability to bounce back from it define you."
—Michael Jordan

Bad credit. It's a term that can strike fear in the hearts of many. It's a financial black mark that can follow you around like a shadow, impacting every facet of your life. I know because I've been there. I've felt the stress, the anxiety, the helplessness that can come from having bad credit. And I've found a way out.

In college, I experienced my first taste of the bitter pill that is bad credit. I had my car, a Hyundai Excel—my very first vehicle—repossessed for nonpayment. That incident, coupled with many late payments and charge-offs from credit cards, as well as accounts that went into collection, ruined my credit.

The hits kept coming. In my late 20s and early 30s, I was swimming in debt, with $100,000 in credit card bills alone. But then, I turned things around. I paid off all my credit card debt in three years, and my credit scores shot up. For the past 25+ years, I've never missed a payment. I learned the hard way about the value of paying on time and managing debt responsibly.

I now also know I wasn't alone in having struggled with credit issues. A study by the Urban Institute found that 64 million Americans have debt in collections, which is a sign of damaged credit. And the Urban Institute's latest research shows that having poor or so-called subprime credit comes with a steep financial cost for the approximately 20% of Americans within the credit system. These individuals often find themselves limited to loans with exorbitant interest rates when they need to borrow. As a result, a significant portion of their income is dedicated to debt payments. In comparison to borrowers with higher, or prime, credit scores, those with subprime credit scores can face additional expenses of nearly $400 in interest for a $550 emergency loan over three months. Furthermore, when obtaining a $10,000 used-car loan over four years, they could end up paying an astonishing $3,000 more in interest. These disparities highlight the significant impact that bad credit can have on a person's financial well-being.

The emotional toll of bad credit is also heavy. The worry about how you're going to pay your bills, the fear of rejection every time you apply for a loan or a credit card, the anxiety every time the phone rings—wondering if it's another call from a debt collector. It's a constant, nagging stress that can make you feel helpless and out of control. When I was deep in debt in my 30s, I never got calls from bill collectors. However, I did certainly worry about my credit card getting rejected when I would use them in stores or restaurants.

Besides the emotional impact and being forced to pay higher interest rates on loans and credit cards—if you can get approved for them at all—damaged credit can also mean being turned down for an apartment or even a job. It can mean higher insurance premiums and security deposits. In short, bad credit can make an already difficult financial situation even harder.

But here's the good news: you can recover from bad credit. I'm proof of that. Not only did I recover from my financial mistakes, but I learned from them. I've spent the past 25+ years maintaining an impeccable credit history, punctuated by a perfect 850 FICO Score—a feat achieved by only about 1% of Americans annually—and I was recently profiled on CNBC-TV for this accomplishment.

Believe me when I say that I understand the pain of bad credit. But I also understand the relief, the sense of accomplishment, and the newfound financial freedom that comes from overcoming it. And that's what this chapter is about. It's about understanding the impacts of bad credit, both emotional and financial. It's about learning from my experiences—and from your own. And, most importantly, it's about providing you with a game plan to overcome your credit setbacks and achieve your own financial success.

In this chapter you will learn:

- How to understand what's on your credit reports;
- How your credit scores are calculated;
- What causes bad credit;
- How piggybacking off someone else's credit can help improve your credit;
- The benefits of using secured credit cards;

- The value of adding rent and nontraditional payments to your credit reports;
- How to negotiate with creditors;
- How to achieve perfect credit;
- Initiating the process: getting creditors to collaborate.

How to Understand What's on Your Credit Reports

A credit report is a detailed summary of an individual's credit history. It is an essential document used by lenders and other entities to assess your creditworthiness and determine your financial reliability. The information in your credit report is typically provided to the three major consumer reporting agencies—Equifax, TransUnion, and Experian—by your creditors. However, it's important to note that not all lenders report information to all three agencies, which can result in slight differences in your credit reports from each agency.

Contents of a Credit Report

A credit report typically includes the following types of information:

Identifying information: This includes personal details such as your name, address, Social Security number, and date of birth. This information is not used to calculate your credit scores.
Credit account information: This information is provided by your creditors and includes the types of credit accounts you've had (for example, credit cards, mortgages, student loans, or vehicle loans), the date those accounts were opened, your credit limit or loan amount, account balances, and your payment history.
Inquiry information: There are two types of inquiries: "soft" and "hard." Soft inquiries result from checking your own credit reports, companies extending you preapproved offers of credit or insurance, or your current creditors conducting periodic account reviews. Soft inquiries do not impact credit scores. Hard inquiries occur when companies or individuals, such as a credit card company or lender, review your credit reports because you have applied for credit or a service. Hard inquiries remain on your credit reports for up to two years and may impact your credit scores.
Public records: This includes details such as bankruptcies, which generally remain on your credit report for seven to 10 years, depending on the type of bankruptcy.

Collections accounts: These are accounts that have been turned over to a collection agency. This can include credit accounts, accounts with banks, retail stores, cable companies, mobile phone providers, doctors, and hospitals. Unpaid rent sold to a collection agency can be included in your credit report for up to seven years. Since July 1, 2022, medical debt that was sent to a collection agency but has since been paid off will no longer appear on your credit reports from Equifax, Experian, or TransUnion.

The Importance of Reviewing Your Credit Report Regularly

Regularly reviewing your credit reports is crucial for a few reasons. First, it allows you to monitor your credit accounts and helps you identify any inaccurate or incomplete information. Second, it's a proactive way to spot any suspicious activity that may indicate potential identity theft. And third, ensuring the accuracy of your credit report is key to maintaining good credit health, as the information contained in it is used to calculate your credit scores.

How Your Credit Scores Are Calculated

A credit score is a numerical representation of your creditworthiness based on the information in your credit report. It's calculated using a complex mathematical model that takes into account factors such as your payment history, the amount of debt you have, the length of your credit history, the types of credit you have, and recent credit inquiries.

A credit score is a three-digit number that lenders use to help them decide how likely it is that they will be repaid on time if they give you a loan or a credit card. Credit scores are designed to predict risk, specifically, the likelihood that you will become seriously delinquent on your credit obligations in the 24 months after scoring. There are many different credit scores available to lenders, and each one is based on a unique calculation, but they are all based on the information in your credit reports at the three nationwide credit reporting agencies—Equifax, Experian, and TransUnion. The FICO Score, one of the most commonly used credit scores, has a range between 300 and 850. The VantageScore—another score developed by the three credit bureaus—also has a range of 300 to 850. Credit scores are calculated using a variety of factors including:

Payment history (35% of the FICO Score): This includes information about whether you've paid your credit accounts on time. Late payments, bankruptcies, and other negative items can hurt your credit score. But a solid record of on-time payments can help your score.

Amounts owed (30% of the FICO Score): This includes the total amount of money you owe and the amount of available credit that you are using. If you are close to maxing out your credit lines, it could indicate that you are overextended and more likely to make late or missed payments.

Length of credit history (15% of the FICO Score): In general, a longer credit history will increase your FICO Scores. It can also help if you have a good mix of new and old accounts.

New credit (10% of the FICO Score): This includes information about how many new accounts you have. It's not necessarily bad to open new credit accounts—it might help your score by increasing your total available credit—but if you open a lot of new accounts in a short time, it could signal risk.

Credit mix (10% of the FICO Score): This includes information about the different types of credit you have, such as credit cards, mortgages, or other loans. Having a variety of credit types does not make a significant difference in your FICO Scores, but it could factor in if your credit report does not have much other information on which to base a score.

As mentioned, your credit score can impact many areas of your life. Lenders, landlords, and even some brokerages check credit scores to assess your financial reliability. Your score can influence whether you're approved for a credit card, a mortgage, or a rental property, and it can also affect the rates you're offered. Some insurance companies also use credit scores as part of their underwriting process.

What Causes Bad Credit

As we delve deeper into the world of credit, it's essential to uncover the factors that can lead to bad credit. It's not just paying bills late—although that's a major no-no. There are other aspects of credit and debt management that can affect your credit rating. Understanding these factors is important for improving your financial health and rebuilding your credit score.

Obviously, bad credit can be a significant obstacle when you're trying to finance a purchase, secure a loan, or even rent an apartment. It's like a red flag to lenders and creditors, signaling that you may not be a reliable borrower. But what exactly causes bad credit? What are the actions or circumstances that can send your credit score spiraling downward?

In this section, we'll explore some of the primary causes of bad credit, including late or missed payments, collections and charge-offs, judgments and bankruptcies, and high credit card utilization or excessive inquiries. By understanding these factors, you can take proactive steps to avoid these pitfalls and maintain a healthy credit score. Let's delve into each of these causes one by one.

Late or Missed Payments

One of the biggest factors that can negatively impact your credit score is a history of late or missed payments. Payment history accounts for approximately 35% of your FICO credit score, making it the most significant factor. When you fail to make a payment on time, it signals to potential lenders that you may be a risky borrower. If you have several late or missed payments, it can significantly lower your credit score. Late payments typically stay on your credit report for seven years from the date of the delinquency. But realize that not all "late" payments count against you in the world of credit scoring. You have to be 30 days late paying a bill before a creditor can report your account as "late" or "past due" to the credit bureaus. So simply being a day or two—or even a week or two—behind in paying an obligation will not affect your credit score. Obviously, you should not take liberties here. Pay your bills on time. But this information is to put your mind at ease in case you've accidentally paid a credit obligation a few days beyond the due date. From a credit standpoint, you don't have to sweat that.

Collections and Charge-offs

When a debt goes unpaid for a long period, the creditor may decide to write it off as a loss; this is known as a charge-off. The debt is typically then sold to a collection agency, which will attempt to collect the debt from you. Both charge-offs and collections are very damaging to your credit score and can remain on your credit report for seven years. It's important to note that paying off a collection account will not remove it from your credit report; it will stay there until the seven years have passed, but it will be marked as paid. Also, if a debt collector comes chasing you down after a lot of years—these are so-called zombie debt collectors because they seem to have come back from the grave with years-old debt—and you pay the collection, simply paying the old account won't erase it from your credit report. And if it's still on your credit files, it's going to still affect your credit score. My advice: negotiate. Before you pay any old collection accounts, first get an agreement in writing from your creditor or the bill collector stipulating that in exchange for you making the payment, they will remove all negative information about the account from the credit bureaus' reports on you. That way, you'll enhance your credit.

Judgments and Bankruptcies

Legal judgments for unpaid debts and bankruptcies are among the most severe negative items that can appear on your credit report. A judgment is a court order to repay a debt, and a bankruptcy is a legal process that helps people who can no longer pay their debts get a fresh start. Both of these items can have a major negative impact on your credit score and can stay on your credit report for seven to ten years.

High Credit Card Utilization

Credit utilization, which is the ratio of your credit card balances to your credit limits, is another significant factor in your credit score, accounting for nearly 30% of your FICO Score. High credit utilization suggests that you're heavily reliant on credit and may have trouble paying off your debts. A high credit utilization ratio can lower your credit score. It's generally recommended to keep your credit utilization ratio below 30%. If it's high, it could be a sign that you're overextended and may be more likely to miss payments or default on your debts. People with excellent FICO Scores in the 760 to 850 point range generally keep their credit usage below 10%.

Excessive Credit Inquiries

Anytime you apply for credit or a loan, a hard inquiry is generated on your credit report. That inquiry stays on your credit report for 24 months. And it counts against you—for the purposes of your FICO Score calculation—for 12 months. While an inquiry generally causes just a temporary ding to your credit score, and it does typically recover after a couple of months, you want to always keep your credit rating as strong as possible and get into the habit of utilizing good credit management practices. This is why you should not apply for credit willy-nilly or just take any credit offer that comes your way. A lot of times, when you're being offered credit in a store, those department store credit cards have much higher interest rates anyway. You're better off financially, and from a credit standpoint, just saying no. Only apply for credit when you truly need it.

Remember, while these are common causes of bad credit, many factors can affect your credit score. It's important to regularly review your credit report and understand what actions can impact your credit health.

Rebuilding your credit can feel like a daunting task, but it's far from impossible. In fact, with dedication and the right strategies, you can gradually repair your credit and improve your financial future. Remember, there's no quick fix for bad credit. It takes time, patience, and consistent effort. But don't worry, this path is well traveled, and many have successfully improved their credit scores using the strategies I'm about to share.

How Piggybacking Off Someone Else's Credit Can Help Your Credit

Piggybacking is a technique that involves becoming an authorized user on another person's credit card account. Typically, this person would be someone who has a good credit score and a history of responsible credit management. As an authorized user, you're allowed to use this person's credit card, and the account's credit history may also appear on your credit report.

There are a few types of piggybacking:

Family or household: This is the most common type, where a family member or someone in the same household adds you as an authorized user to their credit card. This can be beneficial as there is a higher level of trust and mutual understanding.

Friend: A friend can add you as an authorized user, but this requires a great deal of trust as financial issues can strain personal relationships.

Company: Some companies offer services where they add you as an authorized user to a stranger's credit card for a fee. This practice is controversial and might be associated with certain risks. I don't recommend that you do this, as tempting as it might be.

While piggybacking can potentially improve your credit score, it's important to remember that not all credit card companies report authorized user accounts to the credit bureaus. Therefore, you should check with the credit card company beforehand to ensure that your authorized user status will be reported to the credit bureaus.

It's also worth noting that the primary cardholder's actions can impact your credit. For instance, if they miss payments or max out their credit limit, it could reflect negatively on your credit score. Therefore, it's crucial to have open and honest communication with the person whose account you're authorized on.

My husband, Earl, and I have allowed our two oldest children to piggyback off our credit. We've added our daughter to a credit card account we've had for a very long time, and they've both been added onto mortgages with us as well—when we bought them their first homes. Each time, our kids benefited from piggybacking, and they now both enjoy high credit scores in high 700s, even though they are only in their 20s.

The Benefits of Using Secured Credit Cards

One such strategy that has helped many people, including people I've coached, is the use of secured credit cards. Here's what you need to know about secured cards and their pros and cons.

Understanding Secured Credit Cards

Secured credit cards function similarly to traditional credit cards but with one key difference: they require a security deposit as collateral, which serves as your credit limit. That deposit is typically $500 or more. But you might be able to open a secured card with as little as $250. This deposit mitigates the risk for the lender, making secured credit cards an excellent option for those with previous credit problems. The amount you deposit typically determines your credit limit, and by responsibly managing this card, you can gradually improve your credit score and rebuild your financial foundation.

If you're interested in taking this approach, research and compare different secured credit card options to find one that best suits your needs. Websites such as `CardRatings.com` and `BankRate.com` have tons of articles about various credit cards, and they've done a lot of the homework and research for you. Look for cards with reasonable fees, low interest rates, and a solid reputation. Ensure that the card issuer reports your payment history to the major credit bureaus, as this is crucial for rebuilding your credit. This is one potential drawback to certain secured cards: some banks, credit unions, and financial institutions that issue these cards don't report your payment history to Equifax, Experian, and TransUnion. Other institutions report only to one of the credit bureaus. It's best to find a card that gets reported to all three credit reporting agencies. It's pointless and frustrating to get a secured card thinking it will rebuild your credit—only to later discover that the bank doesn't even report your on-time payments. So do your homework before choosing.

Responsible Credit Usage and Timely Payments

Once you have your secured credit card, use it wisely and responsibly. Make small purchases that you can comfortably pay off each month. This demonstrates to creditors that you can handle credit responsibly and are committed to rebuilding your financial health.

It goes without saying that you also want to consistently make your monthly payments on time. Payment history plays a significant role in your credit score, and by consistently paying your bills, you showcase your commitment to improving your creditworthiness.

Gradually Increase Credit Limits

As you make timely payments and demonstrate responsible credit usage, some secured credit card issuers may offer opportunities to increase your credit limit. This can positively impact your credit utilization ratio, a key factor in credit scoring models.

Using secured credit cards strategically provides several benefits if you're recovering from credit problems. First, they offer a valuable opportunity to establish a positive payment history, which can counteract past negative marks on your credit report. Additionally, by utilizing a secured credit card, you can gradually rebuild trust with lenders and demonstrate improved financial habits. Over time, as your credit score improves, you may become eligible for traditional credit cards and other financial products with more favorable terms and conditions. Finally, secured credit cards can serve as kind of a check on excessive spending. If you don't have the money in your account, you won't get approved for the purchase. And because secured cards typically have lower credit limits than regular, unsecured cards, you're less likely to go overboard with your spending.

The Value of Adding Rent and Nontraditional Information to Your Credit Reports

Another strategy that can put you on the path to credit recovery is getting your rent and nontraditional payments reported to your credit reports. By leveraging these alternative payment sources, you can showcase your financial responsibility and potentially improve your creditworthiness. Adding rent and nontraditional payments to your credit report can be a game-changer, addressing your credit concerns and offering you a relatively fast way to significantly boost your credit scores.

Harnessing the Power of Rent and Nontraditional Payments

Traditionally, credit reports have focused on your credit card and loan payments, leaving out other essential financial obligations. However, times are changing, and many credit reporting agencies now consider alternative data, including rent payments, utility bills, and even subscription services. By reporting these nontraditional payments to the credit bureaus, you have the opportunity to showcase a more comprehensive picture of your financial responsibility and potentially boost your creditworthiness.

Research Rent Reporting Services

The first thing to understand is that you can't report your rent or other payments to the credit bureaus by yourself. A third-party company has to do it. So start by exploring credit reporting services that accept rent and nontraditional payment data. Look for reputable agencies that have partnerships with landlords, utility companies, and other relevant service providers. To get you started, here are a few companies that offer rent reporting services: Rental Kharma, Esusu, RentReporters, PayYourRent, and Jetty Credit. Some are free; others charge you or your landlord. Since fees and services can change, look them up online for the latest available information.

When your rent payments are factored into your credit reports, it flows through to some, but not all, of your credit scores. For example, older versions of the FICO Score don't consider rent history. By contrast, newer versions of FICO, such as the FICO 9 and FICO 10, do take into account rental info that's listed in your credit report. The VantageScore likewise considers rent payment information.

Verify Reporting Practice

Be aware that not all services report your data to all three credit bureaus—which is optimal. Ensure that the reporting service you choose sends the data to all three major credit bureaus: Equifax, Experian, and TransUnion. This multi-bureau reporting increases the visibility and impact of your positive payment history.

Consistent and Timely Payments

Just like with traditional credit payments, make it a priority to consistently pay your rent and nontraditional bills on time. Remember, the goal is to form good credit habits, which means that from now on you should strive to pay all bills on time.

Keep Documentation

Maintain thorough records of your rent and nontraditional payments, including receipts, statements, and any correspondence with the reporting service. These records can serve as evidence in case of any reporting discrepancies.

Adding rent and nontraditional payments to your credit report can yield several advantages in your credit recovery journey. For starters, it gives you an opportunity to strengthen your credit history by showcasing your consistent payment behavior in various financial aspects of your life. Moreover, this inclusion of positive rent payments may help offset any previous credit problems in other, traditional credit lines. Finally, rent reporting can diversify your credit profile, which is often viewed positively by lenders when considering your creditworthiness.

How to Negotiate with Creditors

Dealing with credit problems can feel overwhelming, but there are effective strategies that can help you regain control of your financial situation. One such strategy is negotiating with your creditors. By engaging in open and honest conversations with your creditors, you may be able to find mutually beneficial solutions that alleviate your credit burdens. In this section, we will explore the power of negotiating with creditors, providing insights and practical tips to help you navigate this process and pave the way toward a brighter financial future.

Understanding the Importance of Negotiation

When faced with credit problems, ignoring your debts can worsen the situation. Instead, proactively reaching out to your creditors and discussing your financial challenges demonstrates responsibility and a willingness to find a resolution. Creditors are often open to negotiation because they understand that it is in their best interest to recover at least a portion of the debt owed. By engaging in negotiations, you can potentially secure more favorable terms, such as reduced interest rates, extended payment plans, or even debt settlement options. Here's how to approach this challenge.

Assess Your Financial Situation

Start by gaining a clear understanding of your current financial standing. Evaluate your income, expenses, and available resources to determine what you can realistically afford to pay toward your debts.

Contact Your Creditors

Reach out to your creditors directly and express your willingness to resolve the outstanding debt. Be prepared to provide an honest overview of your financial situation and explain any extenuating circumstances that led to the credit problems.

Propose a Workable Solution

Present your creditors with a proposed repayment plan that aligns with your financial capabilities. This may include reduced monthly payments, lower interest rates, or extended repayment periods. Emphasize the benefits of your proposal, such as the guaranteed payment and the potential for a faster resolution.

Be Professional and Persistent

Maintain a professional tone throughout the negotiation process. Keep records of all communication and follow up regularly to ensure progress. Persistence and consistent communication demonstrate your commitment to finding a solution.

Negotiating with creditors offers several potential benefits when you've had credit problems. First, it provides an opportunity to create a manageable repayment plan that suits your financial circumstances, reducing the strain on your budget. Successful negotiations can also result in lowered interest rates, waived fees, or even the possibility of settling the debt for a reduced amount. Additionally, engaging in negotiations allows you to maintain open lines of communication with your creditors, fostering a sense of cooperation and goodwill. Finally, the outcome of a successful negotiation can give you peace of mind and less stress and worry about your debts. Negotiating with creditors is a powerful tool in your quest to bounce back from damaged credit.

How to Achieve Perfect Credit

I mentioned that I've had the good fortune of hitting a perfect 850 FICO credit score–multiple times, in fact. I've written a whole book about improving your credit called *Perfect Credit: 7 Steps to a Great Credit Rating*. As of this writing, my FICO Score is currently 842 points. Woo hoo! Once you start to recover from poor credit, you'll cheer yourself too. You won't just be satisfied with having decent or even good credit. You'll likely want to strive for excellent credit. So let me share with you the seven steps you can take to achieve a perfect credit rating.

What Exactly Is Perfect Credit?

It's important to first define what I mean by "perfect credit." Your credit score provides an objective measure of how well you handle your credit. In my view, individuals with a FICO Score of 760 or higher fall within the range of perfect credit. Therefore, you have perfect credit if your FICO Scores are between 760 to 850 points. Achieving an exact 850 score is not necessary to be considered in the perfect credit range. Sure, that may give you some bragging rights. And if it floats your boat emotionally, strive for it if you want. But I wouldn't chase after an 850 score just to have it. It truly doesn't make any tangible difference financially. The person with a FICO Score of, say, 785 or 820 can still secure the best loan rates and terms offered by creditors and lenders—the exact ones that'll be offered to another person with an 850 score.

Another defining characteristic of perfect credit is your ability to secure any desired loan simply by signing on the dotted line. This ability is based on the strength of your credit reputation, which plays a significant role in determining whether you possess perfect credit. Additionally, being mindful of your debt situation is crucial. Understanding your financial standing empowers you to eliminate excessive debt, and to manage debt wisely. By proactively managing your finances and controlling debt, you contribute to maintaining perfect credit.

The Seven-step Formula to Perfect Credit

If you follow seven straightforward steps in managing your credit and your finances, I can assure you that you'll see your credit scores climb, and you'll get into the perfect credit zone. Here's a quick summary of my unique, seven-step system:

P—Pull your credit reports and credit scores.
E—Examine your files and enroll in credit monitoring.
R—Reduce debt and manage bills wisely.
F—Fix errors and protect your credit.
E—Enhance your credit file constantly.
C—Contact creditors and negotiate.
T—Take time to educate yourself.

Now, here's how to put these steps and this advice into action.

Step 1: Pull Your Credit Reports and Credit Scores

It is truly shocking how many individuals have never laid eyes on their credit files or obtained their credit scores. This lack of knowledge is proving to be a costly mistake. According to a survey conducted by the Consumer Federation of America, this unawareness of credit and how the credit-scoring system functions can cost you thousands of dollars annually.

Without accessing your credit reports and credit scores, you are unable to conduct a proper financial checkup, let alone make improvements to your credit rating. Imagine someone saying, "I've never visited a doctor" or "I've only seen a doctor once in the last five years." Would you treat your physical health so casually? Most likely not. Therefore, it is crucial not to disregard something equally significant—your financial health.

To become a more responsible steward of your overall finances, it's imperative to pull your credit reports and review your credit scores, including your FICO Scores and other scores that provide firsthand information about your credit profile. There are no ifs, ands, or buts about it.

Fortunately, the FACT Act (Fair and Accurate Credit Transactions Act) grants you the right to obtain your credit reports free of charge once every 12 months from Equifax, Experian, and TransUnion. The credit bureaus have simplified the process by allowing consumers to reach all three bureaus simultaneously through a single website (`www.annualcreditreport.com`), a shared toll-free number (877-322-8228), and a common mailing address: Annual Credit Report Request Service, Post Office Box 105281, Atlanta, GA 30348-5281.

In addition to your credit reports, it is also advisable to obtain your FICO credit scores and other scores. Although in some cases, there may be a fee associated with obtaining them, it's worth it because you'll know where you stand. I've met countless people who told me that they were too afraid to look at their credit reports or scores. I sympathize with their concerns, but I also know that keeping your head in the dark about credit problems won't make them go away.

Step 2: Examine Your Files and Enroll in Credit Monitoring

Interpreting your credit report can sometimes be confusing, but it is crucial to actually read and review your reports. Surprisingly, many people who obtain their credit reports fail to go through them thoroughly. Some may simply see it as a task to check off their list, while others postpone it, thinking they'll do it later when they have more time. However, continuously putting it off will result in never delving into your credit files, similar to those who buy books but never read them. Don't let this happen with your credit reports.

The next step toward achieving perfect credit involves two parts. First, you need to examine your credit files. This involves looking at the detailed listing of open and closed accounts reported by creditors. The most crucial aspect is the "Status" section, which indicates whether you have paid your debts on time or have been late, including the degree of lateness. This is the starting point when delving into your account summaries.

Your payment history, as reflected in the "Account Status," "Current Status," "Pay Status," or simply "Status," holds significant importance. Accounts with no delinquencies will show positive comments such as "Pays As Agreed," "Never Late," or "Current." Negative information typically includes 30-, 60-, 90-, or 120-day late payments, as well as references to collections, settlements, or charged-off accounts.

Examining the dollar amounts associated with each credit account is also crucial. Pay attention to summaries such as credit limits/original amounts, high balances, recent balances, recent payments, and monthly payments. These figures provide insight into your credit utilization and payment habits.

In addition to account details, your credit reports may include public records, such as judgments, tax liens, or bankruptcies. Judgments can be dismissed, which improves your credit rating, while tax liens, if unpaid, can have a severe negative impact. Bankruptcies, although they legally discharge debts, are considered highly detrimental to your credit and typically remain on your report for 10 years.

Examining your reports once isn't enough. I suggest you also enroll in credit monitoring, which is an essential tool in managing your credit in today's economy. While some argue it is unnecessary, credit monitoring aids in detecting and minimizing the damage caused by identity theft. While it may not prevent identity theft entirely, it provides early warnings of suspicious activities and allows you to take immediate action to protect your credit.

Credit monitoring also offers benefits such as updated credit reports and scores, improved credit education, legal services and insurance protection, financial reimbursements in case of identity theft, and more. By regularly monitoring your credit, you enhance your financial literacy and safeguard your credit profile.

Step 3: Reduce Debt and Manage Bills Wisely

Your debt and credit share a profound relationship. Since your payment history—specifically, your ability to pay bills on time—is the primary factor influencing your FICO Scores, it is vital to treat debt management with the utmost seriousness. To enhance your FICO Scores, never missing a payment is essential, regardless of the circumstances. This singular action will set you on the path to score improvement.

If you have faced challenges in the past, leading to skipped or late payments due to financial constraints, it's crucial to adjust your budget to ensure timely payment of every bill. And by "every bill," I mean precisely that. Do not neglect utility bills, such as electricity, under the false assumption that local service providers won't report delinquencies to credit bureaus. They can and will.

The same applies to cell phone providers, water companies, and public utilities. Don't be mistaken in thinking that only mortgage payments, car loans, and revolving accounts impact your credit. While those obligations should take priority over less urgent bills, even a 30-day late payment for a telephone bill can have a negative impact on your credit report and potentially lower your credit score.

With Americans collectively owing trillions in consumer and mortgage debt, the opportunity for financial mismanagement and long-term consequences to credit health is greater than ever. Coupled with the unfortunate lack of financial literacy education in our country, this creates a recipe for potential financial disaster.

Understanding the importance of managing debt and its impact on credit health is vital. By prioritizing timely payments and being diligent in debt management, you can pave the way toward a healthier credit standing and long-term financial well-being.

Step 4: Fix Errors and Protect Your Credit

Consumer groups estimate that a staggering 70% of credit reports contain errors. This abundance of misinformation could be costing you money, especially if you're seeking a loan. Having errors in your credit file may lead to higher interest rates than you deserve.

Mistakes in credit reports can occur for various reasons. It could be an inputting error by a clerk who mistakenly types your name, resulting in confusion with someone else. Alternatively, a simple transposition of digits in your Social Security number can lead to inaccuracies. In some cases, family members have discovered that their credit files inexplicably merge with others. Regardless of the cause, it is crucial to address any errors in your credit reports as soon as you become aware of them.

With the immense volume of credit information circulating, it's no surprise that mistakes are routine. Around 100,000 organizations contribute data to credit-reporting agencies, including banks, lenders, collection agencies, credit card companies, leasing firms, utility companies, and any entity involved in extending credit or reporting information about you. The average person's credit report is updated five times a day. Each month, five billion pieces of information are added to credit files, and credit bureaus receive two million credit report orders daily.

While we are familiar with prominent players such as Equifax, Experian, and TransUnion in the credit industry, the United States is home to over 1,000 consumer reporting agencies.

Given the sheer volume of credit-related data, errors in credit files are inevitable. However, when mistakes occur, it falls on you to rectify them. By promptly addressing any inaccuracies in your credit reports, you safeguard your financial well-being and ensure the accuracy of your credit profile.

Step 5: Enhance Your Credit Files Constantly

One essential step in the credit-building journey is to add positive information to your credit file. You can arrange to have the following information included on your credit reports: rent payments, utility bills, credit accounts that appear on one credit report but not the others, and obligations such as car notes or student loans that were paid off but that are missing from your credit files. Doing this has particular value for individuals aiming to establish credit, those with a "thin" file, or those who may have been denied credit due to a lack of credit history altogether.

Let's begin with those who have no credit file or score. There are two common reasons behind this situation. First, you may have never had a traditional credit account, such as a credit card or car loan. This is the case for younger people as well as older individuals—usually women—who haven't had credit in their own names. Alternatively, you may have recently obtained credit, but the account is not yet being reported by your creditor. It can take several months for new accounts to appear on the major credit bureaus' records. In such cases, it wouldn't hurt to reach out to your creditors and ensure that they have reported your accounts.

However, there is a situation where the absence of a credit file or score should raise concern. It occurs when you have indeed opened a credit account, but it does not appear in the records of the credit bureaus. The likely culprit? Someone may have mistakenly listed you as deceased. The Social Security Administration maintains a "Master Death Index" that is accessible to credit bureaus, businesses, and government agencies. If your Social Security number finds its way onto that list, you will be presumed deceased, making it incredibly challenging to obtain credit. Even if you have multiple accounts, a single death notation can potentially wreak havoc on your entire credit file. If you suspect this has occurred, contacting the Social Security Administration (`http://www.ssa.gov`) for assistance in resolving the issue is advisable.

Furthermore, individuals categorized as having a "thin" credit file include young adults, immigrants, and women who have not established credit in their own names. They fall within the classic profile of individuals with limited credit history.

For all these cases, it's essential to take proactive steps to add positive information to your credit file and actively build credit. By doing so, you pave the way for better credit opportunities and financial well-being.

Step 6: Contact Creditors and Negotiate

Never underestimate your power when it comes to dealing with credit card companies, regardless of your outstanding balances. You have more leverage than you might think. Even if you've been making only minimum payments, a credit card issuer does not want to lose your business if you've been consistently paying on time.

By contacting your credit card issuer and indicating that you have a better offer from another financial institution or can obtain one, you're likely to see immediate results. They will probably lower your interest rate or, at the very least, consider reducing it if you maintain timely payments for a continuous period, such as six months. Credit card issuers understand the competitive nature of the market and the constant flood of credit card and balance transfer options bombarding consumers. It is more advantageous for them to contemplate an interest rate reduction than to risk losing your business entirely.

Initiating the Process: Getting Creditors to Collaborate

The most proactive step you can take to engage with your existing creditors is to initiate the conversation. Despite the discomfort it may bring, you must be the one to call them, rather than the other way around. It's time to break the habit of avoiding telephone calls from banks and department stores, or relying on others to claim you're not available. Today, you need to take the initiative to tackle your debts head-on. It all starts with devising a workable plan that aligns with both your needs and the creditor's requirements.

Be honest about your situation. If you have experienced job loss, divorce, illness, or any other circumstances preventing you from working, communicate this to your creditors. Appeal to their sense of fairness and compassion. Remember, you are interacting with another human being, despite the challenging experiences some may have had with debt collectors.

Six Objectives for Creditors' Discussions

When reaching out to your creditors, aim to achieve the following objectives, depending on your circumstances:

- Lower your interest rate;
- Cease late fees;
- Eliminate over-the-limit charges;
- Upgrade your account to "current" status;
- Remove negative entries from your credit file;
- Negotiate a partial payment without adverse effects on your credit.

It is generally more advantageous to engage with current creditors before missing a payment. Creditors are more willing to work with you when you have a track record of timely bill payments. They trust that you will continue to honor your obligations, even if it means making only minimum payments or paying less than the required minimums.

Step 7: Take Time to Educate Yourself

In your pursuit of perfect credit, it is vital to periodically reassess your credit usage and educate yourself on matters impacting your overall financial well-being. There are at least four critical areas that warrant your attention:

Understanding Your Existing Credit Obligations

Take a moment to evaluate all your current financial responsibilities. Consider your mortgage, car loan, cosigned loans, student loans, and those credit cards in your wallet. Do you comprehend the repayment terms, interest rates, and the actions you or your creditors can take if you encounter difficulties in meeting your obligations? Familiarizing yourself with these fundamental aspects is essential for maintaining financial security and increasing your chances of achieving perfect credit.

Knowledge of Personalized Financial Products and Services

Be aware of the nature and terms of financial products, services, and credit-related offers targeted specifically to you. Stay informed about the options available to you and evaluate them carefully to make informed decisions that align with your financial goals.

Staying Current on Credit Scoring Developments

The world of credit scoring is ever-evolving. Stay updated on the latest trends, changes, and best practices in credit scoring methodologies. This knowledge will empower you to make strategic credit decisions and take actions that positively impact your creditworthiness.

Awareness of Credit and Debt Laws

While certain credit and debt laws may not immediately affect you, they have far-reaching implications for consumers in general. Familiarize yourself with the laws that govern credit and debt to ensure you are well prepared for any future changes or situations that may arise.

By prioritizing education in these areas, you equip yourself with the necessary knowledge to make informed financial choices, protect your credit, and strive toward achieving and maintaining perfect credit. Don't overlook these important issues, as they can significantly impact your financial future. Remember, being proactive now will pay off in the long run.

Damaged Credit Resources

1. `AnnualCreditReport.com` – Free credit reports from the nationwide credit bureaus.
2. **Consumer Action** – Education and advocacy on credit issues.
3. **Consumer Credit Counseling Services** – Local credit counselors nationwide.
4. **Credit Builders Alliance** – Fosters financially inclusive communities.
5. **Fair Isaac Corporation (FICO)** – Credit score provider.

6. **LegalShield/IDShield** – Identity theft protection services.
7. **Lexington Law** – Legal help with credit repair.
8. **National Association of Credit Union Service Organizations** – Helps people improve credit at credit unions.
9. **National Credit Reporting Association** – Industry group with credit education resources.
10. **VantageScore** – Credit scores provided from the credit bureaus Equifax, Experian, and TransUnion.

Chapter 11
Dollar Deficits

"The true measure of success is not how high you soar, but how quickly and gracefully you can bounce back from the ground."

—Ellen DeGeneres

Despite relatively low unemployment in the US, the average American is just one setback away from financial catastrophe. Numerous studies show that most Americans have less than $1,000 in savings, too much debt, and pitifully low retirement funds, if any retirement money at all. One huge reason for these financial problems is that financial inequality has widened over the decades, with the rich accumulating vast amounts of wealth while the middle and lower classes struggle to keep up. Additionally, the cost of essential goods and services, from housing to health care, has risen at a rate that outpaces wage growth. Coupled with a lack of comprehensive financial education in schools and communities, many individuals find themselves ill-equipped to navigate these challenges or plan for the future.

Consequently, so many people are just getting by, dealing solely with today's problems and managing their lives from one crisis to the next. That strategy may keep the lights on (in most cases), but it's not a recipe for long-term financial success. To truly take your finances to the next level you have to prevent or overcome the Dreaded D known as "dollar deficits." Think of dollar deficits as living paycheck to paycheck, having difficulties paying your current bills, or lacking sufficient savings for the future. In other words, when you have dollar deficits, your present cash flow is very tight—and candidly, your future finances don't look all that bright either.

That's one reason why you absolutely must build your savings—and even have *multiple* savings accounts to be financially healthy. At first glance, that may seem far-fetched, especially if you're in a financial hole, with no savings or a load of debt. But once you make and commit to a plan to proactively and strategically manage your finances, you'll see that saving more money is totally doable.

Nobody likes to live paycheck to paycheck. It's stressful, depressing, and makes you feel like you're not getting ahead economically. It's even tougher to manage your finances when one crazy bill after another seems to pop up out of the blue. One month your car breaks down, the next month your pet gets sick, and you have costly veterinarian bills. Or maybe something in your house or apartment gets broken and you have to shell out money to fix it. You get the point. Unfortunately, unexpected bills are a common fact of life. It would be great if we could just wave a magic wand and create a perfect life in which nothing happens that wasn't according to plan. But we all know that's just a fantasy. So instead of struggling month after month with a hodge-podge of unforeseen circumstances, the smart thing to do is to rev up your money-management skills and really learn how to implement basic personal finance principles such as proper budgeting, how to wisely stretch a dollar, and practical cash management tips.

In this chapter, you will learn:

- Creative ways to turbo-charge your savings;
- The difference between a "rainy day fund" and an "emergency fund"—and why both are crucial to your financial health;
- Six ways to jump-start your savings;
- What to do if you're approaching retirement and haven't saved enough;
- Strategies for creating and maintaining a realistic budget;
- Four rules to better budgeting;
- How to create a strong financial plan B.

I know that's a lot of ground to cover! But before we get into it, let me give you some inspiration from a woman who faced dollar deficits for a full decade before turning things around. Her name is Chandra Harvey, and she's a chemist. At age 51, she has a remarkable story of having not only survived dollar deficits—but having successfully overcome all 10 of the Dreaded Ds. Chandra has faced downsizing from a job, which resulted in a 10-year ordeal trying to regain full-time employment, a painful, frustrating saga that at times made her wish she was dead. She's been through divorce, endured the death of both her parents, and battled disability and disease coping personally with her own struggles as well as her mom's Alzheimer's. She's confronted disasters, discrimination, debt of all kinds, and damaged credit too. In the midst of these challenges, up until 2021, she also had major dollar deficits, struggling so badly that she didn't know how she was going to keep a roof over her head. If it sounds as if Chandra has been through the wringer, it's because she has. Thankfully, she's now at a point in her life where she's not only found financial strength and emotional resilience from her challenges but also her life's purpose—which came directly out of her biggest struggles. I was amazed at what Chandra was able to endure and overcome, so I hope I can do her story justice. Here it goes.

Chandra grew up knowing she wanted to go into the science field. "I've always been interested in chemistry since I was five years old. My parents took me to the Franklin Institute, and I fell in love with it," she recalls.

After earning a degree in chemistry from Johnson C. Smith University in Charlotte, North Carolina, Chandra had hoped to go to grad school. But she had major academic struggles before finally being diagnosed with ADHD and dyslexia. She did great writing answers and completing essay-based assignments. But she says she flunked out of courses with more traditional assessments. "If it was multiple choice, I got confused and didn't know the answer, but not because I didn't know the information," she explains of her dyslexia. As an undergrad, her learning disabilities had been masked by her getting lots of tutoring and extra support. But grad school was a different matter entirely. After several failed attempts to earn a graduate degree over the years, she finally resigned herself to working in her field without that extra credential.

Indeed, her work life was fine up until January 2010. That's when everything changed. At the time, she was working for Siemens Healthcare Diagnostics in Delaware. "I was sitting at my desk working on something, and I got a call. HR wanted me to come into an office," Chandra says. "I go in there, and they said: 'Your job has just been eliminated,' and I said: 'What?!' I was just so shocked."

No Warning and No Good Prospects

She had no advance warning of the termination, and there had been no issues at all with her performance. And it wasn't just her who got fired. A total of 12 people got laid off, and the company made those same individuals compete for a chance to be rehired, Chandra says.

A couple of coworkers received offers, but she didn't. That downsizing sent her into a decade-long spiral of economic misfortune. First, she lost her condo in Delaware. Unable to keep up with housing payments and ever-rising HOA fees, her home went into foreclosure in 2011. "A lot of my financial problems had to do with the fact that I lost my career," Chandra says. "If I didn't lose my career, I would've been much better off financially, instead of having taken multiple steps back."

But Chandra got married in October 2010 and relocated to the Virginia-Maryland area with her husband. While he worked in IT, she had project work and part-time stints, such as creating science curriculum for students and for the YMCA. When months of searching for a full-time job turned into years, everything started falling apart. Chandra and her spouse divorced in 2017. Though he provided some support, Chandra says she became increasingly desperate to find work and generate income. To make ends meet, she wrote environmental grant proposals for money. She drove for Uber and Lyft for 13 hours a day. And she worked at the National Aquarium teaching the public about marine animals. In fact, in the summer of 2018, she did all three jobs simultaneously.

"I was only making $12 an hour, and I was still mainly living off my 401(k) money. My car died around the same time. I still had bad credit and went to the car place. They said, 'We can turn it into an Uber and Lyft for you. That way you can make some money, and you'll have money to pay for the car,'" Chandra recalls.

Her work at the aquarium came about after she first volunteered there. Coworkers learned of her dire financial straits and "they went and begged the community engagement department for a job for me. They said, 'She's barely scraping by, just give her any job.' And they did."

In her role as a tour guide, Chandra taught the public about the environment and the proper way to handle animals such as jellyfish. She worked with sharks and did dolphin tours, as well as behind-the-scenes tours of coral.

The whole time, however, she kept looking for an in to get back into her work as a chemist—only to find brick walls at every turn due to her long time out of the field.

"A ten-year hiatus as an analytical chemist was the equivalent of losing everything," she says. Employers wanted to hire people who could come on the job with up-to-date skills, and Chandra says she knows her work gap doomed her quest for one potential job after another. "My résumé showed over twenty years of experience, but taking ten years off was a killer. I was no longer employable because I hadn't touched an instrument in over ten years."

She was constantly told no, or to wait for a different opportunity. "It was very frustrating for me, having a chemistry degree and knowing the value that I bring and then being told, 'Maybe you still want to just teach.'"

As it turns out, during the time when she couldn't find a job directly in her field, Chandra did also teach, including STEM programs at schools, to make ends meet. "I spent six years teaching. But it wasn't because I really wanted to. It was the path that I went on because I couldn't find anything else. I was trying to keep myself relevant in the field in some way, shape, or form." She also wrote an oceanography curriculum, which was implemented in four Maryland counties.

Noticing a Pattern Turns into Purpose

Amid all this, there were other difficulties, including losing her mother in 2014 and getting divorced in 2017. Medical debt issues cropped up too, including from her mom's Alzheimer's treatments. "I didn't have money to pay all the bills for years," Chandra says.

Chandra's father had passed at age 68 many years ago. When her mom died at age 80, Chandra used inheritance money received from her mother to start a nonprofit, called ESTEAAM. It stands for environmental, science, technology, engineering, arts, athletics, and mathematics.

At one point, Chandra also worked for an entity called BioEYES, where she taught environmental education to kids in Baltimore County, Maryland. That employment ended amid a discrimination claim on her part, but it also formed part of what became a pattern: teaching.

Chandra now realizes that teaching is her calling and what excites her most in life. That epiphany marks a huge shift in perspective from her darkest times. At her lowest point, Chandra says, "I used to pray to God to just kill me and take me out of this. I used to ask: Can I just die?"

"I couldn't wrap my head around how I had a chemistry degree. I knew people in the mayor's office in Baltimore, Maryland, and I had connections everywhere—yet I couldn't get a full-time job. It just never made sense," she says.

But finally, it's become clear that all those struggles were not in vain. "I found my purpose through all those ten years," she says, noting the irony of it all. "I never wanted to teach," she admits. "My parents *begged* me to become a teacher. I said: 'You get paid no money, and it's a thankless job.' But now I want to open my own school."

That's not the only twist Chandra's life has taken. In March 2019, she was rehired at Siemens—the same company that dismissed her. Her new role came through a referral, another woman who happened to be a manager at Siemens, and who was among the group of 12 people terminated along with Chandra back in 2010. "At my new job at Siemens, I was in the lab, but I wasn't doing the instrumentation I was used to doing." While the new job gave her "a foot in the door," Chandra says she left after nine months for a contract gig with the US government—a role that ultimately led to her current full-time job. After nearly a dozen years of searching, in late 2021, Chandra finally landed an ideal position at PTC Bio, a biopharmaceutical company that focuses on treating rare diseases. She applied for three different jobs at PTC but wasn't granted an interview for the first two. With the last position, she was granted an interview and got the job.

"It took me three tries, but the third was a charm," she says. Chandra now works in quality operations. "I help oversee the manufacturing process for medications we make for our patients," she says proudly. This new, high-paying job has brought career satisfaction and an enormous sense of financial stability. She's relocated for the job from Maryland to New Jersey.

"I feel like I've gone from rags to riches now in a short time," she says. "I thank God every day that I was given this opportunity to be at PTC and to do the work I'm doing."

Still, recently, Chandra said her therapist told her that "when I see you talk about these kids and the science program and what you teach them, you light up. You don't light up like that when you talk about your job." So in 2024, Chandra plans to do both: continue her work as a chemist and jump-start her teaching efforts through her nonprofit, ESTEAAM. "I know that this is definitely my purpose," she says.

To others struggling with dollar deficits and any of life's challenges, Chandra urges two things: persistence and following every opportunity, no matter how seemingly small. She says even during her days driving for Uber and Lyft she met interesting people and talked about science. "Never turn down an open door because you don't know where that door will lead," Chandra says. "Don't doubt yourself. Just go where it leads—and that's your path."

Dealing with Life's Blows

If you feel like you've taken a one-two punch financially, as Chandra did for so long, it's probably not your imagination. In many ways, it's harder to get by these days. The last couple of years were rough. But the years ahead still hold a lot of challenges, and for many people not much of a safety net. During the initial stages of the COVID-19 outbreak, government aid in the form of stimulus payments, improved unemployment benefits, and boosts in child tax credits provided essential support to Americans to help them weather the economic downturn caused by the pandemic. However, currently, most Americans find themselves grappling with high inflation, and bigger costs for virtually everything, with limited assistance available from the government. What this means is: you have to create your own safety net and your own economic backup plan. That's what this chapter is all about—helping you get on solid financial footing so you can be prepared for any eventuality.

Creative Ways to Turbo-charge Your Savings

Have you been short on the rent or mortgage or needed extra time to pay your utilities or car note lately? Wouldn't it be great if you had just a little (or maybe a lot) of extra money each month? Think of what you could do with, say, $250, $500, or even $1,000 or more in your bank account *every 30 days*. You could certainly pay down debt. You could open or start adding to your retirement fund. Or you could finally build some real money in a plain-old savings account—without having to raid your savings for every little emergency. Perhaps you just want a little breathing room and freedom from worrying about all those bills. Well, having enough money to cover all your daily or monthly bills isn't a pipe dream—despite widespread concerns about inflation. You can start bringing in additional bucks *this month*, save more money, and get past your dollar deficits! Here's how.

A Rainy Day Fund Versus an Emergency Fund

Setting aside money in a rainy day fund is a smart move to prepare for unforeseen circumstances that could cost you financially. While similar to an emergency fund, a rainy day fund serves a different purpose. So let's explore what a rainy day fund entails and consider various ways to start building one today.

What exactly is a rainy day fund? When you save for a rainy day, you're essentially budgeting to set aside money for unexpected expenses that may arise. This could be for situations such as car repairs, replacing a malfunctioning washing machine, or any similar occurrences. The funds you save for these events are known as a rainy day fund.

Think of your rainy day fund as you'd think of an umbrella. You have one for those periods of time when it's raining—and maybe you have to run from your car to the office or a store. Or you're out somewhere and it starts raining, and you whip out your umbrella. You know it won't rain forever. But you're prepared for this quick, sometimes unexpected downpour. Likewise, although you can't predict the exact timing of when you'll need money from your rainy day savings, you know that such situations are likely to occur at some point. For instance, even with routine maintenance, your car won't last forever, and certain parts will eventually require repair. While the repair itself isn't unexpected, the timing of it might catch you off guard.

Rainy day funds are primarily designed to cover smaller expenses. Typically, these expenses involve one-time or short-term costs. There's no fixed limit on how much money you can allocate to your rainy day fund, but it should be sufficient to cover expenses of at least a few hundred dollars. Some people prefer to have an extra safety net of up to $1,000. The more money you have saved, the better prepared you'll be when unexpected expenses arise.

It's important to note that rainy day funds should not be confused with emergency funds. Emergency funds serve a different purpose and are generally larger in size as they are intended to cover major unexpected expenses.

An emergency fund is money set aside specifically for financial emergencies. It's not the same as saving money for minor incidents such as a flat tire or a broken washing machine. The purpose of an emergency fund is to protect yourself financially in case of job loss, injury, or a serious illness—long-term situations that won't be quickly resolved just by throwing a few hundred bucks at the problem. You save for potential financial disasters that could cost thousands of dollars or more.

To determine how much you need in your emergency fund, consider the expenses you would face if you lost your job and calculate how much savings would be necessary to cover bills and everyday expenses for three to six months. This will give you a rough estimate of the amount you should aim to save.

Since the scope of events and circumstances covered by emergency funds is broader, there is no fixed limit on how much you can contribute to this fund. You can calculate your income levels for a few months to get an idea of what you might need if you were not working. However, it's challenging to determine the exact amount necessary for unforeseen events such as injuries or serious illnesses. The general practice is to have enough to replace your income for a short period and continue adding more savings as needed.

Don't stress over this process. It's OK to start with nothing and to build slowly. Do know, however, that it's crucial to have both a rainy day fund and an emergency fund. Having separate funds makes it easier to allocate your savings for their intended purposes. If both funds are kept in the same bank account, it becomes challenging to distinguish between them. This could result in unintentionally depleting one fund, leaving you short when you need that money later.

When you have a distinct rainy day and a separate emergency fund, you can avoid accidentally reducing the amount in either fund. If you need money for a broken window, you can directly withdraw it from your rainy-day fund. In the case of a medical emergency like appendix removal, you can utilize funds from your emergency fund if necessary.

Relying solely on a rainy day fund may not provide sufficient resources for significant financial emergencies. Similarly, depending solely on an emergency fund might require dipping into it for smaller expenses such as car repairs or purchasing new appliances. What if you encounter a substantial financial expense while your emergency fund is not adequately funded?

By having both a rainy day fund and an emergency fund, you increase your preparedness for unforeseen expenses, regardless of their size. This comprehensive approach ensures that you are financially equipped to tackle any unexpected situations that may arise.

Six Ways to Jump-start Your Savings

If you've found it hard to save money in the past, try these six ideas to give you an extra boost:

No. 1. Make a commitment and stick to it: You don't need a substantial amount of money or drastic lifestyle changes to start a savings fund. Begin with a modest commitment, such as $25 per paycheck or less, and witness the growth of your fund. Remember, every little bit counts, as long as you contribute consistently.

No. 2. Automate your savings: Let your employer deduct a fixed amount from each paycheck and deposit it directly into your savings. You'll hardly miss the money, and over time, you'll reach your savings goal.

No. 3. Sell unnecessary items: Most people have stuff they no longer need or use. Declutter your house and generate extra cash by selling furniture, electronics, or other items through a garage sale or online platforms. Not only will you bolster your cash cushion, but you'll also create a more organized living space.

No. 4. Utilize windfalls wisely: When unexpected cash flows into your life, such as birthday gifts, bonuses, or tax returns, resist the temptation to splurge. Instead, save these windfalls and add them to your financial reserves.

No. 5. Adjust your paycheck withholdings: If you're getting hefty tax refund checks, that shows that you overpaid your taxes throughout the year. Avoid giving the government an interest-free loan by adjusting the amount withheld from your paycheck. By doing so, you can potentially increase your monthly income by up to $250.

No. 6. Control your spending: No matter what the state of the economy, whether it's in a boom or bust period, try to avoid the urge to constantly engage in excessive spending. Nobody likes to be on spending lockdown all the time, so "frugal fatigue" may tempt you to splurge. But don't make a habit out of doing that. Don't derail your own progress; stay committed to your financial goals.

By following these tips, you'll develop a solid financial foundation and create a cushion that provides stability and peace of mind. Remember, small steps taken consistently can lead to significant financial gains.

What to Do If You're Approaching Retirement and Haven't Saved Enough

Facing the reality that you haven't saved enough money for retirement can be daunting, but it's important to remember that you're not alone. Many people find themselves in a similar situation, and the good news is that there are steps you can take to improve your financial outlook. So don't let a current lack of savings cause you to freeze and do nothing. By implementing effective strategies and making smart decisions now, you can still work toward a comfortable retirement. Here's how.

Assess Your Current Financial Situation

The first step is to thoroughly evaluate your current financial status. Take a close look at your income, expenses, assets, and debts. Determine how much you currently have saved for retirement and compare it to your estimated retirement needs. This evaluation will give you a clear understanding of where you stand and help you identify areas for improvement.

Set Realistic Retirement Goals

While it's important to set ambitious goals, it's equally crucial to be realistic about what you can achieve given your current circumstances. Consider factors such as your age, desired retirement lifestyle, and expected retirement age. Adjusting your retirement goals to align with your financial situation will provide a more attainable target and reduce unnecessary stress.

Create a Budget and Stick to It

Developing a comprehensive budget is essential for effective financial management. Track your income and expenses diligently, identifying areas where you can cut back on unnecessary spending. Allocate a specific portion of your income toward retirement savings. By adhering to a well-structured budget, you'll have a clearer picture of your financial capabilities and be able to allocate resources more efficiently. (See the next section for budgeting tips.)

Maximize Retirement Contributions

Take full advantage of retirement savings vehicles such as employer-sponsored 401(k) plans or individual retirement accounts (IRAs). Contribute as much as possible, especially if your employer offers a matching contribution. These contributions provide a significant boost to your retirement savings and offer potential tax benefits. If you're over the age of 50, consider taking advantage of catch-up contributions to accelerate your savings.

Seek Professional Financial Advice

Consulting with a qualified financial advisor can provide valuable insights and personalized guidance tailored to your specific situation. An advisor can help you develop a retirement strategy, optimize your investment portfolio, and ensure you're making informed decisions. They will assess your risk tolerance, provide long-term projections, and recommend appropriate investment options to help you make up for lost time.

Explore Additional Income Streams

Consider various opportunities to generate additional income streams. This could involve taking on a part-time job, freelancing, or starting a small business. Supplementing your current income can provide extra funds to bolster your retirement savings. Additionally, reinvesting this income into retirement accounts will help accelerate your progress.

Downsize and Cut Expenses

Evaluate your current living situation and determine if downsizing is a viable option. Moving to a smaller home or reducing living expenses can free up funds to contribute toward retirement savings. Assess your monthly bills and identify areas where you can cut back, such as entertainment expenses, dining out, or subscription services. Every dollar saved can make a difference in building your retirement nest egg. By the way, you don't have to wait until the kids are grown and gone to downsize or relocate. Consider doing so earlier if that works for your family. Another tip to cut expenses: use the AARP Foundation's online search tool at `local.aarpfoundation.org`. You simply drop in your zip code and what you need to save money on, and you'll be directed to free and reduced-cost services for food, medical care, job training, and more in your area.

Consider Delaying Retirement

If your financial situation requires it, consider delaying your retirement. Working for a few more years can provide several benefits. I know that's not ideal. Many of us would love to retire early—not have to add more years to our work lives. However, by working longer you'll have additional time to save, your Social Security benefits will increase, and you can continue building your retirement portfolio. Plus, delaying retirement allows your existing savings to grow and reduces the number of years you'll rely on them.

Admittedly, however, not everyone has the ability to retire later. In fact, retirement often does not happen when people think it will. You may face a serious illness or injury that cuts your work life short. You may have caregiving duties, and you're called upon to take care of a sick spouse or aging parent, responsibilities that can make full-time employment nearly impossible. Also, you may be forced to retire at a given age if your employer mandates it, or you get downsized unexpectedly. Because of these realities, only about one in six US workers—17%

of employees—retire when they planned to, according to a recent study from the Employee Benefit Research Institute. On average, people retired 4.3 years *earlier* than anticipated.

Invest Wisely

Make informed investment decisions to maximize the growth potential of your retirement savings. Diversify your portfolio across different asset classes to mitigate risk. Consider a mix of stocks, bonds, mutual funds, and other investment vehicles based on your risk tolerance and time horizon. Regularly review and rebalance your investments to ensure they align with your long-term goals. Not confident about investing? Seek professional guidance in the areas where you lack knowledge or need expert counsel.

Prioritize Health and Wellness

Your health plays a vital role in your retirement plan. Focus on maintaining a healthy lifestyle to reduce medical expenses in the future. Exercise regularly, eat nutritious meals, and prioritize preventive health care. By taking care of your physical and mental well-being, you can minimize the financial burden of health care costs in retirement.

While the realization that you haven't saved enough money for retirement can be unsettling, don't compound your situation by ignoring it or just wishing that things will get better. By assessing your current status, setting realistic goals, and taking the proactive steps outlined above, you can work toward a more secure retirement. It's never too late to start taking control of your financial future and building a nest egg that will support you later in life.

Strategies for Creating and Maintaining a Realistic Budget

Whether you're struggling to stick to your budget or simply want to improve your money management skills, it's crucial to create a realistic budget and set achievable goals that will motivate you to stay on track.

If you find yourself frequently running out of cash and struggling to accurately forecast your monthly expenses, adopting healthy money habits is key. While it may take time to develop these habits, there are several steps you can take to maintain a positive cash flow month after month.

Here are six straightforward steps to help you create a better budget:

Prioritize Your Purchases

Make a list of items you need to buy versus those you simply want. By distinguishing between necessities and luxuries, you can determine what you can truly afford and what you should save up for later. Avoid shopping without a planned list of purchases to avoid unnecessary spending.

Set Realistic Savings Goals

Be honest with yourself about your spending habits. Can you realistically save a certain amount each week on activities such as eating out or entertainment, or are these expenses an essential part of your lifestyle? Identify how much you spend on extras, and determine what you're willing to give up in order to reach your savings goals. Completely eliminating favorite activities may leave you feeling deprived and increase the likelihood of overspending in other areas.

Keep It Simple

Don't complicate your budget spreadsheet. Whether it's an Excel document, online budgeting software, or just plain old pencil and paper, use whatever you like and what's easiest for you. Keep your budget straightforward and easy to reference so that you can quickly consult it when making purchasing decisions or considering big-ticket items. Simplifying your budgeting process will make it more manageable.

Include a Miscellaneous Category

Allocate a portion of your budget for small, unplanned expenses that may arise during the week. This can include last-minute grocery items, additional gas, or forgotten snacks. Incorporating this category will provide flexibility within your budget while still keeping you on track. Neglecting to account for miscellaneous expenses can have a significant impact on your budget, as these small expenses can add up over time.

Track Your Spending

Develop the habit of tracking all your purchases and expenditures, ideally in real time. Avoid waiting until the end of the week or month to review your spending.

Tracking your expenses as you make them will increase your awareness of your spending habits and may even encourage you to spend less.

Adopt a Cash-only Mindset

Break the habit of relying on credit cards and commit to spending only the money you have. Avoid using credit cards for purchases or bill payments until you have your budget fully under control. Your budget should encompass all living and entertainment expenses while remaining flexible enough to accommodate additional expenditures. Relying on credit cards can lead to overspending beyond your monthly budget, so it's essential to resist this financial temptation.

By following these steps and implementing good financial practices, you can regain control of your budget and avoid falling into the trap of relying on credit cards or overspending. Building a strong foundation for your finances will pave the way for a more secure and sustainable financial future.

Understand Four Important Rules of Budgeting

I always tell people who are struggling with budgeting to observe four helpful rules. Heeding these rules will keep you out of a lot of financial problems.

Rule #1: Avoid Overspending

Everyone and their mother knows that it's not wise to live beyond their means, but that doesn't stop people from doing it every day. That's why the first and most important rule of budgeting is simple: you cannot spend more than you earn. While it may sound like common sense, many people overlook this crucial rule. Spending more than your income is a cardinal sin of good financial management because it leads to deficit spending. Whether your annual income is $20,000 or $20 million, if you consistently spend more than you earn, you'll find yourself broke and drowning in debt.

To ensure you're staying within your means, calculate your expenses and compare them to your net income (your actual take-home pay, not your gross salary). If your bills exceed your net earnings, it's time to revamp your budget and prioritize necessities. Start by cutting out luxuries and nonessential purchases to align your spending with your income. No excuses, no exceptions.

Rule #2: Add 20% to Your Planned Expenses

If you're looking for an easy way to stay on track with your budget, let me introduce you to what I refer to as my 20% rule. This simple rule will help you maintain a realistic budget and ensure that you always account for all your monthly expenses.

Here's how it works: Take the bottom-line number you come up with when tallying your monthly expenses and add 20% to it. This will give you a more accurate reflection of your true monthly bills—and your true spending.

Let's say you add up your financial obligations like rent or mortgage, food, utilities, and more, and the total comes out to be $2,500 per month. According to the 20% rule, your actual monthly bills would be 20% more, totaling $3,000.

The reason behind this strategy is that many people tend to underestimate their expenses. When people show me their budgets, I often find that they have overlooked certain categories such as memberships, subscriptions, donations, gifts, year-round holiday spending, and one-time expenses such as car registration fees.

In my experience, I have yet to come across a budget that is 100% complete and doesn't miss any spending categories or expenses that were accidentally overlooked. Even if you consider yourself a skilled budgeter and meticulously track every expense, the 20% rule can still be helpful.

By adding that extra 20%, you create a cushion in your budget. This ensures that your budget isn't too tight, allowing for some flexibility in case of unexpected expenses or fluctuations in your spending.

If you find that you didn't end up spending that extra 20% you budgeted for, consider putting the money into your savings or using it to pay down debts. It's always a good idea to make the most of any surplus funds.

So do yourself a favor and start implementing the 20% rule in your budgeting practices right away. You'll notice a positive difference in your cash flow and overall budgeting efforts. It's a simple yet effective technique that can help you maintain a realistic budget and achieve your financial goals.

Rule #3: Reward Yourself with Treats Along the Way

Here's a little-known secret that successful budgeters swear by: they reward themselves along the way. This practice is especially important for those working with tight budgets and numerous bills to pay. To maintain long-term budget adherence, successful budgeters incorporate planned treats into their financial plans. These treats serve as rewards for practicing good financial behavior.

You have the power to decide what rewards bring you joy and motivate you to stick to your budget. However, it's essential to choose rewards that hold value and won't lead to regretful spending. Let's say you have a passion for photography. Allocate a monthly budget for expenses related to your hobby, such as film, camera equipment, or a photography class. By treating yourself to modest yet meaningful rewards, you won't feel deprived while adhering to your budget.

Rule #4: Include a Savings Category in Your Budget

Did you forget to include a "Savings" category when creating your initial list of expenses? You're not alone. Many people mistakenly assume they can't afford to save or believe there's no room in their budget for savings. However, omitting savings from your budget is a significant financial mistake.

Neglecting to regularly set aside savings sets you up for budgeting failure. Unexpected expenses, such as a flat tire, can quickly throw off your budget or force you to rely on credit cards. Avoid this pitfall by going back and adding a "Savings" category to your budget, regardless of how much or little you can save. Remember, even a small amount contributes to your financial security and helps you handle unforeseen circumstances without derailing your budget.

By adhering to these secrets of successful budgeting, you'll gain control over your finances and set yourself up for long-term financial stability.

How to Create a Strong Financial Plan B

Finally, let's turn to how you can vanquish dollar deficits in the future by creating a strong financial backup plan. If you're ready to improve your overall financial health, there is one simple strategy that can help you achieve economic security and success: creating a financial backup plan, or financial plan B.

The first step is to ask yourself, "What if?" and then come up with preventive or proactive solutions for various potential scenarios. Consider the following situations:

- What if you lose your job? Would you be open to entrepreneurship if reemployment is not an option?
- What if you lose your spouse through death or divorce? Do you have life insurance and a prenuptial agreement in place? Do you have credit in your own name?
- What if you don't get that raise or promotion? Would you regret overspending and not having a cushion to fall back on?

- What if you don't make as much money as you anticipated? Would you still be able to manage your hefty student loans?
- What if your car gets involved in an accident? Do you have the necessary car insurance coverage?
- What if you get sick? Would you lament being uninsured and having no health care coverage?
- What if your child needs surgery? Would medical bills drive you into bankruptcy?
- What if you lose your wallet or your credit cards and personal information get stolen? Would you wish you had looked into identity theft protection?
- What if you lose a big portion or all of your savings/investments? Would you wish you had sought advice from a financial advisor?
- What if you are sued? Would you know how to deal with a lawsuit or court action?
- What if your house is destroyed? Would you be covered with homeowners insurance and know how to avoid contractor scams?
- What if your home needs a major repair? Would you have the extra cash needed to fix things?
- What if your taxes or mortgage/rent payment go up? Would you know how to lower your taxes or consider alternative housing options?
- What if you are fined? Would you know how to earn additional money to avoid living paycheck to paycheck?
- What if your ex stops paying child support? Would you know how to pursue the support that is rightfully due?
- What if the court orders you to pay someone else? Would you have to dip into your retirement funds to meet this obligation?
- What if your wages are garnished? Would you know how to stop wage garnishment?
- What if your employer asks you to relocate, come back into the office full-time or face consequences? Would you have other job or career options?
- What if another financial crisis occurs? Could you and your family survive another recession?
- And finally, what if artificial intelligence takes over the world and kills us all?!

All right, admittedly, I threw that one in there about AI for shock value, but you get the point.

The key takeaway is that the best financial strategy is to do some contingency planning. You need a financial plan B. Consider how you would cope with each scenario and start taking action to mitigate the potential risks.

Today is the perfect day to get serious about fixing your money problems and creating an economic backup plan. Here's how you can start:

Assess your current financial situation: Take stock of your income, expenses, debts, and savings.
Create reserve funds: Set aside a portion of your income specifically for unexpected expenses. Remember: you need both a rainy day fund for one-time events and an emergency fund for bigger, longer-term disruptions to your life.
Develop a comprehensive budget: Track your expenses, prioritize your spending, and allocate funds to savings and future goals. Follow the tips previously offered to become a better budgeter and saver.
Protect yourself with insurance: Review your insurance coverage and ensure you have adequate protection for your home, car, health, and life. This is a huge aspect of financial security!
Diversify your income: Explore additional income streams such as freelancing, part-time work, or starting a side business. Gone are the days when you could just rely on one source of income forever.
Educate yourself about personal finance: Learn about investing, retirement planning, and other financial strategies to secure your future.
Seek professional advice: Consult with a financial advisor to get personalized guidance tailored to your specific needs and goals.
Stay updated on economic trends: Keeping an eye on local, national, and global economic trends can help you adjust your financial strategies accordingly. This might involve making certain investments or avoiding others based on the economic climate.
Maintain a flexible attitude: The financial world is constantly evolving. Whether it's a shift in job markets or the introduction of new financial tools and products, be willing to adapt and make changes to your backup plan as needed.

Creating a financial backup plan is a dynamic process, one that evolves with time and changing circumstances. Continuously reassess your plan, adapt to fresh challenges, and stay proactive in managing your finances. Armed with a robust plan B, you can confidently face the ebb and flow of life's financial tides, ensuring not just survival, but prosperity.

Dollar Deficit Resources

1. **AARP Foundation** – provides referrals to free or money-saving resources.
2. **America Saves** – Builds wealth through encouraging savings.

3. **Community Action Partnership Agencies** – Local resources to help people become financially stable.
4. **Community Development Financial Institutions (CDFIs)** – Offer financial services in underserved areas.
5. **Local Extension offices of colleges** – Provide money management and budgeting classes.
6. **National Association of Personal Financial Advisors** – Has pro bono planners who assist needy individuals and families.
7. **National Endowment for Financial Education** – Provides financial education programs and resources.
8. **Operation Hope** – Helps with financial literacy and money management skills.
9. **United Way Financial Empowerment Centers** – Offers free financial guidance.
10. **Urban League affiliates** – Helps financially empower residents in underserved communities.

Chapter 12
Discrimination

"Challenges may knock us down, but our ability to bounce back is what will ultimately determine our success."

—Oprah Winfrey

Discrimination, in its many forms, is an insidious issue that permeates societies worldwide. Whether blatant or subtle, discrimination is a deeply rooted problem that hinders individuals and communities from achieving their full potential. And discrimination isn't just an ethical or moral issue; it also carries a significant economic impact that is often overlooked in conversations about personal finances. Yet a litany of discriminatory activities can affect you and those you care about.

The gender pay gap that women face—along with employment discrimination against people of color, immigrants, older adults, the disabled—are forms of workplace inequities that lead to substantial income disparities for these groups. Unfair practices such as redlining and mortgage discrimination—both of which still exist—are forms of housing and credit discrimination that sap wealth and disproportionately impact members of Black and Brown communities. Meanwhile, LGBTQ+ individuals must confront bias in employment, which restricts their financial growth and stability.

As you can see, discrimination infiltrates various areas of life and, in doing so, it can weigh heavily on your personal and financial well-being, your work life, and more. That's one thing Mac McAfee has learned after experiencing discrimination early in his profession—and then learning to bounce back from it and make a whole career out of helping others fight such injustices.

McAfee's discrimination story begins when he was just 23 years old, working as a broadcast engineer in a commercial TV station. Having started repairing equipment and wiring at 19, he eventually founded his own company and went on to win a contract to design five TV stations, a multimillion-dollar project funded by the state legislature. In the TV world, he also won a coveted Emmy award. Despite his evident success, McAfee faced significant barriers due to what he calls "longstanding, systemic racism and discrimination."

It started when McAfee hit his first hurdle: he was unable to secure the required bonding insurance for his project. Every place he turned, financial institutions refused to sell him insurance. This was a frustrating reality, especially since the project was backed by a government bond. To get around the issue, he was told he had to work as a subcontractor for a larger, white architectural firm, CDFL. Under the arrangement, he could rely on the insurance provided by the architectural firm. "I didn't like what that felt like, because it felt like sharecropping," McAfee recalls. Though he detested the structure of the deal, he went through with it.

But his difficulties didn't end there. McAfee then found himself facing financial issues due to delayed payments, a process caused by federal and state laws requiring net 30 or 60 days for payment to subcontractors. Despite being under CDFL's rider, payments were delayed up to 180 days, driving McAfee into further financial distress and risk of foreclosure.

Desperate for resolution, McAfee demanded a $10,000 check, but this only led to the discovery that CDFL had a $500,000 bank line of credit, which they'd used to float their own expenses. Meanwhile, struggling to keep afloat, Mac found himself on the verge of bankruptcy and even had his wages garnished. He took his case to court where the judge acknowledged the validity of his bond and contract, thus ensuring he was paid all his dues.

Yet, the struggle didn't end there either. When McAfee requested a line of credit from the bank, he was met with the shocking revelation that his own company was not legally incorporated, despite having operated, paid taxes to, and received payments from the state of Mississippi for four years. An investigation revealed that an ex-employee of the Secretary of State had pocketed McAfee's incorporation fee, leading to his application never being processed. The Secretary of State wrote a letter confirming the misdeed. Nonetheless, without incorporation, the bank refused to provide McAfee with credit.

McAfee's story highlights the challenges many minority business owners face. Despite designing successful TV stations and showing exceptional skills, he still grappled with financial instability and discrimination. He likens this to redlining and gentrification, perpetual and systemic barriers that disadvantage racial and ethnic minorities. That situation didn't deter him though. Far from it. The incident served as a catalyst for his lifelong work and activism.

Today, McAfee advocates for and represents a host of clients when these individuals face various race-related violations, discrimination, or predatory practices. In many ways, his role is part strategic counselor, part business advisor, and part fixer—due to his dogged determination in overcoming obstacles he or his clients encounter. "I'm here to accelerate change and positive outcomes," he says. In both his personal life and his work life, McAfee is keenly aware of the setbacks and struggles that persist but refuses to let them define him or his success. He cites a series of 2023 Supreme Court cases—including one banning affirmative action in higher education—as examples of how progress for African Americans has always been met by legal challenges and the "rolling back" of any gains secured.

As a result, "Bouncing back is a perpetual process if you're Black in America," McAfee says. "When you get out of one frying pan, you're constantly in another." But it's not the economic hardship that he considers most damaging. "What racism and discrimination does in demoralizing a human is way more significant than its financial implications. It's unquantifiable," McAfee notes.

No one person's story can ever capture the fullness of discrimination, given the diversity of human experiences. And these are complex issues, to be sure. But by understanding at least the main issues confronted by marginalized groups, we can foster empathy and promote much-needed awareness for action. Additionally, by presenting these topics in a straightforward and accessible manner, it's my hope that you'll grasp an inkling of the full scope of the problem and its profound financial implications. Ultimately, I want you to be aware of the discrimination barriers you have faced or continue to face, what others face, and what you can do about these issues. Even if you've never experienced an ounce of discrimination in your life, I hope that some of what you read here will inspire you to be a part of the solution.

In this chapter, you will learn:

- How discrimination hurts us all;
- All about employment discrimination and the gender pay gap;
- Some facts about redlining and mortgage and housing discrimination;

- An understanding of racial discrimination and its financial impact;
- Why age discrimination is wrong and its financial impact;
- All about gender discrimination, shattering the glass ceiling, and the "pink tax";
- Some insights into LGBTQ+ discrimination;
- Facts about disability discrimination and financial access;
- Five strategies for dealing with discrimination;
- A framework for healing from workplace discrimination.

How Discrimination Hurts Us All

Various forms of discrimination don't just affect a person's wallet—it also produces harmful outcomes that affect everyone.

Where there's discrimination, entire communities get left behind. That's the case, for instance, in low-income neighborhoods where there's a lack of banking services, which causes a ripple effect of financial disadvantages. Where there's credit discrimination, underrepresented entrepreneurs lack access to capital and financing—stifling economic growth and innovation. Where there's health care discrimination, individuals from marginalized groups face barriers to accessing quality medical treatment, preventative care, and insurance coverage. This leads to poorer health outcomes, higher mortality rates, and increased public health risks that affect entire communities. And where gender discrimination exists, say, in STEM fields, society loses out on the unique perspectives and innovations women too could bring.

And that's not all. Discrimination disrupts social cohesion and trust. Discrimination breeds animosity, mistrust, and division among different groups within a society. It perpetuates stereotypes, fosters misunderstanding, and hampers the building of relationships and cooperation among diverse communities. Such divisions can lead to social unrest, conflict, and even violence, affecting the overall stability and peace in the society. This harms everyone, as people live in constant tension and fear.

Discrimination also has significant economic costs. When discrimination exists in the workplace, it often results in job dissatisfaction, decreased productivity, and increased turnover. These factors can adversely impact the profitability of businesses and, on a larger scale, the economy. Furthermore, dealing with lawsuits and settlements related to discrimination can be financially burdensome for businesses and the state. Ultimately, the economic costs of discrimination are borne by everyone in the form of decreased economic output, lower incomes, and increased prices.

In short, discrimination is not just an issue for those directly affected by it, but it has wide-ranging repercussions for everyone in society. It can inhibit societal progress, undermine social cohesion and trust, and create economic burdens. Consequently, by reducing discrimination, we can bring about a more equitable, harmonious, and prosperous society.

All About Employment Discrimination and the Gender Pay Gap

Discrimination in the workplace is a widespread issue that affects millions worldwide. It comes in many forms, each with its own financial implications. The gender pay gap, racial and ethnic discrimination, discrimination based on sexual orientation, and more, all contribute to an unequal workplace that not only hampers individual employees but also families, communities, and the overall economy.

Let's start by examining the gender pay gap. The gender pay gap is a stark indicator of discrimination, representing the difference in median earnings between men and women. According to the latest data from the US Census Bureau, women in America earn 82 cents for every dollar earned by men. For many women of color, the pay gap is even wider. For example, Black women earn only 64 cents and Latina women earn just 54 cents for each dollar earned by their white male counterparts. This discrepancy isn't just about fairness—it translates to a significant financial loss for women over their working life and into their golden years. Because women are getting shortchanged on the job, we retire with 30% less money than men—or a potential $1.6 million less in retirement savings, according to the financial services firm TIAA.

Employment discrimination doesn't stop there. Racial and ethnic discrimination, for example, also has significant financial implications. Imagine being as qualified as anyone else for a job but being turned down because of your race or the color of your skin. Or consider the reality for many people with ethnic-sounding names whose applications are overlooked—a phenomenon known as name bias. Likewise, discrimination based on sexual orientation can negatively impact job opportunities and wages. The Center for American Progress found that between 11% and 28% of LGBTQ+ workers reported losing a promotion simply because of their sexual orientation, and transgender individuals have unemployment rates three times higher than the national average.

Workplace discrimination also impacts individuals with disabilities. Despite possessing qualifications and capabilities, these individuals often face employer doubt and unwillingness to make reasonable accommodations. This is disability discrimination, akin to being an excellent swimmer but being barred from competition because the pool lacks an accessible entrance.

Further, gender and age discrimination still persists. Picture a woman in a male-dominated field, overlooked for promotions or given less-challenging assignments despite her qualifications. Or envision an older worker, valuable for their experience and wisdom, but neglected by employers favoring younger, cheaper hires. These scenarios represent gender and age discrimination, respectively, and they're as unjust as a strong runner being confined to slow heats or a skilled football player left on the bench due to age.

So how can we promote workplace equality? Implementing comprehensive anti-discrimination policies, fostering a diverse and inclusive workplace culture, and ensuring transparent and unbiased hiring and promotion processes are key steps. Moreover, enforcement of equal pay laws and commitment to pay transparency can significantly bridge the gender pay gap. At an individual level, if you encounter workplace discrimination, you can also speak out against it or challenge policies that unfairly disadvantage one group to another.

Some Facts About Redlining and Mortgage and Housing Discrimination

Housing discrimination is a pervasive issue with far-reaching financial consequences. From redlining and mortgage discrimination to the appraisal gap, predatory lending, racial steering, exclusionary zoning, and disability discrimination, these practices create unfair hurdles for many individuals, especially among minority and low-income populations, when trying to secure a home.

Redlining, a practice that began in the 1930s, involved banks and other financial institutions refusing or limiting loans, mortgages, and insurance within specific geographic areas, often inner-city neighborhoods predominantly occupied by Black communities. Despite being officially illegal since the 1960s, forms of redlining continue to exist. For instance, insurers may charge higher premiums to customers in certain areas based on data like credit scores, indirectly leading to discrimination against low-income or minority communities.

Another form of housing discrimination is the appraisal gap. This refers to when a property, typically in a predominantly Black or Hispanic neighborhood, is undervalued compared to similar homes in predominantly white neighborhoods. This undervaluation can impact homeowners looking to sell or refinance their homes, potentially leading to significant financial loss over time. The appraisal gap can also strike Black homeowners when they live in predominantly white neighborhoods. That's exactly what happened to me when my husband, Earl, and I lived in an upper-middle-class town called Mountainside, New Jersey. We were once looking to get a home equity line of credit (HELOC) on our home in Mountainside but experienced blatant appraisal bias. Here's what happened.

My Experience with Appraisal Bias and the Appraisal Gap

Before obtaining the HELOC, our home needed to undergo an appraisal. However, as soon as the appraiser arrived, we sensed that things were not going to go smoothly. The appraiser, an elderly Caucasian man, arrived at our doorstep, quickly assessed us, and hurried through the process of measuring, evaluating, and photographing our three-bedroom, three-bathroom house. Mountainside, New Jersey, is a well-to-do suburb located about 45 minutes away from New York City. And our home was a very nice property, complete with a full basement and pool.

Whenever we tried to ask questions or offer information about the upgrades and improvements we had made, we were met with dismissive and abrupt responses. Sadly, we were not entirely surprised when the appraiser's report returned with a valuation that was approximately $100,000 lower than the recently sold prices of comparable houses in our neighborhood, despite the fact that we had just invested $40,000 in renovating our kitchen. As African Americans, we were aware that it was not uncommon for homeowners like us to receive undervalued appraisals due to bias.

Fast-forward to early 2022, during the peak of the real estate market just before it began to soften. We had since moved to an affluent suburb of Houston, Texas. Our close friends, who are Hispanic, were also seeking a HELOC for their five-bedroom home during the first half of that year. When they provided the appraiser (another elderly Caucasian man) with data about a nearly identical property right across the street that had recently been sold, the appraiser responded, "Oh, you don't want me to compare your house to that property."

Their appraisal returned with a value of approximately $53,000 lower than similar homes that had sold, and the appraiser used outdated sales data and less relevant properties in his report.

In both instances, we and our friends appealed these underestimated appraisals, strongly believing that we were initially victims of racial discrimination by the appraisers.

In our case, after we filed an appeal for the appallingly low initial appraisal, a second appraiser was assigned, surprisingly a Black man. We never mentioned to him what had happened previously, but he seemed to intuitively understand the underlying issue. He meticulously took photographs, carefully measured our property, and then he offered us some advice that left us astounded: he suggested removing all the pictures of our Black family that adorned our walls.

My husband was furious at the mere thought of complying with this request. It felt profoundly unjust—an erasure of our identity and an absurd tactic to combat toxic racism. Initially, Earl contemplated refusing and asking the appraiser to leave our home. In the end, he reluctantly relented. We took down the pictures, begrudgingly allowing the appraiser to capture images of our "neutral-looking" house. When the appraisal was finally completed, the value came back $100,000 higher.

If you do an Internet search of the phrase "appraisal bias," you'll find tons of stories of Black homeowners who've had similar experiences.

The Pitfalls of Predatory Lending

Predatory lending is also a significant issue. This practice involves lenders targeting racial minorities and low-income individuals with loans that have high interest rates or hidden fees. The financial burden of these loans can lead to financial instability and, in some cases, foreclosure.

Racial steering involves real estate agents showing homes to potential buyers based only in certain neighborhoods and steering them away from others based on their race or ethnicity. This practice can limit the housing choices available to minority homebuyers and contribute to residential segregation.

Exclusionary zoning involves local zoning laws limiting the construction of multi-family or low-income housing units in certain areas. This practice often disproportionately affects people of color and low-income families, restricting their access to affordable housing.

Disability discrimination in housing refers to situations where homes aren't accessible to people with disabilities or landlords refuse to make reasonable accommodations. This form of discrimination can make it difficult for people with disabilities to secure suitable housing.

Mortgage discrimination involves banks offering harsher loan terms or outright denying services based on an applicant's race. Like redlining, this practice has contributed to racial disparities in homeownership and wealth accumulation.

Combating Housing Discrimination

Combatting these forms of discrimination involves a range of strategies, from policy reform and regulatory enforcement to community advocacy and public education. For instance, the Fair Housing Act of 1968 prohibits discrimination in the sale, rental, or financing of housing based on race, color, national origin, religion, sex, familial status, or disability. However, enforcement of this law can be inconsistent, and many instances of discrimination go unreported or unresolved.

Furthermore, recent research has highlighted the role of technology in perpetuating housing discrimination. For example, online advertising platforms such as Facebook have been criticized for their role in facilitating discriminatory advertising practices. Although Facebook profiles do not explicitly state users' race or ethnicity, research has shown that Facebook's advertising algorithms can discriminate based on these factors. This can lead to the exclusion of certain demographic groups from seeing housing or employment ads, a violation of civil rights laws. In response to these issues, Facebook has faced lawsuits and has made some changes to its ad targeting system, but concerns remain about the potential for discrimination.

To fully address housing discrimination, it's essential to tackle these issues on multiple fronts, from strengthening and enforcing anti-discrimination laws to scrutinizing and reforming the practices of financial institutions and technology companies. By doing so, we can work toward a future where everyone has an equal opportunity to secure a safe and comfortable place to live.

An Understanding of Racial Discrimination and Its Financial Impact

Racial discrimination refers to the unfair treatment of individuals based on their race or ethnicity, leading to disparities in various aspects of life, including education, employment, housing, health care, and access to financial resources. By examining the economic consequences of these various forms of discrimination, we can work toward dismantling systemic barriers and promoting racial equity for all.

Racial discrimination in housing also denies individuals from racial minority groups the opportunity to live in desirable and resource-rich communities, impacting their access to quality schools, health care, and economic opportunities. Consequently, racial discrimination contributes to a significant wealth gap, with individuals from racial minority groups facing limited access to wealth-building opportunities such as homeownership, business ownership, and intergenerational wealth transfer.

Unfortunately, from an economic standpoint, a lot of racial discrimination against vulnerable populations can be found through various forms of financial services discrimination.

Consider the unequal treatment and limited access to financial services experienced by individuals from racial minority groups. Racial discrimination in the financial sector can manifest in higher interest rates, stricter lending criteria, and limited access to credit and investment opportunities.

Banking Deserts in Low-income Neighborhoods

Imagine living in a neighborhood where there are no banks or financial institutions within a reasonable distance. This is the reality for many individuals and families in low-income neighborhoods, commonly referred to as banking deserts.

It's tough trying to manage your finances without access to traditional banking services. In banking deserts, people often resort to alternative financial services such as check-cashing stores, payday lenders, or pawnshops, which often charge high fees and offer limited financial products. This can lead to increased financial vulnerability, a cycle of debt, and limited opportunities for savings and wealth building. But we don't have to just accept these conditions. There are some strategies we can use—and advocate for—to improve banking access in underserved areas.

Each of the following ideas can help address the issue of banking deserts and improve banking access in low-income neighborhoods:

Community development financial institutions (CDFIs): CDFIs are specialized financial institutions dedicated to serving underserved communities. These institutions can provide affordable banking services, loans, and financial education tailored to the needs of the community.

Mobile banking and financial technology: The implementation of mobile banking and financial technology solutions can bridge the physical distance between individuals and traditional banking services. Mobile banking apps and digital platforms can provide convenient access to basic banking services, allowing individuals to manage their finances, make transactions, and save money without the need for a physical bank branch.

Partnerships between banks and community organizations: Collaborations between banks and community organizations to establish banking services in underserved areas can and do also work. By working together, banks can gain insights into the specific needs of the community and tailor their services accordingly.

Financial education and empowerment: Another necessary component is financial education programs targeted at low-income neighborhoods, providing individuals with the knowledge and skills to make informed financial decisions, manage their money, and build wealth.

Policy initiatives: Lastly, we can all advocate for the development of policy initiatives that incentivize banks to establish branches in underserved areas and ensure equitable access to banking services.

Why Age Discrimination Is Wrong and Its Financial Impact

Age discrimination refers to the unfair treatment of individuals based on their age, particularly in the workplace. This happens in a variety of ways. Imagine being a highly skilled and experienced worker but finding it increasingly challenging to secure employment due to age bias. Age discrimination can limit job opportunities for older workers, leading to lower-paid work, prolonged unemployment, and financial instability. In many cases, older workers subjected to workplace discrimination find themselves working alongside colleagues who perform similar tasks and have comparable qualifications. However, due to age discrimination, the older worker consistently receives lower compensation or is denied pay raises and bonuses compared to their younger counterparts.

Now imagine having the ambition to climb the career ladder and take on more senior roles but facing barriers and biases that prevent you from advancing due to your age. In such a workplace, training and development opportunities are predominantly offered to younger employees, while older workers are overlooked. All this age discrimination can result in limited access to skill enhancement programs, leaving older workers at a disadvantage in a rapidly changing job market. It's like being a dedicated runner, committed to improving your technique, but being denied access to coaching and training resources. Ultimately, age discrimination hinders career progression, denying older individuals their rightful opportunity to maximize their earning potential and financial growth.

All About Gender Discrimination, Shattering the Glass Ceiling, and the Pink Tax

I've explained how women earn far less money than men for doing the same job. But that's not the only form of employment discrimination that can hurt a woman's pocketbook. There's also the problem of occupational segregation. We've all seen this. It's a workforce where certain industries or positions are predominantly occupied by individuals of a specific gender. Occupational segregation perpetuates gender discrimination by limiting women's access to higher-paying or male-dominated fields, leading to restricted earning potential and financial inequality.

Even though in some ways, more women are shattering the glass ceiling, there is still a lot of work to be done to gain anything resembling parity in the workplace. That's why operating in mostly male environments is nothing new to some women, particularly those who aspire to reach leadership positions within an organization. As of this writing, there are 52 female CEOs in the Fortune 500, meaning women now helm 10% of America's biggest companies. This may sound great. But 12 of these CEOs were just hired in the past year or so, marking the highest number of female-led companies to date. For many years, though, there were only a handful of these female chief executives, according to *Fortune* magazine. These stats alone suggest that women are constantly encountering invisible barriers that prevent their upward mobility. The glass ceiling represents the unspoken limitations and biases that hinder women's career advancement, limiting their access to higher-level positions and accompanying financial rewards.

Now consider the "pink tax," a phenomenon where products marketed toward women, such as personal care items or clothing, are priced higher than similar products marketed toward men. The pink tax represents an additional financial burden for women, as they are forced to pay more for essential products solely based on their gender.

To fight back against the pink tax you can do any of the following seven actions:

Be a conscious consumer: Compare prices of similar products across different brands and gender classifications. Don't let gender-based marketing guide your buying choices. If the men's version of a product is cheaper and essentially the same, don't hesitate to buy it instead.

Support equal pricing brands: Encourage businesses that practice gender-neutral pricing by choosing to buy their products over those with a pink tax.

Show your support for these brands and spread the word about them among your social networks. Case in point: CVS Health in 2022 announced a 25% price cut on its own brand of menstrual products, including pads, tampons, liners, and menstrual cups, in stores nationwide. Furthermore, the company is covering the sales tax on these products in 12 states, countering the practice of many states that tax menstrual products as "luxury items."

Speak out: Use your voice and platform to raise awareness about the pink tax. This could be through social media, blogs, or even conversations with friends and family. The more people know about this issue, the more pressure there will be on companies to eliminate discriminatory pricing.

Advocate for legislative change: Contact your representatives or participate in advocacy campaigns to call for laws that ban gender-based pricing. Some areas have already enacted laws against the pink tax, and your activism could help expand these protections.

Educate others: Many people are unaware of the pink tax and its impact on women. By informing others, you can help grow a community of informed consumers who resist gender-based price discrimination.

Report discriminatory pricing: If your local jurisdiction has laws against gender-based price discrimination, report violations to the appropriate government agency.

Support women-owned businesses: Women-owned businesses are more likely to be aware of the pink tax and less likely to participate in discriminatory pricing. By supporting these businesses, you contribute to a marketplace that is fairer and more equitable.

These actions can help combat the pink tax, but ultimately, widespread change will come from concerted effort from consumers, businesses, and lawmakers.

Some Insights into LGBTQ+ Discrimination

Imagine a world where you can't be your authentic self, where you face prejudice and discrimination simply because of your sexual orientation or gender identity. LGBTQ+ individuals often confront various forms of discrimination, including employment bias, limited access to health care, and unequal treatment under the law. You might be a talented professional seeking a new job. However, when employers learn about your LGBTQ+ identity, they hesitate to hire you or offer you promotions.

Unequal Access to Health Care and Other Services or Opportunities

Now, imagine needing health care but being met with health care providers who refuse to treat you or provide necessary services due to their personal beliefs or biases. This is unequal access to health care, and it puts your physical and emotional health at risk. It might also cost you money—if you have to schedule additional doctors' appointments with other practitioners or drive out of your way just to find someone who will treat you.

Picture yourself searching for a place to live, too, but landlords deny you housing because of your LGBTQ+ identity. LGBTQ+ individuals often face housing and rental discrimination, making it difficult to find safe and welcoming homes.

You might even have the desire to build a family through adoption. LGBTQ+ couples may encounter adoption agencies that refuse to work with them or discriminate against them based on their sexual orientation or gender identity.

All these forms of discrimination have significant financial consequences for LGBTQ+ individuals and families. Limited employment opportunities, unequal access to health care, housing discrimination, and barriers to starting a family can hinder financial stability and wealth accumulation.

To foster a more inclusive society, it is essential to promote LGBTQ+ rights and fight against discrimination. This includes advocating for comprehensive antidiscrimination laws, workplace policies that protect LGBTQ+ individuals, and inclusive health care practices. Creating safe and affirming spaces, supporting LGBTQ+-owned businesses, and fostering education and understanding are also vital steps toward inclusion. By dismantling discriminatory practices, we can build a society where LGBTQ+ individuals can thrive financially and be their authentic selves. With these steps, hopefully we can one day create a more just and inclusive society that celebrates the diversity and contributions of all individuals, regardless of sexual orientation or gender identity.

Facts About Disability Discrimination and Financial Access

You'll recall the chapter on disability and the story of Chris Powell. He's working at a college, but in some ways, his achievements are the exception rather than the rule, as discrimination faced by individuals with disabilities is rampant. Imagine navigating a world where you're judged based on your physical or cognitive abilities rather than your skills and talents. Individuals with disabilities face various forms of discrimination, including limited employment opportunities, unequal access to public spaces, and societal stigma.

Barriers to Financial Access

Picture yourself needing to open a bank account or obtain a loan, but the bank doesn't have accessible facilities or the staff lacks disability awareness. This lack of accessibility creates barriers to financial access for individuals with disabilities. It's like being ready to start a race but being told that the starting line is only accessible to certain participants.

Limited Employment Opportunities

Now, imagine having the skills and qualifications for a job, but employers hesitate to hire you because of your disability. This is employment discrimination based on disability, and it's like being an excellent cyclist but being denied the opportunity to compete because of the type of bike you ride.

Promoting Disability Rights and Financial Inclusion

It is crucial to promote disability rights and foster financial inclusion for individuals with disabilities. This includes advocating for accessible financial services, encouraging inclusive employment practices, and raising awareness about the abilities and potential of individuals with disabilities. Creating accessible physical and digital environments, providing financial literacy programs tailored to individuals with disabilities, and promoting disability representation are important steps toward fostering financial empowerment and inclusion.

Discrimination faced by individuals with disabilities creates significant barriers to financial access and stability. By advocating for disability rights, promoting inclusive practices, and fostering financial inclusion, we can work toward a society where individuals with disabilities have equal opportunities to participate in the economy and achieve the financial well-being that they deserve, just like everyone else.

It's important to recognize that discrimination is not a series of isolated incidents, but a web of systemic biases woven into the very fabric of our society. These discriminatory practices not only hinder individual progress but also perpetuate intergenerational cycles of inequality. They erode trust, stifle innovation, and hinder our collective potential for economic prosperity.

However, there's power in advocacy, policy reform, and collective action in dismantling discriminatory structures and promoting equality.

To move forward, we must continue the dialogue, challenge the status quo, and actively work toward a more just and inclusive society. We must advocate for fair housing policies, equal employment opportunities, and comprehensive anti-discrimination laws. We must push for inclusive financial systems that provide equal access to credit, banking services, and insurance. We must invest in education, health care, and social programs that address the root causes of systemic discrimination.

Change starts with awareness and empathy. I asked you to picture yourself as various individuals to help you put yourself in someone else's shoes. It's a far cry from what marginalized individuals deal with on a daily basis. But it's a start. By understanding the financial consequences of discrimination, we can better comprehend the urgency of dismantling these barriers. We must strive for a society where every individual, regardless of their race, gender, sexual orientation, disability, or age, can access equal opportunities and fulfill their personal and financial aspirations. Financial stability is a right, not a privilege.

Five Strategies for Dealing with Discrimination

I understand that being a victim of discrimination is a deeply hurtful experience. Here are five strategies that you can use to fight back and heal emotionally:

Speak up: Don't let fear silence you. When you encounter discrimination, whether it's based on your race, gender, religion, or other aspects of your identity, take a stand. Document and report the incident to the relevant authorities, such as your school or workplace management, or law enforcement if necessary. You can also share your experiences with friends, family, or a supportive community who can help you through this difficult time.

Find support: Connect with people who understand your experience. This could be a support group, counselor, or organizations that work with people who have experienced similar forms of discrimination. They can offer guidance, empathy, and resources to help you cope and fight back against the discrimination you're facing. African Americans can also join a healing community for Black people such as Therapy for Black Men or Ethel's Club. For African American professionals, joining Black mental health organizations is an effective way to find a community of others who can identify with your issues and make you feel seen and heard. If you can afford therapy, seek out Black psychologists and psychiatrists as well.

Take care of your mental health: Experiencing discrimination can take a toll on your emotional well-being. It's important to prioritize self-care. This can take different forms for different people but may include activities such as exercising regularly, maintaining a balanced diet, getting enough sleep, and engaging in relaxation techniques such as meditation or yoga. Seek professional help if you feel overwhelmed or have symptoms of anxiety or depression.

Aja Evans, the therapist who specializes in financial matters, notes that many Black women who have suffered various forms of discrimination—such as being followed in a retail store—may unconsciously act in ways that don't serve their best interest, such as choosing, to buy an expensive purse—just to show that store clerk or owner following you around that you can afford it. "With microaggressions, the things you internalize tend to show up in what you do with your money," Evans says.

When facing a stressful situation such as discrimination or any other Dreaded D, Evans says that after acknowledging your feelings about the circumstances, self-care should be a priority. She urges women, in particular, to adopt a more expansive view of taking care of themselves, noting that getting your hair and nails done isn't the only way to pamper yourself.

"Journaling, gardening, dancing, listening to music, and even just talking to a good friend—anything can be a coping skill and a form of self-care if it's helpful or calming to you," Evans says.

Educate yourself and others: Knowledge is power. Educate yourself about your rights and the laws that protect you against discrimination. This information can empower you to take appropriate action when you face discrimination. Equally important is educating others around you about the harmful effects of discrimination. You can initiate conversations, share your experiences, and challenge stereotypes to foster understanding and empathy.

Engage in activism: Channel your experiences into making positive changes in your community. Join or start advocacy initiatives to address the issue of discrimination. This could be through awareness campaigns, policy changes, or supporting organizations that fight against discrimination. It's a proactive way to regain control and fight back against the discrimination you've experienced, while also preventing others from experiencing similar hurt.

Remember, it's crucial to not let the discriminatory actions of others define your self-worth or limit your potential. Be patient with yourself as healing takes time, and you should always seek professional help if the emotional burden becomes too overwhelming. You are not alone in this fight.

A Framework for Healing from Workplace Discrimination

Minda Harts is a career development specialist and the author of *Right Within: How to Heal from Racial Trauma in the Workplace*. In *Right Within*, Harts shares a tool for navigating harm in the workplace, called The Affirmation Pyramid. The pyramid has five components with corresponding strategies she recommends. Here are Harts's five suggestions, in order, for healing from workplace discrimination:

Pause. Give yourself the space and grace to process what happened. You do not have to immediately move into action.

Acknowledge. Acknowledge to yourself that what happened was wrong and harmed you regardless of another person's intention. You don't have to make excuses for others.

Document. This is primarily for yourself. This will allow you to trust yourself, recall specifics, and trust what happened even if others doubt you. Documentation can also help later, legally, if you need it.

Redirect That Energy. We often hold on to the harm and can get stuck in thought spirals. This can impact your stress and mental health. Ensure you are releasing this stress in healthy ways, such as therapy, exercise, or meditation.

Affirm. Constantly remind yourself that you deserve human dignity, equity, and respect in the workplace. You did not do anything to cause the harm done to you.

With this five-step framework, Harts provides actionable advice for processing and moving forward after experiencing discrimination at work. By pausing, acknowledging, documenting, redirecting energy, and self-affirming, you can begin to heal and regain your sense of self-worth.

Congratulations and an Invitation

We've come to the end of *Bounce Back*. Congratulations on completing this book! Financial recovery and emotional renewal are ongoing processes. They require patience, perseverance, and a positive mindset. There may be times when you face additional setbacks or encounter unexpected obstacles. Remember that setbacks are not failures but opportunities for growth and resilience. Trust in your ability to adapt, problem-solve, and find creative solutions.

This journey wasn't just about bouncing back from a specific Dreaded D—such as downsizing, divorce, or debt—but also about finding a renewed sense of purpose, redefining your priorities, and embracing the possibilities that lie ahead. Use the knowledge and tools you have acquired to create a life that aligns with your values, passions, and goals.

As you conclude *Bounce Back*, I encourage you to also pick up a copy of *The Bounce Back Workbook* to do a personalized deep dive into different concepts and to customize various insights according to your unique circumstances and needs. It's my prayer that in doing so, you'll carry with you the lessons learned, the strength you have cultivated, and the aspirations that fuel your spirit. You have the power to shape your future and build a life of security, purpose, and fulfillment. But when things get tough, remember that you are not alone on this journey. During times of change—and when you're in transition, trying to process that change—reach out to family and friends for support, seek external guidance from professionals when needed, and draw upon the inner resources that reside within you as well. Believe in and be kind to yourself, embrace your challenges as opportunities, and continue to move forward with confidence, hope, and resilience.

Let me extend one final offer of support and encouragement. I'd love to hear your tale of resilience and growth and cheer you on. So I invite you to email me any feedback you'd care to share, any lessons you've learned from *Bounce Back*, or any progress you've made to recover from a Dreaded D emotionally or financially. You can message me at `info@AskTheMoneyCoach.com`. Please put "Bounce Back reader" in the subject line so I can prioritize these messages.

Here's to you bouncing back stronger than ever!

Discrimination Resources

1. **AARP** – Addresses age discrimination.
2. **Anti-Defamation League** – Fights against anti-Semitism and bias.
3. **Asian American Justice Center/Asian Americans Advancing Justice** – Advances the civil and human rights of Asian Americans.
4. **Disability Rights Education and Defense Fund** – Advances the rights of the disabled.

5. **Equal Rights Advocates** – Provides gender discrimination legal help.
6. **GLAAD** – Advocacy for LGBTQ community.
7. **Mexican American Legal Defense Fund** – Advocacy for Latino civil rights.
8. **NAACP** – Seeks equality for people of color.
9. **National Urban League** – Community Empowerment for African Americans.
10. **National Women's Law Center** – Advocates for policies helping women and families.

Research Resources

Introduction

LendingTree study on bad credit: https://www.lendingtree.com/personal/credit-scores-financial-products-survey/.

Pew Charitable Trusts research on financial shocks affecting 60% of US households Pew Charitable Trust report – Oct. 2015: https://www.pewtrusts.org/~/media/assets/2015/10/emergency-savings-report-1_artfinal.pdf.

Pew Charitable Trust report – Nov. 2015: https://www.pewtrusts.org/-/media/assets/2015/11/emergencysavingsreportnov2015.pdf.

Pew Charitable Trust report – Oct. 2017: https://www.pewtrusts.org/-/media/assets/2017/10/rs_financial_shocks_put_retirement_security_at_risk.pdf.

President Biden signed Executive Order 14058 in December 2021: https://www.whitehouse.gov/briefing-room/presidential-actions/2021/12/13/executive-order-on-transforming-federal-customer-experience-and-service-delivery-to-rebuild-trust-in-government/.

New York City study of Gender Pricing: https://www.nyc.gov/assets/dca/downloads/pdf/partners/Study-of-Gender-Pricing-in-NYC.pdf.

California Senate Committee research on the pink tax: https://sjud.senate.ca.gov/sites/sjud.senate.ca.gov/files/2.18.2020_sjud_gender_pricing_info_hearing_background_paper.pdf.

Chapter 1: Resilience and Grit in the Face of Adversity, Transition, and Change

John Elway and "The Drive" in front of 80,000 fans in Cleveland: https://www.denverbroncos.com/news/legend-and-legacy-the-drive-14983643.

Additional Background on Elway and "The Drive": https://www.cbsnews.com/news/john-elway-the-drive/.

William Bridges's 1979/1980 book, *Transitions*, along with the 40th-anniversary book (Dec. 2019), and info about the author and wife Susan Bridges: https://www.amazon.com/Transitions-Making-Sense-Lifes-Changes/dp/0201000822/ref=monarch_sidesheet https://www.amazon.com/Transitions-Making-Sense-Lifes-Changes-dp-0738285404/dp/0738285404/ref=dp_ob_title_bk.

William Bridges's 1991 book, *Managing Transitions*: https://www.amazon.com/Managing-Transitions-Making-Most-Change/dp/0201550733/ref=pd_vtp_h_vft_none_pd_vtp_h_vft_none_sccl_1/140-6199958-8158105?pd_rd_w=qlz26&content-id=amzn1.sym.a5610dee-0db9-4ad9-a7a9-14285a430f83&pf_rd_p=a5610dee-0db9-4ad9-a7a9-14285a430f83&pf_rd_r=CVY4RZN2WCSMZZJ1R5W6&pd_rd_wg=Ru57m&pd_rd_r=794f18ba-52c0-415a-b15a-1681312ec2ce&pd_rd_i=0201550733&psc=1.

Sudden Money Institute founded in 2000: https://www.suddenmoney.com/our-story.

Sudden Money Institute Transitions Journal: https://s3.amazonaws.com/kajabi-storefronts-production/sites/177943/themes/2148847918/downloads/nMyHCFyORfyRxDxbRc92_SMI_Transitions_Journal.pdf.

Research of Psychologist Angela Duckworth: https://angeladuckworth.com/research/.

Financial Resilience Institute definition of financial resilience (p. 9): https://prospercanada.org/getattachment/News-Media/News/The-Financial-Resilience-Institute-releases-two-ne/Financially-Vulnerable-Ecosystem-Report_Jan10.pdf.aspx;?lang=en-US.

Financial Resilience Institute findings that 78% of Canadians are financially vulnerable and not financially resilient (p. 60): https://prospercanada.org/getattachment/News-Media/News/The-Financial-Resilience-Institute-releases-two-ne/Financially-Vulnerable-Ecosystem-Report_Jan10.pdf.aspx;?lang=en-US.

Financial Health Network estimates that 70% of Americans are not financially healthy (p. 14); and measures of financial health related to saving, spending, borrowing, and planning (p. 11): https://finhealthnetwork.org/research/financial-health-pulse-2022-u-s-trends-report/.

Bankrate survey abound banking fees disparities: https://www.bankrate.com/banking/checking/checking-account-fees-disparity-survey/.

McKinsey study on bank fees charged in Black vs. white neighborhoods (p. 18): https://www.mckinsey.com/~/media/mckinsey/industries/public%20and%20social%20sector/our%20insights/the%20economic%20impact%20of%20closing%20the%20racial%20wealth%20gap/the-economic-impact-of-closing-the-racial-wealth-gap-final.pdf.

Economist Daniel Kahneman won Nobel Prize: https://www.apa.org/monitor/dec02/nobel.html.

Nobel Prize winner Daniel Kahneman's research and others showing 80% to 90% of financial decisions are emotional: https://www.nobelprize.org/uploads/2018/06/kahnemann-lecture.pdf https://baritessler.com/2021/04/85-of-our-money-decisions-are-based-on-our-emotions/ https://savology.com/the-psychology-of-money.

AI Replika – the artificial intelligence: https://replika.com/.

AI Replika marketing on App store as "a friend with no judgment, drama, or social anxiety": https://apps.apple.com/lt/app/replika-virtual-ai-gpt-friend/id1158555867.

Researcher Dr. Michael Ungar: https://www.michaelungar.com/.

Research Kenneth Ginsburg: http://www.fosteringresilience.com/about.php.

Chapter 2: Building Your Resilience

Ben Hardy book, *The Gap and the Gain*: https://www.amazon.com/Gap-Gain-Achievers-Happiness-Confidence/dp/1401964362.

Saundra Davis, founder of Sage Financial: http://sagefinancialsolutions.org/ https://www.linkedin.com/in/saundradavis/.

CivicScience poll with nearly half of Americans admitting they don't drink enough water: https://civicscience.com/forty-seven-percent-of-americans-dont-drink-enough-water-plus-more-h2o-insights/#:~:text=The%20latest%20CivicScience%20polling%20shows,drink%20more%20than%20eight%20glasses.

Additional Background info on strategies to promote resilience, journaling and self-care.
Source: Khoury, B., Sharma, M., Rush, S.E., and Fournier, C. (2015). "Mindfulness-based Stress Reduction for Healthy Individuals: A Meta-analysis." *Journal of Psychosomatic Research*, 78(6), 519–528: https://doi.org/10.1016/j.jpsychores.2015.03.009.
Source: Emmons, R.A., and McCullough, M.E. (2003). "Counting Blessings versus Burdens: An Experimental Investigation of Gratitude and Subjective Well-being in Daily Life." *Journal of Personality and Social Psychology*, 84(2), 377–389. https://doi.org/10.1037/0022-3514.84.2.377.
Source: Pennebaker, J.W., and Seagal, J.D. (1999). "Forming a Story: The Health Benefits of Narrative." *Journal of Clinical Psychology*, 55(10), 1243–1254. https://doi.org/10.1002/(SICI)1097-4679(199910)55:10<1243::AID-JCLP6>3.0.CO;2-N.

Chapter 3: Downsized from a Job

Harvard Business Review citing research that 40% of Americans have been laid off at least once: https://hbr.org/2023/01/managing-your-emotions-after-being-laid-off#:~:text=In%202021%20alone%2C%20there%20were,of%20Americans%20have%20layoff%20anxiety.

US Bureau of Labor Statistics data—layoffs and discharges top 20 million 2002–2019 (p. 18): https://www.bls.gov/opub/mlr/2020/article/pdf/job-openings-hires-and-quits-set-record-highs-in-2019.pdf https://www.bls.gov/opub/mlr/2020/article/job-openings-hires-and-quits-set-record-highs-in-2019.htm.

World Economic Forum "2023 Future of Jobs Report": 75% of employers plan to use AI (p. 5); an estimated 42% of all business tasks will be automated by 2027 (p. 6); positions most at risk and expected to lose 26 million jobs by 2027 (p. 33): https://www3.weforum.org/docs/WEF_Future_of_Jobs_2023.pdf.

Goldman Sachs report on AI replacing 300 million jobs globally; and BBC report on the same https://www.goldmansachs.com/intelligence/pages/generative-ai-could-raise-global-gdp-by-7-percent.html

Goldman Sachs 2023 "Disruptive Technology Symposium" describes generative AI/Chat GPT as more disruptive than the COVID-19 pandemic: https://www.goldmansachs.com/intelligence/pages/stability-ai-ceo-says-ai-will-prove-more-disruptive-than-the-pandemic.html.

Organizational psychologist and behavioral scientist Chris Argyris (July 16, 1923–Nov. 16, 2013): https://www.psychologicalscience.org/publications/observer/25at25/chris-argyris.html https://news.yale.edu/2013/12/11/memoriam-chris-argyris-authority-organizational-behavior.

Chris Argyris first applied Psychological Contract to workplace; Denise Rousseau expanded on it: https://academic.oup.com/book/4256/chapter-abstract/146113033?redirectedFrom=fulltext.

Denise Rousseau, professor at Carnegie Mellon: https://www.heinz.cmu.edu/faculty-research/profiles/rousseau-denisem.

Maggie Mistal's book, *Are You Ready to Love Your Job: Making a Great Living through Soul Search, Research and Job Search*: https://www.amazon.com/Are-You-Ready-Love-Your-ebook/dp/B0BKTLCKNB.

Rob Barnett's book, *Next Job, Best Job: A Headhunter's 11 Strategies to Get Hired Now*: https://www.amazon.com/Next-Job-Best-Headhunters-Strategies/dp/0806541482#:~:text=Book%20details&text=Rob%20Barnett%20is%20an%20innovator,disrupt%20the%20job%20search%20industry.

"Dawn Kelly named to New York City Small Business Advisory Commission in 2022": https://nyc-business.nyc.gov/nycbusiness/article/small-business-advisory-commission.

"Lynnette Khalfani-Cox profiled on CNBC for having a perfect 850 FICO score": https://www.cnbc.com/2022/10/13/finance-coach-how-i-got-to-a-perfect-850-credit-score.html.

Chapter 4: Divorce

US Census Bureau data on divorce and stats from Divorce.com: https://divorce.com/blog/divorce-statistics/.

American Academy of Matrimonial Lawyers survey on women paying alimony and child support: https://www.prnewswire.com/news-releases/big-increase-of-women-paying-alimony-and-child-support-300647725.html.

Chapter 5: Death of a Loved One

Secondary or Ancillary losses explained: https://speakinggrief.org/get-better-at-grief/understanding-grief/secondary-losses https://www.psychologytoday.com/us/blog/writing-between-the-lines/202107/crash-course-in-grieving.

Chapter 6: Disability

CDC data shows 61 million Americans—or one in four people—have a disability: https://www.cdc.gov/media/releases/2018/p0816-disability.html https://www.cdc.gov/ncbddd/disabilityandhealth/infographic-disability-impacts-all.html.

Council for Disability Awareness report showing more than 25% of today's 20-year-olds will become disabled before retirement; and long-term disability lasting 34.6 months on average: https://disabilitycanhappen.org/overview/.

Bureau of Labor Statistics data showing only 35% of civilian employees have access to LTD plans: https://www.bls.gov/opub/ted/2020/short-term-and-long-term-disability-insurance-for-civilian-workers-in-2020.htm.

Social Security Administration info on SSDI earnings caps for blind and non-blind individuals: https://www.ssa.gov/redbook/newfor2023.htm.

Social Security Administration info on qualifying criteria for SSDI: https://www.ssa.gov/benefits/disability/qualify.html.

The Center on Budget and Policy Priorities statistics on SSDI and SSDI recipients: https://www.cbpp.org/research/social-security/social-security-disability-insurance-0.

SSA data on disability overpayments: https://www.ssa.gov/policy/docs/ssb/v79n2/v79n2p65.html.

Chapter 7: Disease

CDC data on chronic disease prevalence: https://www.cdc.gov/chronicdisease/resources/infographic/chronic-diseases.htm https://www.cdc.gov/chronicdisease/pdf/infographics/chronic-disease-in-america-H.pdf (p. 1).

CFPB report on medical debt: https://s3.amazonaws.com/files.consumerfinance.gov/f/documents/cfpb_medical-debt-burden-in-the-united-states_report_2022-03.pdf.

Chapter 8: Disasters

NCEI data on billion-dollar disasters: https://www.ncei.noaa.gov/access/billions/.

American Lung Association tips on returning home after disaster: https://www.lung.org/clean-air/emergencies-and-natural-disasters/returning-home.

Team Rubicon info: https://teamrubiconusa.org/about/.

VOAD info: https://www.nvoad.org/.

FEMA info on disaster recovery and emotional fallout: https://www.fema.gov/pdf/areyouready/recovering_from_disaster.pdf.

Federal Government "Life Experiences" Initiative: https://www.performance.gov/cx/projects/ https://www.performance.gov/cx/projects/facing-a-financial-shock/ https://www.performance.gov/cx/assets/files/FCXI-Journey-Maps-Disaster-Survivor.pdf https://www.performance.gov/assets/cx/files/OMB-Life-Experiences-Cross-Project-Overview.pdf https://assets.performance.gov/cx/files/life-experiences/2022/CX-2022-Life-Experience-Charter_Financial-Shock.pdf.

Chapter 9: Debt

Federal Reserve Bank of New York data on consumer debt: https://www.newyorkfed.org/microeconomics/hhdc.

Pew Charitable Trusts debt data: https://www.pewtrusts.org/en/research-and-analysis/issue-briefs/2020/08/a-look-at-americans-debt.

Urban Institute report on Americans with debt in collections: https://www.urban.org/urban-wire/nearly-one-three-americans-have-debt-reported-collections.

Biden Administration new efforts to provide student loan forgiveness: https://www.whitehouse.gov/briefing-room/statements-releases/2023/06/30/fact-sheet-president-biden-announces-new-actions-to-provide-debt-relief-and-support-for-student-loan-borrowers/.

Attorney Lyle D. Solomon website info about him becoming the "payday loan crusader": https://www.ovlg.com/attorneys/lyle-david-solomon/.

IRS info about installment payments: https://www.irs.gov/payments/payment-plans-installment-agreements.

Office of Personnel Management federal student loan repayment program: https://www.opm.gov/policy-data-oversight/pay-leave/student-loan-repayment/.

Consumer Federation of America credit scoring survey: https://consumerfed.org/press_release/consumer-knowledge-about-credit-scores-has-steadily-declined-over-the-past-eight-years/.

Chapter 10: Damaged Credit

Urban Institute report on the cost of credit for subprime and prime borrowers: https://apps.urban.org/features/credit-health-during-pandemic/.

FICO Score formula: https://www.myfico.com/credit-education/whats-in-your-credit-score.

Chapter 11: Dollar Deficits

N/A

Chapter 12: Discrimination

Census Bureau data on pay gap between women and men as cited by the GAO: https://www.gao.gov/products/gao-23-106041#:~:text=For%20example%2C%20in%202021%3A,18%20cents%20on%20the%20dollar.

TIAA retirement inequality data: https://retireinequality.com/.

Center for American Progress data on LGBTQ discrimination: https://www.americanprogress.org/article/widespread-discrimination-continues-shape-lgbt-peoples-lives-subtle-significant-ways/.

Fortune Magazine data on women CEOs: https://fortune.com/2023/06/05/fortune-500-companies-2023-women-10-percent/.

Kiplinger report on CVS Health efforts to combat the pink tax: https://www.kiplinger.com/taxes/cvs-will-pay-pink-tax-and-drop--period-product-prices.

Index